TAKE A
FINANCIAL
LEAP

The 3 golden rules for financial and life success

TAKE A
FINANCIAL
LEAP

The 3 golden rules for financial and life success

BIG SKY PUBLISHING
www.bigskypublishing.com.au

Pete Wargent

Copyright © Pete Wargent

First published 2015

Copyright remains the property of the authors and apart from any fair dealing for the purposes of private study, research, criticism or review, as permitted under the Copyright Act, no part may be reproduced by any process without written permission.

All inquiries should be made to the publishers.

Big Sky Publishing Pty Ltd

PO Box 303, Newport, NSW 2106, Australia

Phone: 1300 364 611

Fax: (61 2) 9918 2396

Email: info@bigskypublishing.com.au

Web: www.bigskypublishing.com.au

Cover design and typesetting: Think Productions

Printed in China by Asia Pacific Offset Ltd

National Library of Australia Cataloguing-in-Publication entry (pbk.)

Author: Wargent, Peter, author.

Title: Take a financial leap / Pete Wargent.

ISBN: 9781925275322 (paperback)

Subjects: Finance, Personal--Australia.
             Saving and investment--Australia.
             Success.
             Self-realization.

Dewey Number: 332.02401

National Library of Australia Cataloguing-in-Publication entry (ebook)

Author: Wargent, Peter, author.

Title: Take a financial leap / Pete Wargent.

ISBN: 9781925275339 (ebook)

Subjects: Finance, Personal--Australia.
             Saving and investment--Australia.
             Success.
             Self-realization.

Dewey Number: 332.02401

10 percent of the author's proceeds will
be donated to the *McGrath Foundation* in aid of
furthering breast cancer research and support.

This book is just like Pete: clear, organised and intelligent with an easy-going style. The valuable information within is actually a how-to manual or blueprint for how to escape the rat race and live a life of financial freedom… written by someone who's actually managed it. What an achievement!

Michael Yardney, #1 Amazon best-selling author and voted Australia's leading property investment advisor.

After thoroughly enjoying Pete's first two books, I once again learned effective strategies to get ahead of the game. Pete conveys his messages in simple terms that are easy to understand and gives you the tools to create long term wealth. Another great read!

Jonathan Giles, AFL player, Essendon Bombers.

Congratulations on your decision to buy this book! If like me you've read Pete's previous books, you'll have high expectations…and you won't be disappointed! Expect sensible, practical, and well-articulated strategies to follow all the way to financial freedom, from a man who has done it himself.

The first time I met Pete, he told me very simply that 'investing is fun'. Whether or not you agree, it shouldn't be a mystery. And with this book in your hand, it no longer is. I'm excited for you. Big things lie ahead!

Jacquii Alexander, four time elite fitness World Champion, and owner of a multi-million dollar property portfolio.

Contents

Part One
3 Golden Rules For Multiplying Results

1
What Do You
Desire?

1

'Compound interest is the greatest mathematical discovery of all time.' – Albert Einstein.

The life of your dreams

We all have a dream of the way we would like our life to be. All of us want to experience happiness and to lead a great quality of life. Yet for too many, dreams become watered down over time by the realities of everyday life or even forgotten about completely. Instead of trying to figure out ways to accomplish their dreams, people too often become side-tracked by trivialities and fail to recognise the bigger picture or put detailed plans in place to achieve their longer term goals.

All of us would like to chase our dreams, but life just seems to get in the way. People do not seem to have enough time, money, enthusiasm or holidays. Jobs can be unfulfilling and instead of experiencing the true pleasure of living a life once dreamed of, people compare with envy the quality of their lives to that of their peers.

There are 3 golden rules for multiplying your results.

In order to maximise your awesome potential and multiply your results, you need to understand why this occurs and exactly how to action the changes you need to make in order to design the life that you once dreamed was possible. You need to raise your standards above the mediocre or humdrum, change the limiting beliefs that are holding you back from maximising results and implement specific new strategies that can help you to achieve your ultimate goals.

There are three golden rules which you can use to multiply your results - not only when investing in property or shares, but also in business and indeed in all areas of your life. If you can master these three golden rules, what you can achieve may be almost limitless. These three golden rules are:

- Golden Rule **#1: The 80/20 Principle** - most of your results will be derived from a handful or 'vital few' of your decisions and actions;

- Golden Rule #2: **Snowballing** your results - understanding and then using compound growth; and

- Golden Rule #3: **The Pleasure-Pain Principle** - what you link pleasure and pain to will determine the way in which you act and thus your results.

In this book I will show you how you can first understand and then apply these three golden rules across all areas of your life in order to massively improve and then continue to multiply your results to a level above and beyond what you may have believed to be possible.

Getting out of the rat race

I am the author of two previous books on personal finance and investment, the co-founder of a property buying business with offices at Mayfair in London and Martin Place in Sydney, and an investment mentor. I built a significant net worth for myself from scratch, quit my career job when I was 33 and have been a business owner since that time. Over the years of mentoring and coaching my clients, if one question seems to be asked of me more than any other, it is this:

'How quickly can I be financially free and retire?'

Now here is the thing - I believe that the traditional concept of retirement is old fashioned and somewhat out of date. In decades now past folk typically worked from a young adult age until they hit 65, often in one career or even in only one job for one employer, and then retired on their pension for a short while before shuffling off this mortal coil.

That is not really how it works any more, and nor should it be! It occurs to me frequently that if your goal in life is retiring as early as possible, then it is quite likely that you are working in the wrong career, or at the very least you are engaged in a job or role which does not genuinely inspire you. The part of your life which is your work should be something which gets you out of bed each morning excited, passionate and raring to go!

How can you make your vacation your vocation?

The true goal of this book therefore is to offer you a practical guide for how you can design the life you want to lead, how you can build and compound the wealth you require to take your focus away from a dependence on your full time job or pay cheque, and how you can then choose to make your vacation your vocation through turning your passion into your business. As Mark Twain once observed, the person who is able to make their vacation their vocation will never feel as though they have 'worked' a day in their life. In my experience that is absolutely true.

As you will have gathered from the book title, there are three golden rules which you must be aware of and resolve to master if you are to multiply your results, and these three themes will be returned to throughout this book. This is a lot of ground for us to cover in a relatively short space, so let us get straight into it.

A bit about this book

I was originally a Chartered Accountant by profession, but this is not a book that will be filled overwhelmingly with numbers. Although the numbers *80* and *20* will feature prominently because of my belief in the colossal power and reach of the 80/20 Principle, I will not spend pages analysing figures which will make your eyes glaze over. Instead, I will show you some simple yet powerful principles which:

- Help you to set huge, thrilling and inspiring goals

- Show you how to get the power of compounding growth or 'snowballing' working in your favour in order to generate significant wealth throughout your lifetime

- Understand the psychology of life success and how to achieve emotional mastery

- Easily understand how to become a long-term successful share market investor

- Create very substantial and sustainable wealth through real estate

- Make your vacation your vocation by turning your passion into your business

- Help you to escape the rat race to design and live the life you choose, rather than one which is dictated to you by your boss, your job or your mortgage.

Yes, we will cover how to invest successfully in property and shares. But this book is so much more than that. It is also a motivational tool which will help you to set big goals, teach you how to transition from paid employment towards financial freedom (and if you so desire working for yourself in a line of business which gets you out of bed each morning, passionately excited and champing at the bit), and how to improve the quality of your life, health and relationships.

And a bit about me...

So why listen to what I have to say as opposed to all of the other motivational books out there? There are plenty of them on the shelves, to be sure! The problem I have with a lot of motivational books when it comes to building wealth and designing your ideal life is that they are very heavy on motivational content but light on the practicalities of so doing. That is not too surprising in some regards, as plenty of wealth creation and success books are written by those from a positive thinking background, such as personal trainers and the like.

> It all starts with getting your personal finances in shape.

In contrast, my background is in finance. From the first day of my career when I trained as a Chartered Accountant in London, I have only ever worked in financial employment as well as being an investor in financial markets and the co-founder of a property investment advisory business based in London and Sydney. Simply put, investment, business and finance are what I do.

In my late twenties, I was still working as a Chartered Accountant in Sydney with one of the Big Four accounting firms, but I knew something was not quite right in my life. I spent a great deal of time in the office or working with clients, and had very little free time. Perhaps the majority of my week was consumed by people who were a drain on me, rather than those who added vitality to my life or inspired me to be the best that I could be.

My career paid well enough and I quite enjoyed most of it, but I was never genuinely passionate about it and therefore I was never likely to be an outstanding or inspirational performer myself. Thanks to a vital few smart investment decisions made with my wife (who incidentally is also a Chartered Accountant, and a much more diligent one than me) we became relatively well off at a young age. It is notable looking back that the great bulk of our net worth at that point in time was attributable to only a vital few smart decisions and successful property and shares investments that we had made, and very little was due to our salaries.

Learn to harness the power of the 80/20 Principle.

I was able to continue making radical improvements to my life once I began to fully comprehend the power of the 80/20 Principle. It eventually became more and more clear to me that tinkering around with my life at the margin was simply not going to fit the bill. Working harder and more efficiently as an accountant - as they used to advise us to do in training courses - would have had very little meaningful impact on my life.

I had originally thought that being a Chartered Accountant was the ideal career for me. I was almost right, but not quite. I loved working with numbers and was hugely passionate about economics, finance and investment, but the daily travails of working in professional practice and then later working in the mining industry as a Financial Controller did not genuinely excite me.

I worked for the one of the world's largest accounting firms, but was not particularly well suited to working for a massive organisation, and I certainly never had a great deal of interest in office politics, appraisal reviews, efficiency drives or clambering my way up the career ladder. I ultimately resolved this by first establishing my own financial security as an investor and then subsequently founding a business around my passion which directly assists others in how to achieve the results that I have. Now *that* is something which excites me and gets me out of bed each morning raring to go! These days I cannot wait to wake up and start the day.

Success in life is achieved by snowballing your assets and doubling down on your successes...growth upon growth.

As I will show you in this book it is possible to use the power of focus and the 80/20 Principle to create a large and snowballing net worth which allows you to escape from the reliance on a career job or pay cheque and to understand how to create business income from a relatively small number of clients. I made these dramatic changes to my life through designing the life that I wanted to lead and then building a specific plan to transition away from the rat race of paid employment and towards a life following my passion.

Living the 80/20 way does not mean only doing the important stuff which is getting you results and forgetting everything else. It is a far more empowering concept than that. Instead following the principles of 80/20 living requires you finding out which strategies are working best for you and *doubling down* on them. It means focusing on your passion, because what you are passionate about you will also excel at, and importantly, this will also bring vitality and happiness to your life.

> The 80/20 Principle dictates that you should recognise what is working and do more of it.

Almost by definition therefore, when it comes to your personal finances and investing it may not be the smartest thing to do to take the financial advisor's advice and invest a little bit in everything. That will at best lead to average or ordinary results. Instead, why not become an expert in one or two strategies and use them to invest as an expert? I will show you in this book that this can be relatively straightforward to do if you understand a few basic rules and seek professional advice where necessary. The 80/20 Principle holds that through the power of focus you can attain results far in excess of what you previously believed to be achievable.

Your childhood dreams

Think back to your childhood. Did you have dreams of how life might pan out? I suppose that you did. Has it turned out the way you expected? The problem for most of us is that over time, small piece by small piece childhood dreams are gradually chipped away or battered down by the realities of everyday life, and gradually people come to accept that life will be not be the way they dreamed it would in younger years.

> You can make a decision today to follow your dreams.

You do not have to accept second best if you choose not to. You can choose to design the life you want to lead, and through applying the 80/20 Principle to identify how to achieve those results, you can live it too. One word of warning, however. You have to be able to commit to changing. As the old saying goes, if you keep doing what you have always done, then you can expect to keep getting what you always got.

A short parable in the book *Who Moved My Cheese?* explains how important change is to us as individuals.[1] Whether we like it or not, change happens in the world. The inescapable conclusion of this is that we need to be able to anticipate and monitor change, be adaptable to change ourselves, and further, to actually enjoy doing so. If you can be flexible enough to adjust to change you can flourish, but if you fail to adapt your life could become moribund or stagnate.

In fact this parable is even more poignant than that – you need to adapt to change but you also need to embrace it and make it work for you. You need to become a *master* of change by taking back control. I can remember back in my career days daring to dream that I would be able to become a multi-millionaire and escape from my job as an accountant, and all the way through my journey, I heard one phrase, or a variation of it, continuously:

'That is not possible. You can't...'

If there is one thing that is more or less certain in life, it is that if you believe you cannot do something you will fail to achieve it in any sustainable way. This is precisely why motivational books spend so much time considering mind-set and the psychology of success. Looking back, the people who said that my goals were not achievable have almost without exception not achieved remotely the level of success that they might have done in their careers, lives or personal finances. Their doubting inner voices became self-fulfilling and they have not always maximised their undoubtedly limitless potential.

Who is to say that you cannot achieve financial freedom and choose to live the life you want? Of course you can do it. Other people continue to achieve it, so why not you? I suggest here that a very good starting point in achieving the success you want is to surround yourself with positive and like-minded people, and conversely gradually move away from people who light-heartedly take the rise out of you for daring to dream big. Think about it - why would true friends ever need to drag their peers down?

Another key point to understand is that success is not a mountain to be scaled. You can start to live a happy, successful life now, right here today. It is true that one reason people do not achieve great long-term financial results is that they focus too much on short-cuts, short term plans and immediate outcomes. This is why it so important to understand the concept of compounding growth, a snowballing effect of your investment returns and life results. The ability to multiply your results through snowballing is the second golden rule which we will consider in more detail in chapter 3 and beyond.

Make a genuine decision

The first thing you must do if you want to escape from the rat race of dependence on a pay cheque and begin to live the life you truly want to lead is to make a genuine <u>decision</u> to do so. What does it mean to make a real decision? The word is derived from the Latin *decider,* meaning to *cut off.* To make a real decision means that you have literally chosen to cut off all other alternatives. And that is how it is when it comes to building wealth and designing the life you want to lead. You need to make a decision to cut yourself away from the choice of failure.

> Making a decision to achieve a goal means
> cutting off all other alternatives.

Why is this so vital? The reason is that in the life of every person there will necessarily be failures and setbacks. What separates the winners from the rest therefore, is a total and absolute commitment when things do not go as planned to resolve to get back on the horse and never, ever give up. The ultimate goal of this book is to guide you on how to get from where you are today to where you want to be, but whatever plans and strategies you implement you will of course always encounter obstacles to success. Only you can decide if you have the burning desire and commitment to overcome them.

True wealth

> 'I hate to be a failure. I hate and regret the failure of my
> marriages. I would gladly give all my millions for just
> one lasting marital success.' – J. Paul Getty.

For all of the above, it is important to recognise that happiness and success is rarely derived solely from material possessions. In previous years I spent a lot of my time living and working in East Timor, known to locals as Timor-Leste. Timor has had a challenging history having been through war, occupation, civil unrest, genocide and mass starvation. As a result, the country today remains one of the poorest on the planet. While it may be a *cliché*, one thing I learned as a result of living with the wonderful people of Timor is that material wealth and possessions are not in themselves what cause people to be happy or otherwise.

This is one of those things that you hear people say regularly, and I can assure you it is absolutely true! In order to be happy, what we actually need are meaningful human relationships, our health and, importantly, a true purpose and meaning to our lives. So while this book in part shows you specifically how to build financial wealth and discusses the practical challenges of building a successful business, its true scope is much wider than that. As well as snowballing or compounding your wealth, I want to inspire you to compound your education, your quality of life, to widen your horizons and to find a real meaning for your life and a means of contribution.

Wealth comes in many different forms.

It has always been interesting to me how some people are quite content to stand still or meander through life doing more or less the same thing. Routine is comfortable to them, travel is not a significant draw-card and job security tends to be paramount. There is nothing inherently right or wrong with that, but I was simply not built that way. I have often felt that if I was not moving jobs or moving house every couple of years then I was somehow missing out on the opportunity to do something new, experience new horizons or learn new skills. Interestingly, I was always quite happy with repetitive work provided that I could see that my overall career was still progressing.

Persistence pays.

Too often today people lack persistence and are always looking for short-cuts or are not prepared to put in the hard yards. I have also come to realise that restlessness can be a hugely effective character trait when it is used and channelled in the right way and is utilised as a tool for constant improvement. The second golden rule of this book alongside the 80/20 Principle relates to the power of compounding, snowballing or growth upon growth. Compound growth is such a powerful force that it nearly always seems to defy logic.

While my expertise is in the realm of personal finance and investment, I want you to consider not only building wealth for the sake of becoming rich, but also to understand how you can grow and compound the quality or your life. Think of all the areas of your life which impact the quality of your existence. Here are a few, in no particular order:

- Friendships

- Relationships

- Your career or business

- Your home and living environment

- Family

- Nutrition

- Exercise

- Physical and mental health

- Spirituality

- Financial wealth

- Charitable giving or volunteering

I have only scratched the surface here and naturally there are many other areas besides these. When you stop for a moment and consider all of these various parts of your life, do you think that it is drawing too long a bow to say that you could aim to improve the quality of your life by say, 5 percent each year, however that may be measured? Of course not! If you set yourself big and inspiring goals and then resolve to chase them like a dog with a bone, you can easily improve your life quality by 5 percent each and every year. In reality you can achieve much, much more than that.

I have come to understand over the years that snowballing or compounding does not only create awesome and magical power in terms of your financial health. You can compound your wisdom, your self-worth and your sense of contribution. Small gains at first can become larger gains later through building upon past successes. In fact, you can compound the quality of your entire life. And if you start to do it now, imagine how different your life in the future could be from the alternative path of periodically taking two steps forward only to then take three steps back. And no, it does not matter if you are not 21 anymore. Resolve to start today!

By committing to making constant small improvements to the way you live, work, save, invest, exercise and socialise each day and each week through your life, the snowballing effect can and will see the quality of your existence improve dramatically over time. At first the changes may seem to be marginal, but over time the impacts will begin to have far-reaching consequences that you may never have anticipated when you started out. So start today!

Figure 1.1 – Constant improvement

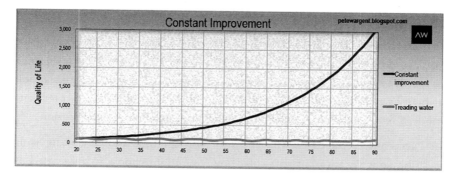

Following your passion

What if you could get out of bed each morning passionate and raring to go because you are doing what you really always wanted to do? Well, you can! And that is what this book is here to help you with, to help you design the life you want to lead, establish the financial base you need to allow you to follow your passion, and then to turn your passion into your business. This book comes in five short parts, as follows:

In **Part One** of the book I will discuss how you can use the power of compounding in all areas of your life in order to achieve greater things than you may ever have believed possible. I will spend some time discussing the psychology of life success and how through setting huge and inspiring goals you can excite and infuse yourself with the energy required to take decisive and committed action daily.

We will also take a look at the third golden rule for multiplying your results, the Pleasure-Pain Principle. The Pleasure-Pain Principle is vitally important because it can help you to understand human behaviour and the reason we behave in the way that we do. If you can become a master of this concept in concert with an understanding of the 80/20 Principle and the ability and understanding of how to compound or snowball your results, the potential of what you can achieve can be boundless.

In **Part Two** we will then take a look at your personal finances and investments and specifically how you can go about building a portfolio of assets which will keep going out to work for you *as long as you live*, even *beyond* your own lifetime. Though acquiring quality, appreciating assets for the long term you can begin to build and snowball your net worth and gradually shift your focus away from a reliance on a pay cheque and towards following your life passion.

In **Part Three** comes a closer look at the practicalities of investing and how you can deal with adversity and the inevitable false starts and setbacks, since in life there will always be such hurdles to negotiate. We will also take a look at how to re-prioritise your life, including moving away from the prevalent modern mind-set of mass consumption and towards one of contribution.

In **Part Four** I will cover why and how you might consider making your vacation your vocation, in particular how you might choose to get started in business or self-employment from a small base, and the practical logistics of how this can be done. That is, to follow your passion so that you can wake up each morning thrilled with the excitement of being able to do what you are truly passionate about.

Finally in **Part Five** we will look at living the life that you have designed for yourself and how this can be sustained in a meaningful way. Throughout the book I will refer to the three golden rules and how you can continue applying these and multiplying your results throughout your life. Remember these three golden rules which we will look at in turn are:

- Golden Rule #1: **The 80/20 Principle**
- Golden Rule #2: **Snowballing** your results
- Golden Rule #3: **The Pleasure-Pain Principle**

Let's go!

As with all my books, I have intentionally kept this book relatively succinct and to the point. It is not intended to be an encyclopaedia on everything there is to know about personal finance, investing, the psychology of success and setting up a small business. Rather it is a book which aims to show you the power of focus and just how much can be achieved if you focus intensely on the things in life which really make a difference. After all, that is what living the 80/20 way is all about. All set? Good, then let's get going!

Introduction

» Most of the big results in life come from a vital few key decisions, and therefore you need to get the big decisions right

» The 80/20 Principle holds that you should actively recognise the strategies that are working you, and resolve to replicate them

» The most powerful force available for all us all to use is compound growth – growth upon growth

» The snowballing effect can be utilised in and applied to most areas of your life

» This is a book about designing the life you want to lead, and then living it

» Through setting inspiring goals which excite you enough your persistence will naturally follow

» Persistence pays off!

2
Golden Rule #1
Living The 80/20 Way

2

The Universe is unbalanced

The Universe is not balanced. It's out of whack. Although it is fashionable today to speak of the importance of balance or the twin concepts of *yin* and *yang* from Chinese philosophy, successful people intuitively understand that in truth the dice in business, investment and in life are loaded.

The first of the three golden rules to understand and then use to your advantage is the 80/20 Principle, a concept which was first written about more than a century ago. Way back in 1906 the Italian economist Vilfredo Pareto noted that 80 percent of the land in Italy was owned by only 20 percent of the population.[1] It often also proves to be the case that more than 80 percent of the wealth of a nation is held by fewer than 20 percent of its inhabitants.[2] The world we all inhabit is curiously, yet surprisingly consistently, unbalanced.

A small number of inputs cause most of life's outputs.

Pareto went on to develop his principle by observing that 20 percent of the pea pods in his garden contained 80 percent of the peas, and the famous *Pareto Principle* was born. Today, people often instead refer to the 80/20 Rule or the 80/20 Principle (or sometimes even the Law of the Vital Few), but the name you prefer to attach to this concept is of far less importance than how you choose to apply it to your own life.

Consider the potentially huge implications of this simple rule! Most of your personal wealth will likely be derived from only a handful of your investment decisions. In business it is often the case that only 20 percent of customers account for 80 percent of revenues and profits. Meanwhile 80 percent of customer complaints are frequently derived from only 20 percent of the customers (and guess what – it is unlikely to be the same 20 percent of customers that are generating most of your turnover!). The examples go on and on.

So what does the 80/20 Principle really mean for us as individuals? In short, nearly all of the genuinely significant results in your life will be derived only from a vital few of your actions. On the other hand, most of what you actually do achieves very little. The significance of this is that if you can harness the power of this simple concept and apply it across the way you live, work and invest, you can radically improve the quality of your life including your wealth, health, relationships, happiness and more.

Better still, if you can make a few good decisions, observe very carefully what is working most effectively for you and then resolve to double down by doing *even more* of it, your results can get better and better. The 80/20 Principle can be a phenomenally powerful tool when it is thoroughly understood and applied effectively, and it represents the first of the three golden rules which are recurrent themes throughout the course of this book.

Getting it 80 percent right

One of the reassuring things about the 80/20 Principle is that there can be plenty of headroom for mistakes. You do not have to get everything right all of the time. This is fortunate, because we are all human and we all make mistakes every day. I know for sure that I do!

This is one of the important facets of the 80/20 Principle. You by no means have to be perfect, and nor should you necessarily even try to be. After all, to err is human. However, you do need to resolve to learn from genuine mistakes, ensure that you get the big decisions right and, above all, aim to be the best *you* that you can be. The majority of your most important results will come from getting the basics right. The rest is just fine tuning!

> 'Tell me and I forget, teach me and I may remember, involve me and I learn.' – Benjamin Franklin.

Remember, living the 80/20 way does not mean only taking the key actions which are getting you results and ignoring other parts of your life. The 80/20 Principle is a more empowering concept than that which requires that you study which of your strategies are achieving results and *doubling down* on them. The 80/20 Principle also implies that you should focus on your passion. This is in part because what you are passionate about you are likely to become a great expert in, and just as crucially, this is because doing what you are passionate about should also make you happy and fulfilled.

Investment mentor

Having invested heavily in real estate and stock markets over the years, I suddenly found myself in my early thirties in the happy position of being surprisingly wealthy. What is remarkable as an investor is how the small but satisfying gains which you generate in the early days can grow and compound until the gains become larger than you had ever anticipated or even dared to dream when you started out. I began mentoring others on how to replicate my successes and side-step the inevitable pitfalls which I encountered.

'The most powerful force in the Universe is compound interest.'
– Albert Einstein.

This snowballing effect is the second of the three golden rules of this book which we will consider further in the next chapter and beyond. You can make huge strides as your life progresses far in excess of what you believed was possible at the beginning of your journey. The gains you make later in life can total more than the sum of all of your preceding results combined - your second million will be considerably easier to make than your first. A commitment to consistent and never-ending improvements can also start a chain reaction in to other areas of your life.

Upon realising with relief that I no longer was compelled to work full time in my professional career as a Chartered Accountant in order to chase an ever-higher salary - half of which was lost in taxes anyway - I went to travel the world for 18 months visiting more than 25 countries. This gave me an awful lot of time to think and reflect on what strategies had worked for me and which courses of action had been less effective.

Thereafter, I gradually shifted via a period of part-time contract work, from employee to business owner. Today I am the co-owner of a property business with offices in London and Sydney. And in this book I will provide an in-depth explanation of how you can achieve a similar goal of rotating out of the workforce in order to follow your passion and you can do so sooner than you might believe.

Transitioning away from reliance on a pay cheque is challenging but achievable with patience, time and discipline.

What became clear to me through my mentoring sessions with clients was that so many everyday people have the same - or at least very similar - questions about how to get started and how to be successful in investment. While the specifics of each question always differed a little, very similar themes cropped up over and over again. The years of mentoring my clients has given me a deeper understanding of the most common challenges and hurdles people face and how they can overcome them.

'History doesn't repeat itself...but it does rhyme.' – Mark Twain.

I therefore set out to present to you here a simple one-stop shop of how to first design and then live the life you dream of, using simple principles to master the share markets, how to become a substantially wealthy investor in real estate and how to turn your passion into your business to free you from the shackles of employment. In particular, I have looked at all times to cover off those key questions that seemed to keep being raised by my clients.

'But I don't have the time?'

Have you ever heard of the concept of opportunity cost? Here is an example. When companies calculate their cost of their capital, they understand that it would be nonsensical to undertake projects which return less than the cost of financing them. A mining company might elect to invest one million dollars in a new piece of crushing equipment which could increase its throughput rates. Before it does so, however, the company will generally need to look at what that money might be doing for them instead.

If that $1 million could alternatively be invested at a risk-free return of, say, 5 percent per annum, then it could be said that the crushing equipment has an opportunity cost of $50,000 in year 1. The crushing equipment should therefore be increasing throughput sufficiently to return additional cash flows more than the equivalent of an extra $50,000 each year over its useful economic life. Put another way, before you spend some money or invest it, it is first useful to know what you are foregoing or missing out on by so doing. Companies do this all the time when they analyse projects.

Opportunity cost can be intuitive.

Whether you realise it or not, opportunity cost applies to your personal finances. Each time you spend your hard-earned dollars on a treat or a luxury, there is a twin cost attached to it. Firstly, once you spend your dollars, you do not have that money in your pocket or bank account any longer. And secondly, those dollars spent could have been invested in assets which might earn you many more dollars in the future.

What is perhaps slightly less obvious is that opportunity cost also applies to your time. It is truly amazing how often you hear people say that they do not have time to sort out their personal finances, get started in investing or attempt to chase the life of their dreams. The fact is that you have 24 hours in a day and 7 days in a week, just the same as I do. What is more, Richard Branson and Bill Gates have the same number of hours in a day that we have.

Therefore it does not really make sense to say that we don't have the time to do something, for by definition we all have the same amount of time as each other. What we are really talking about is how we prioritise our time. Remember that 80 percent of our results come from only 20 percent of the causes or inputs, so by focussing on what is important, we should all be able to free up some time to dedicate to investing.

Donald Trump is an example of someone who takes the concept of opportunity cost to its ultimate extreme. He sees life as a competition as to who can be the richest and biggest businessman and therefore only sleeps for four hours each night. Sleep is seen as wasted time in the great competition of life. Clearly I do not recommend such an extreme approach but it seems to work for Trump as he confesses that he loves the competition aspect of life.[3]

While the concept of opportunity cost might be seen to induce stress, it need not. Whether or not we realise it, we all weigh up opportunity cost almost every time we make a decision. Each time you elect to work overtime instead of going to the pub, go to the football or go shopping, or choose a slice of cake instead of going to the gym, you are intuitively weighing up the costs and benefits of each decision.

Opportunity cost can impact careers too.

By way of a practical example, over recent years an increasingly tough choice has faced many youngsters. With the introduction of expensive university tuition fees, would-be students must balance up the benefits of a university education which may see them incur considerable debt against the long-term benefits of attaining a degree or higher education qualification.

By the time a student has graduated with a debt burden, his or her school-friend who shunned higher education may have worked for three, four or even five years and saved a significant amount towards buying their first house. A graduate might earn a higher salary but they probably need to do so in order to pay off their student debts! Of course, these can seem to be impossibly difficult decisions to make at such a young age.

When I was younger a colleague at the accounting firm I worked for, Deloitte, said to me that he couldn't see the point in owning a large portfolio of properties and shares as I did, as it would be stressful and take up too much time. The irony of this is that working in professional practice can be such an all-consuming career itself, with employees often working 40, 50 or even 60 hours each week for one heavily-taxed income. There is very little leverage in that unless you are earning some serious dollars, and all of those hours of employment can have the greatest opportunity cost of all if you are missing out on living life.

The internet age brings new opportunities

It seems almost hard to imagine now, but not so long ago there was no internet and no email. People communicated face-to-face, over the phone or sometimes by fax. Imagine the difference that this technological revolution has made to the way in which we do business and the way, for example, in which people trade shares so much more frenetically. In my profession – accounting - book-keeping was until relatively recently recorded in actual books. The ledgers were handwritten. When complex consolidated group accounts were prepared the auditors pored over seemingly endless worksheets which folded outwards and outwards…and outwards. Today the thousands of journal entries can easily be encompassed in a simple spreadsheet.

Information moves ever more quickly today.

There was a widespread assumption that the advent of electronic communication would make the accounting profession infinitely more efficient and free up more time for accountants to focus on other things. Some even felt that auditors would become obsolete, since everything would be recorded so efficiently and accurately that the human element would become surplus to requirements.

It never happened, of course. Certainly ever more information and data got emailed or pinged around, and more and more data travels today with previously unthinkable velocity. In certain ways the world has become less efficient rather than more. A whole new mini-industry sprang up – 'Time Management' - which aimed to help middle managers utilise their time more effectively. *Prioritise the key tasks* was one of the key suggestions. *Think marginally about your time* was another. I can't remember any others, but I am sure there were plenty of them which we learned about in lengthy training sessions that took up lots of valuable...well, time.

For most professionals and employees today there seems to be less and less time in the week. Indeed, the modern world is seemingly becoming polarised between those who earn good money yet have little or no free time in which to enjoy it, and those who are under-employed and thus have all the time in the world to do stuff, but no money with which to do it!

The internet can be used to leverage your time.

It is important to understand that the internet and information age has also brought with it great benefits for those who understand how to leverage the new technology. Information is more freely available than ever before, should you choose to seek it out. The world and information moves more quickly, which can be a huge benefit to those who know how to utilise it and benefit from it. Better still, the internet age has made going into business or becoming self-employed far more accessible with lower overheads than has ever been the case before. Young internet entrepreneurs have built multi-million dollar and sometimes even billion dollar businesses from ideas they first conceived in their own bedrooms.

What might you be able to achieve if you can identify in life what you are truly interested in and passionate about, what makes you happy and in what areas of life you have a natural advantage? What if you can double down and do even more of what you excel at and what excites you? Can this bring greater results and more happiness? We spend the majority of our time – perhaps as much as four-fifths of it - on matters which achieve very little of any importance and bring us little happiness. How can you instead grasp the 80/20 Principle and use it to your advantage? There is little point in tinkering around at the edges with the management of your time. Instead, you need to consider how and where you can achieve results and happiness and apply time to that field with gusto.

To escape the drudgery of the rat race or dependence upon a pay cheque, you first need to build a portfolio of assets.

To escape from a total reliance or dependence upon a pay cheque, paid employment or a career which you do not find inspiring, first you need to build a portfolio of quality income-producing and appreciating investments that will bring you income and capital growth in perpetuity - for as long as you live.

I want you to learn how to invest in quality assets which you never have to sell because they will keep on going out to work for you in perpetuity. Then, for ongoing cash flow or income you can choose to make your vacation your vocation by turning your passion into your business. It is worth making the point here that although Part Four of this book goes into some detail about how to make your vacation your vocation by turning your passion into your business, there is equally no reason that you cannot fulfil the same goals by working in a paid job in your area of passion.

Modelling the 80/20 way

One of the most useful and effective tools in your entire armoury if your goal is improving your life is that of *modelling*. That is, to find someone who has achieved the goals that you want to achieve and to model what has worked for them - to learn from what has worked so effectively for them and what has not and apply the learnings from their experiences yourself.

If your goal is to become the CEO of a large company or a Partner in a professional services firm, find CEOs or Partners who have achieved the success you want, and study how they became successful. If instead your ultimate goal is to found and then run a football coaching school, find someone who has achieved just that. Through modelling their most effective actions, strategies, performance and demeanour you can begin to achieve the same results, perhaps even more quickly and effectively than they did themselves. You can learn from them the potential traps and pitfalls too.

Having established myself as a property investor in London and in Sydney, one of the key mentors I chose in order to take my property investing skills up to the elite level was the best-selling author and leading property expert and advisor Michael Yardney.[4] Why did I choose him above all of the other possible real estate gurus? Mainly because he had a proven track record of achieving results over a period of forty years and was most certainly not a flash in the pan.

Find mentors who have already achieved your goals.

There were plenty of other real estate experts selling their wares, but many of them seemed to be relatively new to the property game or were claiming to have discovered some new angle or fad. That is definitely not what you want from an investment mentor. Instead you want someone who has been there and done it over a prolonged period of time, through the highs and the lows of many market cycles. The full gamut of their experiences, which have been gleaned through good times and bad, can be priceless. I do not even know whether he realises it himself or not, but I still learn something new from Michael every day.

In the world of share markets and investing, I have read and learned from hundreds of books over the years and probably tried each and every approach to investing and trading at some point in time. And my word, there are lots of them! Eventually I came across one short book by top-selling author and investor Peter Thornhill which brought it all together and made share investing make perfect sense.[5]

I quickly realised that Thornhill must be a man worth seeking out, and having got to know him I learned more from his words of wisdom than from reading thousands of pages of moderately useful information elsewhere or watching the endless dozens of talking heads on the television. This is a superb example of the 80/20 Principle in action! What this book helped to clarify for me is that the share markets have become plagued by speculators, always wondering, hoping or praying that they know which way the market will dive next. His book puts into black and white what I had intuitively felt. Investing need not and *should not* be that hard.

Invest in shares to compound your income as well as growth. Invest in properties to snowball your asset base and equity.

Shares are an income asset. Great companies will pay you dividend income every year. If you can find an investment product which invests in a well-diversified range of great companies and has a proven track record over multiple decades of paying investors increasing dividends each and every year, then you can focus on the ever-increasing income stream and not on the day to day gyrations of the share price. Instead of spending each day or week worrying about what the stock market is up to, you can continue to receive your dividend cheques safe in the knowledge than when a company increases its dividends each and every year, over time, the share price will also take care of itself.

The best time horizon for holding a quality investment is forever.

What I learned from these true experts in their respective fields was that true power and peace of mind can be found in quality investments which can be held forever. Continuing to accumulate income-producing, appreciating investments is the simplest, most efficient and most effective method of becoming wealthy. This is an example of using shortcuts to success using the 80/20 rule.

As I will consider in the next chapter, gains can grow and compound unimpeded by transaction costs or capital gains and your wealth can snowball while you sleep.

Using experts

One of the great things about you having picked up this book is that you have made a choice to educate yourself in how to become financially free, how to design the life you want to live and to escape from the daily grind of the rat race. Do not underestimate the power of taking this step!

As I will note in more detail later in the book, one of the key reasons I was able to achieve my own financial freedom at the age of 33 is because I realised that this was a goal I wanted to achieve and I read prodigiously, some hundreds and hundreds of books in total. Granted, some books were considerably less useful than others, but over time having educated myself through huge amounts of reading I was able to choose a number of key mentors I could learn from to help me achieve my goals.

'Not all readers are leaders, but all leaders are readers.'
– Harry S. Truman.

While it may not be feasible or even desirable to read hundreds of books, I do recommend that you attempt to read regularly and commit to learning new things. The world is ever-changing and evolving, and while the principles of success remain the same the specifics do shift subtly over time. It also sometimes makes sense to employ the use of an expert in investment.

In fact, most employees actually already do so by paying for a fund manager to manage their pension fund. They may not physically pay the cash, but the fees are simply deducted from the fund each year, regardless of whether the fund managers have made money or lost money for the fund.

Others, including myself, deem the value to be added by fund managers as unacceptably low and thus elect to self-manage our pension and invest in different share market products which do not attract hefty or punitive fees, as I will explain clearly and simply in chapter 10. When it comes to investing in the share markets, I believe there is a solid case for considering investment companies which incur only very low management and administrative costs, or simply investing in index funds.

Experts can help in investment.

Does that mean I would never pay for expert assistance in investment? Definitely not. In some instances, such as when investing in property, it absolutely makes sense to have a team of experts on your side: a property buying agent or expert investment advisor, a solicitor or conveyancer, a chartered surveyor, a building inspection professional, an accountant and a property manager, for example. While it is always admirable to take action and to determine to learn from your mistakes as you go, using leverage to buy real estate is too big a deal to get wrong.

Statistics show that the overwhelmingly majority of property investors never progress beyond owning only one or two properties, which is certainly not enough to achieve financial success for most people. One of the salient reasons for this is that they simply do not get it right in the early days – through inexperience they do not carry out the right research in order to buy the right property. They become disillusioned and never create the equity they need to generate new deposits for investment in further properties and therefore snowball their wealth. The other main reason is that investors too frequently and mistakenly sell appreciating assets!

If you make a successful property investment, however, the power of leverage can see you attain returns that can be leveraged relatively quickly into further investments through redrawing the equity created. That is why you simply must get it right and why I recommend that you should probably enlist the help of an expert to ensure that you do so.

The principle reason that property investment is such a powerful tool when it is done well is that the leverage involved can be such that a relatively small number of investment properties can make a huge difference to your personal finances. What this does mean, however, is that if you are potentially only going to own half a dozen investment properties, you cannot afford to get those investment decisions wrong if you want to accelerate your results.

Chapter 2 summary

- » The 80/20 rule holds that most of your results will come from a minority of your decisions – make a few great decisions and follow them with fervour!

- » Modelling is the strategy of finding someone who has achieved your goals and resolving to follow, or even improve upon, their path

- » Choose great mentors and make a decision to learn from them

- » Aim to build a portfolio of quality assets which will continue to work for you around the clock

- » The best assets to acquire are those which continue to build wealth for you *forever*

3
Golden Rule #2
The Snowball

3

'Compound interest is the eighth wonder of the world. He who understands it, earns it. He who doesn't, pays it.' – Albert Einstein.

Get excited for a moment!

Over the coming chapters I am going to spend some time looking at setting goals and the psychology of wealth creation. But first I want to get you excited about what you can really achieve when you fully understand the power of compounding and how to use it as an investor. Great results in life are achieved by setting huge, exciting and inspirational goals.

If you set yourself inspiring goals then the motivation to put into practice the massive action required to reach those goals becomes so much easier to source. When we talk about compound growth, what do we really mean? Let us take a look at a short real-world example or two of compounding in action. Once you understand the principles you can use them to multiply your earnings and create potentially boundless wealth.

Compounding like rabbits

Thomas Austin was a rather gung-ho Englishman who enjoyed hunting rabbits for sport back in England in the mid-19th century. Upon his arrival Down Under in Australia, Mr. Austin mused that the introduction of a few wild rabbits could do little harm and in October 1959 he released just 24 wild bunny rabbits on his property near Winchelsea in Victoria, with the idea of using them for a quiet spot of hunting.

It's well known via colloquial expression that rabbits have a tendency towards breeding with a certain enthusiasm, yet it is nevertheless unlikely that anyone could have foreseen the sheer scale of the subsequent explosion of the rabbit population in Australia. Because the Antipodes did not play host to the freezing winters that were commonly experienced back in Blighty, those lucky few rabbits were able to breed all year round which only served to accelerate the outlandish growth in their numbers.

Within a decade the Australian rabbit population had spread so voraciously that two million rabbits could be shot or trapped each year with no noticeable effect on the surviving population. It was the fastest recorded spread of any mammalian population anywhere in history. That, in short, is compound growth. Each pair of coupling rabbits could produce several more rabbits, and the *growth upon growth* continued to escalate wildly.

> Compound growth outstrips linear growth,
> so it must only be used wisely.

This short tale of short tails demonstrates two things rather neatly. Firstly, where growth is compounding in its nature rather than linear or arithmetic, its reach and impact can be beyond staggering. Secondly, while compounding growth can be an incredibly powerful force where it is used to your benefit, the unintended consequences from the misuse thereof or poor planning can also potentially be devastating. Despite the construction of three colossal rabbit-proof fences, those seemingly-innocent bunnies continue to destroy millions of dollars of crop value every year. The compounding effect has seemingly taken on a life of its own.

What I want you to take away from this is that it is entirely possible to get your dollars breeding for you if you know what you are doing in order to multiply your wealth. If you can resolve to invest your earnings rather than spending them on consumer goods, each and every dollar you earn and then save can be sent out to breed more dollars for you and keep bringing more money back to you...forever. You can achieve this if you learn to acquire the right assets.

Once you understand this, it becomes easier to make the paradigm shift from an earn-and-spend mentality to an earn-save-and-invest lifestyle. Typically, for every 100 dollars you earn the taxman takes perhaps a third, and most (if not all) of the rest gets spent on necessities and luxuries. What if you could find a way to invest your income before the taxman gets his hands on it? What if you could grow and compound every dollar you earn in *perpetuity*?

A fair day's pay

While I was living in East Timor, I became great friends with a young local chap who owns a coffee plantation in the mountains. Coffee plantations are a tough industry to make profits in, and one day he asked me to come and try picking coffee for a day. Always game for a challenge I spent a weekend picking coffee on the plantation.

It was tough work in the extremely humid dry season climate, and I was consistently amazed with the speed with which the locals could pick coffee. Even the elderly ladies could easily pick three times the volume of beans that I could. The owner of the plantation explained to me that locals could be paid around one US dollar for each day of work.

This all reminded me of an old story – more of a fable really – wherein a young man goes to work on a farm, and the farmer offers him thirty dollars pay for thirty days of work. The young man smiled and instead offered the farmer that he would work for just one cent per day, providing that for each day of quality work he completed, the farmer would agree to double his pay.

Sensing a potential bargain the farmer accepted the offer and in the first few days he was happy enough as the boy's pay doubled to two cents on day two, then four cents on day three, and then eight cents for the fourth day. You may be able to guess where the story is heading. Had this been a true story rather than a fable, the farmer would have quickly been sent bankrupt and the boy would have become a very wealthy young man because by the thirtieth day the farmer would have been paying the boy more than 5 million dollars for only one day of work!

This is an amusing little parable but the theme comes back to one of the most powerful forces in investment - compounding. Any number of examples could be given. If you come somehow fold a piece of paper a couple of dozen times it would be thick enough to reach the moon. If you placed one grain of rice on the first square of a chessboard, and two on the second, four on the third, and so on, by the time you had reached the final square all of the rice in India would not be enough to cover the number of grains needed.

Salary income is linear – it does not compound.

These examples are important to the extent that they demonstrate the tremendous force that can be applied through a comprehensive understanding of compounding. The problem with a salary is that - unlike in the story above where the boy is able to double his pay each day simply by asking his boss – earned employment income tends to be linear. Each day starts afresh and you must start earning again the next morning.

As an employee you are paid for your time, and should you decide or are forced by circumstance to stop turning up for work you will quite quickly find that you are no longer getting paid. Since there are only so many hours in a year, salary income is capped at the level of your pay per hour multiplied by however many thousand hours you decide to commit to hard graft.

Income from investment and business need not be linear. In fact, if you can understand how to use compound growth to your advantage in investment then you can generate wealth beyond what may presently be your wildest dreams. In the forthcoming chapters I am going to show you in some detail how you can compound your wealth using property and share investments, and also how you can also compound your education and your quality of life.

The Snowball

The Snowball is the title of a book by Alice Schroeder within which she wrote in great detail about the life of perhaps the greatest share market investor in history, Warren Buffett.[1] Buffett is the perfect example of how compounding growth can work to create massive wealth, because he truly and comprehensively understood how continuing to own and invest in assets which create an income and grow in value over time can create stupendous returns. Here is a quote from Schroeder in her book:[2]

'The most important thing to understand is the value of time - and this is something that has come from observing Buffett, learning his story and learning that time compounds. What you do when you are young (and as you use time over your life) can have an exponential effect so that if you are thoughtful about it, you can really have powerful results later, if you want to.

Also, that is a reason to be hopeful, because compounding is something that happens pretty quickly. If you are 50 or 60, it is not too late. He said to me one time, if there is something you really want to do, don't put it off until you are 70 years old...do it now. Don't worry about how much it costs or things like that, because you are going to enjoy it now. You don't even know what your health will be like then.

On the other hand, if you are investing in your education and you are learning, you should do that as early as you possibly can, because then it will have time to compound over the longest period. And that the things you do learn and invest in should be knowledge that is cumulative, so that the knowledge builds on itself.'

Warren Buffett is an optimal example of an investor who understands the force of compounding. His company Berkshire Hathaway was able to produce 20 percent per annum returns over a period of decades from investments, and due to the compounding effect Buffett became a multi-billionaire as well as one of the wealthiest men and greatest ever charitable givers.[3]

Buffett understood compounding so well that even as one of the wealthiest men to have ever lived he drove a second hand car. Of course, had Buffett felt that buying a new car would make him a happier person he would doubtless have gone out and bought one, but with a strong sense of opportunity cost and what he could achieve with that money instead, he opted for the value proposition. Once you understand the opportunity cost of money spent on luxury items, this should automatically help to curb your spending habits.

The rule of 72

I noted previously that although by profession I am a Chartered Accountant, I will resist the temptation to overwhelm you with numbers in this book. I will use a few numerical examples, of course, but the numbers will be relatively simple in nature.

Compounding growth can occur where a return is generated on a growth investment for which ownership is retained, whether it is shares, property or your business. For example, if you had a bank account which had $10,000 in it and the bank was offering a return of 5 percent per annum, at the end of the first year and assuming no tax, you would have $10,500. If you added no additional funds to this account, but simply relied on the interest being paid by the bank, your $10,500 would then turn into $11,025 by the end of the second year.

Savings can be eroded by inflation and taxes.

Unfortunately interest income in a bank account is usually taxed and inflation tends to eat away at the purchasing power of the balance, so money in the bank is rarely an effectively tool for compounding your wealth. As you can see from the short example above, the rate of return and the time in which the money is invested determines how much money you are going to accumulate over the life of the investment. Crucially, note how if you can find investment whereby your unrealised gains are not taxed the compounding interest in year two will be higher than that in year one – the returns are very gradually starting to snowball.

The simplest way to calculate how compounding will impact an investment is to use the Rule of 72. This rule uses a very simple formula which divides the number 72 by the compounding annual rate of return in order to calculate how quickly an investment will double in value.

The below table gives an example of several different rates of return and how many years it would take to double the value of the investment based upon the Rule of 72. For example, if you bought a house which increased in value by 6 percent per annum, in just 12 years it would have doubled in value (72/6 = 12). Intuitively you might expect an asset which increased in value at 10 percent per annum to double in value in a decade. But in fact, due to the compounding effect – growth upon growth – in only 7.2 years the asset would have doubled in value (72/10 = 7.2).

Figure 3.1 – How quickly an investment doubles in value

Rate of return (percent)	Years for investment to double in value
5	14.4
6	12
7	10.2
8	9
9	8
10	7.2
15	4.8
20	3.6

The implications of this are very powerful. If you can learn the skills to invest in high value assets which appreciate at a rate of around 8 percent per annum, they will continue to double in value in every 9 years, and this can make you very wealthy.

6 to 8 percent returns

I am going to use an assumption through this book that you can learn the skills to attain returns of 6 to 8 percent from your investments. In share markets, historically it has been possible to attain average returns of a significantly higher figure than 8 percent, and it may be possible that you can continue to do so into the future. Over long periods of time, it has been possible to generate returns at double digit levels in percentage terms.

However, generally speaking we have likely transitioned into an era of lower inflation, lower economic growth and lower gross returns, so to be conservative I will assume that an investment in a well-diversified equities product can generate returns of 8 percent – approximately 4 percent from dividends (which can be taken as income or reinvested in more shares to compound your wealth) and 4 percent from capital growth.

The nature of stock markets is such that you will not see these returns every year. Some years will likely be amazing and others possibly quite dire, but over the course of a market cycle you should be able to compound returns by at least 8 percent per annum, with potentially a pleasant surprise to the upside.

> Investment returns can be volatile from year to year,
> but quality assets can compound over time.

Returns from property investment are a hotly debated subject. I am going to assume in this book that you can learn the skills to generate 6 to 8 percent capital growth per annum from investment property. Now straight away people will leap in here and suggest that it is not possible for the price of property to outpace the growth of household incomes in perpetuity and therefore this figure is unrealistic.

And in one sense, they would be exactly right. I wholeheartedly agree that is not possible for the price of all property to outpace incomes forever. That would not make any sense, because if property prices kept increasing ahead of income growth eventually only those with existing equity could afford to buy.

However, I most certainly do not suggest buying *any* property. I only recommend buying the property types in locations which will easily outperform the averages over time. Over the last two decades I have gradually been forced to change my opinion on returns from investment property, as I will explain in a little more detail below and in later chapters of the book.

> Times have changed since the subprime crisis.

When the global financial crisis hit, various certain markets around the world which had become overheated, including various housing markets in Ireland, the US and Spain, collapsed quite dramatically. This led many pundits to declare the household debt super-cycle to be over and that residential property is a dud investment. This appeared to be a logical conclusion, and no doubt if you bought property at the peak of the market in Ireland you may take that viewpoint. But it is partly quite wrong.

Several housing markets from around the globe which had been in bubble territory did crash, of that there is no doubt, but quality, well-located investments in continually strong demand areas just kept on rising. In the United Kingdom for example certain regional and remote property markets corrected sharply and took fully seven or more years to recover even in nominal terms. In real terms, when adjusted for inflation, property prices in many areas have gone backwards.

Yet property prices in certain key suburbs of central London where I invest, and had always recommended investing, simply kept on rising. In fact, price growth accelerated with the median London house price gaining an astonishing 25 percent in the year to June 2014.[4] Similarly median prices in certain key suburbs of Sydney appreciated by well over 50 percent in the half decade after the financial crisis.[5] Because my portfolio of investment properties was largely focused on Sydney and London, my returns have actually accelerated since 2007. Depending on when you are reading this book, the best cities to invest in property may have changed.

We have moved into a new economic era since the financial crisis.

Clearly property prices do not continue in that vein forever, but if you know what you are doing, if you can apply some market timing skills, and in particular if you can learn to carry out the research which I will show you in this book, it can be possible to attain capital growth of 8 percent per annum over time which can compound your wealth.

Notably, it has become more and more clear that certain types of prime location real estate in global cities are being used as a store of wealth by international investors. If you can understand where these capital flows are increasingly being directed, as well as demonstrate the ability to time the market through buying investments counter-cyclically when sentiment is weak, you can comfortably outperform the median price growth of national property markets.

Just as in the share markets, you will not see that level of capital growth in each and every year, but averaged out over market cycles, it can be done.

My wife and I have been doing exactly that for the past two decades with our property portfolios, and that includes straight through the middle of the greatest global financial crisis since the Great Depression of the 1930s. Due to the power of leverage – using borrowed funds – even if your returns are lower than this you can still multiply your wealth year after year in order to generate very substantial equity over time. However, since leveraged investing introduces risk, you must get the research right if creating property wealth is to be your goal.

Changing times

When the latest financial crisis was triggered when the US subprime fallout hit, experts were out in force to declare the end of the world for residential real estate, yet because of where my property investments were located in quality inner suburbs of cities such as Sydney and London, low interest rates actually saw the rate of capital growth on my investments accelerate.

In short, times have changed. The world has gone through a structural shift and entered an era of low interest rates, lower inflation, and slower global economic growth and, for many developed countries, weaker national and household income growth. In order to achieve outperforming returns you do need to be able to analyse property markets in some detail and I will explain in this book some of the key demographic shifts and the dramatic changes in the use of household debt which you need to understand in more detail.

In particular it is no longer good enough to simply wait for currency depreciation to inflate away the value of mortgage debt and nor is it sufficient to pray for rising household debt to float the price of all real estate even higher. Those days are gone and are well behind us. The financial crisis and crashing share markets has changed the way the world views real estate as a potential store of wealth, and if you can understand where global capital will flow you can benefit from this huge structural shift.

That said, I cannot do it all for you and make explicit recommendations in this book, because what is right for one investor is not necessarily right for another. You will ultimately need to either learn how to analyse property markets at a localised or micro level, which I discuss later in the book, or engage a professional who can do that for you.

Belief systems determine everything.

Your belief systems are everything when it comes to investment and life. This is a great case in point. If you believe that it is not possible to create great wealth through shares and property, then this will be true…for you. Yet others will continue to do so as they have throughout the course of modern human history.

This may seem esoteric, but I have seen with my own eyes time and again how belief systems affect investment strategy. Someone who believes that property can be a good investment can buy a quality asset and hold it through the inevitable bear markets and cyclical downturns in sentiment. On the other hand someone who does not believe it is possible to create wealth through real estate will panic and sell at the worst possible moment, that being the nadir of the cycle, thereby inevitably confirming their own belief that property is a dud investment.

Owning property and the land which sits underneath it will be an incredible investment over the next few decades, but only if you own land and the right types of properties in the right locations. You must learn how to recognise demographic trends to invest in the outperforming property types and locations or engage an expert to do so for you, but I assure you it most certainly can and will be done over time.

With the advent of the internet, there will be of course predictions of property crashes every year, without fail. And in some years there will indeed be property market corrections. Of that there is no doubt. But if you can learn to understand economic data, demographic trends and household formation rates, you can still make outstanding returns from property markets through the cycles, while the corrections will present buying opportunities for the educated investor.

Making money while you sleep

When you invest in great assets, it is said that you make more money while you are asleep. Why? The answer to this is closely aligned to Warren Buffett's points on the snowballing of returns – the longer your own quality assets for, the greater the opportunity for the snowballing or compounding effect to work its magic. The problem for so many people is that they invest in shares in companies and then watch them daily or even hourly as the share prices first tick up and then tick back down again. They fret over every news report and worry that they will become the next victim of a stock market crash.

It is important to build a strategy which brings you peace of mind.

This is the wrong approach to investing for most people. Instead, you need to have an approach to investment that gives you total peace of mind so that you do not need to watch the markets every day. I will discuss later in the book how to do this, firstly through investing regularly which averages out your entry cost, and secondly through owning great assets that you do not need to worry about over the long term. These include assets such as index funds, quality, low-cost Listed Investment Companies (LICs) and well-located residential property.

It is said that you can make more money from quality investments while you sleep. It's true – but why is this so? Because while you are asleep quality assets that you own continue to work for you and since you are not worrying about them you are far less likely to mistakenly sell in a panic!

How quickly can I be financially free?

Over the years while undertaking mentoring of clients there is one question which I have been asked more than any other:

'How quickly can I be financially free and retire?'

My advice is usually to try to think a little differently. Instead of having it in mind to create a certain amount of wealth at which point you will quit your job and retire to the Caribbean, a caravan park or a cruise ship (depending upon how and where you set your goals), instead to try to consider how you can build a plan to snowball your wealth for the rest of your life…and even *beyond* your own lifetime.

This is a major mind-set shift for most people to make, but I believe that it is a vitally important one. One of the major challenges facing people today is to stop thinking of money as something to be earned and then spent. Instead, try to consider how the money you earn can be invested in assets which will grow and compound for you in perpetuity. If you can identify quality assets which will continue to generate return for decades and decades into the future, suddenly you can begin to maximise your wealth-creation plan. There will never be a need to sell and you can continue to multiply your wealth for as long as you live.

Using this information practically

I have introduced some ideas in this chapter, but how can you use them practically? I am going to suggest that if your goal is to escape from the rat race of reliance on a pay cheque relatively quickly you probably need to use a buy-and-hold approach investment property as well as equities products, and in this short section I will show you a handful of charts to explain why.

In chapter 5, I will go on to consider how the number of dollars you would be likely to earn from a lifetime in employment could be far higher than you might intuitively expect, and consequently it is not so much a question of whether you can earn a couple of million dollars. Rather it should be a question of whether you can *keep* that amount!

How can you accelerate your returns?

What if you want to achieve financial freedom sooner than the traditional retirement age? The ideas already introduced in this chapter should tell you that what you need is a portfolio of quality assets or investments which you can hold on to forever, which will continue to grow and compound for as long as you live. Then, if you so wish you can also begin to focus on building a business to gradually replace your salary income rather than focusing on chasing an ever-higher salary which accrues ever-higher tax liabilities.

Let us look at some simple numbers. Suppose you were able to invest $5000 in the share market and attain average returns of over 8 percent per annum, reinvesting your dividends, and each year you are able to invest an extra $5000 per annum. This is one of the most efficient forms of investing, because by not trading (continually buying and selling in a bid to try to time the market) you do not incur unnecessary transaction costs and you do not become liable for capital gains taxes each time you sell for a profit.

> Buying and holding quality investments is the most efficient way to build wealth that exists.

Even by only investing the same amount each year, the gains of 8 percent per annum keep growing and compounding so that the size of the portfolio gradually begins to accelerate. Of course, the returns will not be as smooth as this because share markets are liquid - they are easy for investors and traders to buy into and sell out of as suits them - and therefore tend to be fairly volatile.

However, for those with a long term outlook share market gyrations need not be a major concern. Indeed, the averaging effect of buying a set dollar amount of shares at regular intervals means that you effectively buy more shares when the market is depressed and has careered lower, and correspondingly acquire fewer shares when the market is exuberant and has bolted higher.

While the principle here is more important the absolute numbers, which will naturally vary depending upon your income and the amount of money you can make available to invest, you can see that over time it is easily possible to build a reasonable net worth. In fact, if you are planning to remain in the workforce for decades, you can easily adopt this approach of buying a diversified portfolio of quality shares hard and often and holding them for the long haul. It is a proven and time-tested long term route to wealth.

Figure 3.2 – Investing $5000 per annum in equities

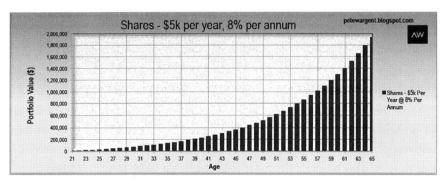

What if you could get money to work for you sooner and for longer? The results are quite surprising because of the sheer power of the compounding effect. In the above example $5000 has been contributed to the portfolio each year, and thus total contributions come to $225,000.

What if you could simply invest $100,000 in the stock market today and leave it there for the long term? Surprisingly, over the course over a typical working career that amount invested could grow and compound to around $3 million, even with no extra funds invested. This is where the phrase 'money goes to money' comes from. The dice are very much loaded in favour of the wealthy who have more financial capacity to invest in quality assets for longer and they become richer and richer with each passing year.

Figure 3.3 - $100,000 invested at 8 percent per annum

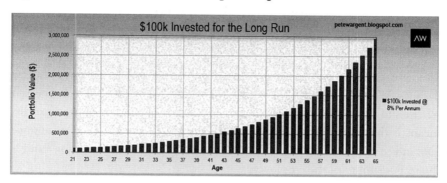

The vital point to take away here is that if you want to achieve financial freedom sooner, then you will likely need to invest as hard as you can as young as you can. You need to have as many dollars as you can working for you as long as possible. When you consider the chart above, it makes one wonder how it can be that so few people truly retire wealthy. How is it that the average pension balance at retirement is so meagre and so many rely on government assistance after they retire?

One of the reasons is that life simply gets in the way. A redundancy happens, or some emergency expenditure comes along. Increasing numbers of people these days become separated or divorced, which is one of the most effective ways of destroying your net worth. Growing up in a broken family myself I have seen first hand the dramatic difference that divorce makes to the financial health of a household.

I once had a boss, the CEO of a firm that I worked for, who said to me: 'Pete, the single best piece of financial advice I can give you is this…don't get divorced!' I suspect that he may have been talking from a position of personal experience. Regardless, he was spot on! The concept of compounding or snowballing your wealth is many times more powerful if you do not allow a major life event such as this to get in the way of your results.

> Spend less than you earn, and invest the
> difference in compounding assets.

Another reason that retirement balances are often so paltry is that so few people truly understand the impact of compounding and therefore are quite content to spend every cent they earn and then some. Expensive holidays are particularly easy to justify after a hard year of work. New cars are seen as a necessity instead of what they actually are, which is a proven destroyer of wealth, a depreciating asset which declines in value from the moment you trundle away from the garage forecourt.

The nature of pensions has also changed quite dramatically over the last few decades. We have lived through a structural shift from defined *benefit* pension schemes to defined *contribution* or accumulation schemes. In short, what this means is that while pension amounts to be received at retirement were once guaranteed by the employer or by the government, today the pension fund is the responsibility of the employee.

Your pension is your own responsibility.

People are often confused on this point, thinking that because the management of their pension is delegated to a fund manager their pension is someone else's responsibility. This could not be further from the truth! Your pension balance is your own responsibility and you must decide how it is managed and by whom, or whether you decide to manage it yourself. Another of the reasons that people do not successfully build for their retirement is that the pension system is not really set up for you to win. Firstly, this is because the dollar amounts invested are not allowed to grow and compound in the most efficient manner, with pension funds churning over stocks repeatedly in a vain attempt to beat the market. Since institutional funds in aggregate largely *are* the market, this achieves very little except for generating transaction costs and triggering capital gains tax points.

Secondly, pension fund managers clip out management fees in good years and in bad with the management fee typically based upon a percentage of the amount you have invested, which means that the fees charged tend to increase over time as your pension balance increases. It is therefore little wonder so many pension balances at retirement are such a puny reward for decades spent in the workforce and the hundreds of months of contributions paid in.

If you want to become financially free sooner, the way in which this becomes possible is to invest as much as you can as young as you can in assets that you never need to sell. This very simple point is precisely why I believe that - if you want to escape the rat race of reliance or dependence on a pay cheque - you ideally need to own or invest in residential investment property. For the average investor the leverage you can use is generally so much greater than that available in any other asset class that you can achieve results more quickly, provided you invest with an appropriate level of detailed research and skill.

To become financially free sooner...you need to invest more, sooner.

Take the below example where instead of investing $100,000 in the share market, the investor has used that amount as a deposit to invest in a $1 million property which appreciates at 8 percent per annum. For the sake of simplicity we have ignored transaction costs here, which can be a material dollar figure when in investing in residential property.

Due to the snowballing or compounding effect the property doubles in value in only 9 years (remember the Rule of 72) and after a decade is worth $2.15 million, generating equity or net worth of well over $1.25 million. The investor is comfortably a millionaire in only one decade through the use of leverage and allowing the value of the property to grow and compound totally unimpeded by transaction costs or capital gains taxes.

Figure 3.4 – Becoming a property millionaire?

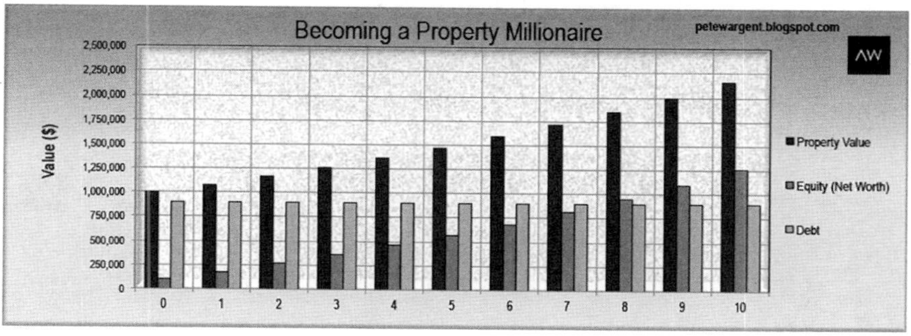

Of course, just as in the share market price gains do not occur in such a linear fashion, so it is with residential property. Instead in a typical market cycle capital city property prices tend to be flat or declining for a period of some years before entering a recovery and then ultimately booming, before again returning to a downturn phase. And indeed, the asset selected might take significantly longer than nine years to double in value. No matter, for now it is the principle here that is important, in particular because the investor who builds equity is typically able to redraw a portion of it to invest in other assets.

Recurrent property market cycles tend to repeat due to the nature of housing market economics, whereby construction increases in response to rising prices until the market is fully supplied or over-supplied, putting downward pressure on the market. The cycles are also partly due to the human emotions of fear and greed, which are always in evidence in financial markets. The chart back in Figure 3.2 showed the tremendous impact of being able to invest more money sooner, which, all things being equal in terms of returns and holding period, achieves results far in excess even of the sensible approach investing smaller amounts regularly over the years.

So what if you could learn how to invest millions of dollars safely? The short answer is that you can generate more wealth than you may ever have believed possible. This is true even if you cannot generate 8 percent capital returns as the chart below clearly shows. In fact, if you use the newly created equity to acquire more investments the equity you can build over a lifetime could potentially be boundless, providing that you are sensible and always resolve to maintain a healthy buffer for the inevitable market downturns.

Of course, people tend to scoff as such obviously over-simplified examples. However, note that if there is one single trait that all of those doing the scoffing often have in common, it is that they have never successfully built a portfolio of investment properties themselves.

Figure 3.5 - $3 million invested for the long haul

Observe how where a consistent growth rate is achieved on an asset, the dollar value of returns are not constant - your wealth does not go up in a straight line. It accelerates because of the compounding effect. The implications of this are several. Firstly, if you want to achieve financial independence at a young age you probably either need to be investing in residential property or you need to be able build a big business.

Now don't get me wrong, shares can be a wonderful investment when you know what you are doing, and contrary to popular belief shares are also a *safe* investment for building wealth slowly but surely. If you are planning on earning a regular salary income for decades to come there is no safer way to build wealth that I know of than to invest consistent dollar amounts into a diversified share market portfolio or product regularly.

> Leveraged investing in an extremely powerful tool,
> but also a double-edged sword.

And the simple fact of the matter is that to invest millions of dollars into any market quickly introduces a level of risk which must be managed correctly. However, the way in which it becomes possible to use millions of dollars safely is by investing in the right type of property which appreciates in value, to draw out *some* of the equity to use on further investments, but always maintaining a sizeable buffer.

At various times in the lending markets it has been possible to use 100 percent mortgages (or even sometimes 105 percent mortgages). This can certainly work as a strategy over the long haul and I have even used 100 percent mortgages myself previously. However, what the global financial crisis demonstrated neatly is that when banks are starting to throw around 100 percent mortgages this is also likely to be the period in the cycle when there is an elevated level of risk in the market.

It is far better to take your time and always maintain a reasonable buffer of cash to protect against market downturns or an unforeseen period of unemployment. You should also always maintain an equity buffer between the value of your property portfolio and investment mortgages to protect against adverse market movements.

More than anything else, it is important not to buy rubbish. There have been a proliferation of real estate books over the years which have taught 'investors' how to buy rubbish properties in one-horse regional towns with miserable economic prospects due to the seemingly attractive rental yields. This is totally the wrong approach to investing in property. Instead you should invest in quality properties in landlocked and thriving capital city locations where the population of the city and demand for property is guaranteed to increase for as long as you live.

The vital importance of buy and hold

In every economic cycle and financial markets cycle it will be said that buy and hold is dead as a concept and in the future you will need to be cleverer by trading in and out of markets faster than everyone else does. In aggregate, of course, this is not possible for all investors to do since it is a zero sum game and most traders achieve very little. Only the skilful and experienced traders with great money management skills will win at this game and everyone else gets 'ticket clipped' or wiped out entirely.

The problems with trading financial assets are threefold. Firstly, there are transaction costs involved in buying and selling most assets, such as brokerage fees, stamp duty or agent fees. Secondly, there are capital gains taxes to pay on the sale of an asset where you have made money. And thirdly, most people are generally far less skilful at timing the market than they think they are, this being a deceptively challenging skill to master.

> Success happens neither overnight, nor in a straight line.

Building a retirement portfolio should be a relatively straightforward exercise. Buy quality assets and hold them for the long term. So how then, do so many folk end up requiring a state pension? In most cases this is because for some reason compounding growth has not been allowed to work for them. Perhaps they traded their house half a dozen times and the transaction costs involved in doing so kept on piling up.

If you came from a split family as I did, you will sadly know only too well the financial complications and setbacks that can eventuate from a divorce or other such significant life event such as a period of unemployment. During recessions jobs can be lost and financial buffers are eroded while a new job is sought. Other people simply spend every dollar they earn, which is the one sure-fire way to achieve very little financially!

For many reasons, wealth is not always built successfully throughout a working lifetime. The best chance you have of continuing to compound your wealth is to invest in assets which you never have to sell because they will keep earning you ever more income and continuing to grow in value for as long as you live.

Designing the life you want to live

I have talked a little about my investing philosophies in this chapter, but this is not only a book about investing. It is also about how you can design the life that you want to lead and how you might consider turning your passion into your business, either through you setting up a business of your own or getting a job in your field of passion.

However, it is nevertheless true that life can be far more satisfying if you have your financial future secured before you replace your paid employment career with your passion. Simply put, securing your financial future first takes the pressure of that particular area of your life. The numbers in this chapter merely form a broad overview of what might be possible, and later in the book I will show you how in practical terms you can achieve these outstanding returns. What this chapter does demonstrate is the power of getting more money to work for you sooner and therefore for longer.

Chapter 3 summary

» The sooner you invest in quality assets, the better your results will be over time

» The most efficient form of investment is to buy and hold quality assets for the long term

» Asset classes which you can use to snowball your wealth include shares and well-located capital city real estate

» If you want to build a large portfolio more quickly, residential property is the asset class which gives you the leverage to achieve this

---

4
Golden Rule #3
The Pleasure-Pain
Principle

4

'There's a very fine line between pleasure and pain. They are two sides of the same coin, one not existing without the other.'
– E.L. James.

Your past does not equal your future

It is all too easy to believe that because in the past you have not necessarily fulfilled your potential then it must always necessarily be so. Nothing could be further from the truth! The past need not in any way equal the future. Look at the lives of the most successful people in their fields and you will often find that before they achieved great success they also ground down many of the same challenges that face lesser mortals.

Famously the great British author J. K. Rowling saw her initial *Harry Potter* manuscripts rejected by a dozen publishers before finding a publishing house executive who was wise enough to let his nine year old daughter proof-read the draft manuscripts for him, thus allowing the true magic of her work to be discovered.[1] And as the popular media never tires of reminding us, Rowling had previously battled through family illness and feuds and other personal traumas. There was to be no shortage of people willing to come forward and discuss how apparently limited her talents were in younger years.

Yet J.K. Rowling went to on to produce one the most popular book series ever written, at the same time amassing personal fortune of well over half a billion pounds. Today, she is recognised as one of the most prolific charitable givers in British history. Of course, there was a a stream of people who came forward to tell us how unremarkable J.K. Rowling was before she found fame and success - if anything, this only underscores the fact that persistence pays off. The take-away point is that your past need not equal your future. This has been proven time and time again.

Not random creatures

The Pleasure-Pain Principle is important because it can help you to understand human behaviour and therefore how to be more successful in *everything* that you do. While the behaviour of individuals may at times appear to be quite random, it is not so. Importantly, if you can understand the Pleasure-Pain

Principle you can also begin to comprehend why you are achieving satisfactory results in some parts of your life, but poor results in others. More excitingly, you can use the Pleasure-Pain Principle as a tool to change the results that you are getting in life dramatically.

It is vital for all of us to realise and then understand that we as humans are not random creatures. Everything which we do, every choice we make and each action we take, happens for a reason. We may not always be aware of the reasons for our actions, of course, and often times we just seem to *do* stuff without really thinking about it. But whether it is conscious or unconscious, nevertheless there is an underlying driver for our behaviours.

What stops you from saving your income, from starting a business, from building a portfolio of investments for the future or from aiming for the goals and life of your dreams? What stops you from following your passion? Usually procrastination ultimately comes back to an inherent imbalance between pleasure and pain. Often the pain of uncertainty seems to outweigh the potential pleasure of achieving our goals through taking what may appear to be great risks.

Think about the following question for one moment - what do all of us actually want to achieve in life? Is it not to change the way that we *feel* about life? I believe so. It is true for everyone through history from most bullishly aggressive of Gordon Gecko types to the most caring of Mother Teresa characters. As diverse as these apparently contradictory character traits may appear to be, just like us they have focused on what brings the most pleasure to their lives such as doing large business deals and helping less fortunate people.

Strange though the example may seem, they are also driven to avoid pain. Megalomaniac business types cannot stand coming second at anything in life, seeing life a race to be won – to them people who sleep for more than four hours a day are wasting their time. Mother Teresa could not stand the pain in seeing others suffer, and so devoted her life to ensuring as few people as possible continued to do so.

We all ultimately reach pain thresholds.

In areas of our lives, we can all ultimately reach pain thresholds where we finally decide that change is necessary. In fact, humans will generally go to greater lengths to avoid pain than they will to achieve pleasure. How long will it be before you hit the pain threshold and decide to change? In a job?

In a relationship? In your personal finances? At some point the pain of not changing begins to exceed the short term relief and apparent comfort of the maintaining the status quo.

Perhaps the most interesting and also important aspects of the Pleasure-Pain Principle is that we will most often do more to avoid pain than we will to do whatever it takes to achieve the ultimate pleasure of sustained success. We frequently take short term measures to dodge relatively small individual instances of pain, but this approach rarely works towards our long term advantage.

Why do people drink to excess, chain smoke or take drugs every day? Is it for the pleasure? Perhaps in the first instance. But there must surely be little pleasure in a drug addict living in a squat desperately fumbling for a syringe to take away the agonising withdrawal symptoms. Is a smoker really enjoying their thirtieth cigarette of the day? Probably not. The addiction is caused by the pain of withdrawal, which keeps the smoker coming back again and again to avoid it. This is only one simple analogy but similar patterns are repeated throughout our existence on this planet.

'Numbing the pain for a while will make it worse when you finally feel it.'
- J.K. Rowling, *Harry Potter and the Goblet of Fire.*

Indelibly linked to the Pleasure-Pain Principle is the fact that far too often people adopt a short term approach to life instead of focussing on long term results, and thus they drift through life with no firm plan, as if carried on a river with strong flow. Anthony Robbins, a leader in the science of peak performance, coined the phrase *Niagara Syndrome* to describe this phenomenon.[2]

People are so often carried along by a current through life with no real plan of where they are trying to get to. Instead they focus on avoiding the next rock and keeping their head above water, until eventually they are dragged close to the edge of the waterfall. At this stage they may try to swim against the tide, but it is often too late and they are destined for a big fall, be it emotional, financial, a relationship crash or another type of fall.

It does not have to be that way, but you need to take control of your future by setting some inspiring goals and then putting together a specific plan to reach those goals. The alternative is to allow your life to be carried along in a haphazard manner which will necessarily lead at best to haphazard results.

So many of the world's crises can be explained by these insightful analogies. You may not necessarily equate the global financial crisis or sub-prime meltdown to the Pleasure-Pain Principle, yet the global economic crash was a classic case in a long human history of pleasure and pain influencing decisions adversely throughout the entire debacle, leading ultimately to catastrophe.

Global financial crisis

Rewinding to around the turn of the century, the dotcom bubble finally burst and stock markets crashed. In the US the Federal Reserve slashed interest rates in an attempt to stimulate the economy and save the US from the *pain* of a recession. As can often be the case, low borrowing rates fuelled an apparent boom in real estate. The returns on fixed interest investments such as US Treasury Bills consequently became very low and therefore investment capital had to look elsewhere for a worthwhile return.

> Humans will frequently do more to avoid short term pain than we will do to experience longer term and lasting pleasure.

Bank executive remuneration and compensation schemes are meant to be designed to encourage long term planning. In reality, executives are often far too motivated to take short term risks in order to meet their immediate targets and secure annual bonuses. And so it was in the run-up to the subprime crisis.

Within this framework of short termism and a hungry drive for profits, the private sector understood that the one sector of the market where they could create serious in-roads was subprime lending, being the issuance of higher risk loans. In a tragic case of the 80/20 Principle being chronically misunderstood, 80 percent of the subprime mortgages that were written came from private sector lending, with some 12 million mortgages written worth an astonishing $2 trillion in 2006.[3]

> Continually attempting to avoid short term pain can be severely counter-productive over the long term.

With private sector and non-bank lenders bringing new and innovative products to market, it was then the turn of the commercial banks to feel the pain of missing out until they too felt forced to get creative. Huge entities with strange sounding nicknames derived from acronyms like Fannie Mae

(FNMA) and Freddie Mac (FHLMC) joined the subprime party in order to avoid missing out on the short term profits and gains.

A fear of missing out is what drives irrational exuberance in markets.

Meanwhile, with interest rates significantly lower than they had been in times past, asset managers felt increasingly starved of yield and also felt the pain of lower profits and lower compensation payments. They became compelled to conceive of new ideas to generate the equivalent level of profits that had once come so much more easily, and through some apparently clever creative thinking came up with the idea of *bundling* mortgages as a way to link mortgages to investors. After all, a mortgage is simply another form of bond, so why not treat it like one?

With interest rates still stuck at relatively low levels in 2006, Wall Street firms were able to utilise significant levels of cheap credit or leverage in order to snaffle up bundled mortgages which investment banks packaged together into what were known as CDOs which could seemingly be made safer through the use of a type of insurance known as Credit Default Swaps (CDSs). Unfortunately, the complicated web of transactions disguised that these new products were potentially toxic yet the credit rating agencies ranked them at their highest available rating of AAA mistakenly believing that the insurance made them a safer prospect.

Notably it was also felt that ultimately a mortgage ought to be a relatively safe product since if the homeowner defaulted then the house could be liquidated in a fire-sale in order to cover the outstanding mortgage balance. In other words, while a person who defaults on their mortgage might be able to disappear, a house and land is unlikely to be going anywhere. While this is essentially fine in theory, what this overlooks was that if the housing market collapses and there are no buyers, then there will still be insufficient value left in the house. This, incidentally, is why I never recommend buying property in illiquid regional markets and implore investors to instead look at well located capital city property for which there is always a strong demand.

Fund managers dived in and bought the newly created investment products with inadequate due diligence or consideration of the consequences, while banks had had their capital requirements loosened by the Securities and Exchange Commission (SEC) which simply added fuel to the increasingly raging fire.

Avoid investing in highly illiquid markets at all costs.

When the dam burst it was soon discovered that investments held in mortgages which defaulted were not worth a great deal. Those who had bought CDOs faced a similar predicament and as illiquid banks collapsed the insurance was also rendered useless. The financial crisis spread from institution to institution and the US government was forced to step in with its controversial bailout package and the ultimate *pain* was trillions of dollars of taxpayer money. Unfortunately, the taxpayer is the end of the line when it comes to avoiding pain, since there is no-one for the taxpayer to pass the pain on to.

What does this mean for us?

This is an oversimplified view of just a few of the actions which ultimately caused the global financial crisis to play out. In reality, it was an infinitely complex affair with a web of complex derivatives unravelling, but the key point is that the underlying causes are largely explained by human behaviours and in particular the way in which we interact with pleasure and pain. Over and over again people look for ways to avoid short term pain instead of deciding what they need to do in order to achieve longer term pleasure.

You need to link pleasure and pain correctly
to achieve optimal results.

If you can understand what makes people tick and act the way they do, and especially, why *you* act as you do, then you can become the true master of your own destiny. How? Through linking massive *pain* to potentially destructive behaviours and enormous pleasure to those which will bring you the results you truly desire over the long term.

Pleasure and pain in politics

While I have used the subprime crisis as one simple example of the role of pain in human actions and behaviours, and how attempting to avoid short term pain can lead to potentially unthinkably desperate problems later, the same principle can be seen again and again across all spheres of human existence.

Another great example was the arms race between the United States and the Soviet Union. Nuclear weapons were seen as an important tool in gaining national power as well as ensuring defence. After 1947, under President

Truman, the US adopted a strategy aimed at the containment of communism. During the last 18 months of the Truman presidency until 1953 his defence budget quadrupled and the seeds of the end of the Cold War were born. Later the Russians experienced similar problems as Gorbachev found that his arms budget was crippling the country.

> When people associate pain to damaging behaviour patterns, lasting change becomes possible.

While there so many well-meaning folk who campaigned long and hard for nuclear disarmament, the arms race only really began to dissipate when the financial *pain* for the respective governments became too great. This is another superb example of how as humans we often do not make key changes to our lives until the pain has become too great to force us to make key changes. We see similar trends playing out repeatedly, in politics, war, sport and practically any other arena you might care to mention.

Why is this principle so important?

The reason that this is important is because it is perfectly possible for us to train ourselves to link pain and pleasure to the key issues facing us in our lives. If, for example, you have a problem with overeating or consuming too much junk food, it is entirely achievable that you can correct your behaviour patterns over the short term through willpower or abstinence. However, it is less likely that you will achieve long-term success until you can link enough pain to the old pattern and enough equivalent pleasure to a stimulating or empowering new alternative. The same applies to quitting smoking, gambling, consuming too much alcohol, indulging in retail therapy and all manner of other damaging behaviour patterns.

> The Pleasure-Pain Principle can be used scientifically to achieve your ultimate goals.

How exactly can we utilise this knowledge to change our behaviours in order to achieve success? Firstly you need to write down what it is you truly want to achieve, whether it be to become a multi-millionaire, to run your own business or whatever else your ultimate goals may include. Then you must list the limiting behaviour patterns which have prevented you from achieving your goals in the past especially and what this will cost you if you fail to make the required changes. Remember that pain can be a greater driver of change than the pursuit of pleasure. Next, you must list beside those limiting behaviour patterns a new list of empowering alternatives which will allow you to achieve your goals.

Once you have made your list you then need to consciously associate massive pain to the old behaviour patterns until the point that they become utterly unthinkable for to you to continue indulging in. At the same time you need to be able to associate huge and overwhelming pleasure to the new and empowering behaviour patterns. This all sounds great in theory, of course, but how might it work in practice?

Short term versus long-term goals

This all sounds straightforward, so why then do we so often link pleasure and pain to the wrong things? The reason is that we as humans tend to draw immediate associations between pleasure and how we are feeling at that given point in time. Reaching for a bar of chocolate can be a great comfort, and the sweet taste and sugar hit can result in a pleasurable feeling. And I say that as someone who loves chocolate (albeit dairy-free)!

The fact of the matter is, however, that few of our problems are likely to be solved by eating confectionery, and if we keep eating sugary products too regularly, the longer term outcome could indeed be painful, perhaps for your health or even to your hip pocket if a costly trip to the dentist is needed.

Anything which is worth having in life rarely comes easily, and long-term pleasure usually requires short term sacrifice.

The trouble is that too many people get this completely back to front by taking short term pleasure for relief which results in longer term pain. Willpower might only get you so far, so what you need to be able to do is set an inspiring alternative goal which you can work towards and link pleasure to that. Now you understand the principle, the true challenge is to use this to your lasting advantage. In chapter 6 and beyond I will consider the practical use of the Pleasure-Pain Principle in greater detail and in particular how it can be applied to designing compelling and exciting targets for your future in all areas of your life.

Pleasure and pain in investing

The Pleasure-Pain Principle also has great relevance when it comes to how you approach your personal finances and investing. One of the greatest problems I see with my clients and mentees today is that people are focussing on shorter and shorter timeframes, so when markets move down they feel pain. They are always trying to avoid the next rock, but in the meantime they are drifting downstream at alarming speed towards the waterfall. What exactly do I mean by this? By way of an example, take a look at the online coverage of financial markets:

- *'Stocks plummet by 2 percent on profit-taking'*
- *'Share markets recover on value hunting'*
- *'Goldman sees sell signal'*
- *'Gold is in a bearish triangle pattern'*
- *'Analyst recommends rotating from banks into mining stocks'*
- *'Short covering sees weekly trend reversal'*
- *'Analysts warn of property downturn'*
- *'Dwelling prices decline by 0.1 percent in July'*
- *'Is it time to buy property or shares?'*

The jargon that has been invented to describe what is essentially a share price or index moving up or down has expanded beyond belief, from 'head and shoulders patterns' to 'bullish homing pigeons' to 'double bottoms'. I am sure you have also seen the headlines about billions being *wiped off* the market by profit takers, before *bargain hunters* see prices revert upwards again (although billions never seem to be wiped *on* the market, of course).

The language used by the media is particularly noteworthy, frequently preferring to emphasise the negative. Take the British tennis player Andy Murray. Has he ever *lost* a game of tennis in a Grand Slam tournament? Apparently not according to the popular press - he always *crashes out*!

So much time and energy is wasted on guessing what the stock markets and other financial markets are going to do next. And make no mistake here, the overwhelming majority of it is guesswork. Ask ten different fund managers, as they do on the business television channels frequently, and you will get ten different opinions or essentially guesses on what the markets will do next.

What this means is that almost half of the time investors are associating the market with *pain* and not pleasure. Yet a cursory glance at the long-term direction of share markets should tell you most of what you need to know. That is, you should buy quality profit-making and dividend-paying shares and hold them for the long term to benefit from income and capital gains.

Figure 4.1 – Dow Jones 114 year chart

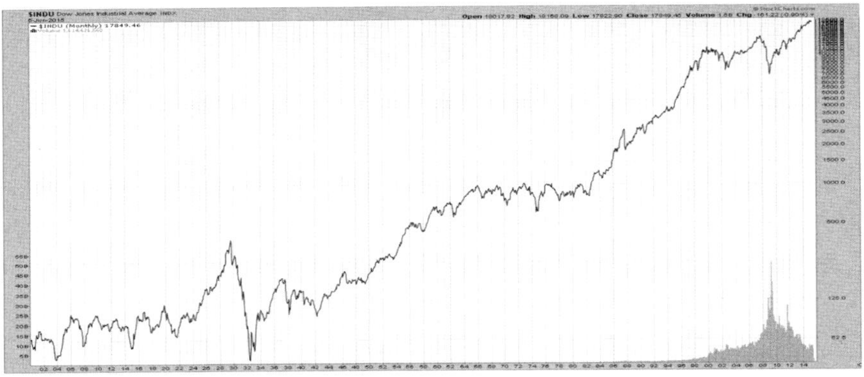

Perhaps the second most common questions I am asked by clients and mentees include these:

'Is it a good time to buy shares?'

'Should I invest in property now?'

The answer, obviously, is 'that depends upon what your strategy is'! If you are buying shares with a view to trading them and selling them in a short timescale, your odds of achieving any success at all are pretty much going to be 50:50. In fact, by the time you deduct your transaction costs, the odds are likely to be even worse than that, and your long-term odds of success with such a strategy are quite likely to be close to nil. The world increasingly seems to have lost sight of the whole point of investing and most amateur investors instead speculate on what prices will do next.

Investing should be about buying shares in a company or a portfolio of companies which generate profits and pay you dividend income. Over time, a profitable and successful company should also see its share price increase, so a long-term investor in successful ventures benefits in more ways than one.

Later in the book, I will discuss the best ventures and products to invest in to achieve this.

Plenty of people these days also like to talk about 'investing' in gold or silver. I have some good friends who are very keen on precious metals, and placing a small part of your net worth in silver or gold might be a sound idea as a hedge or for diversification purposes. But focusing too much on precious metals makes no sense to me. Gold does not actually do anything. It just sits there. It does not make a profit or pay you an income. So, really, buying gold or silver is just pure price speculation - a guess as to what prices will do next or over the long term.

The basic theory put forward by gold-bugs is that the supply of gold is relatively speaking fixed, with only one or two percent added to the total stock each year. Therefore if demand increases, particularly from China or India, then the price must rise over time - provided no huge new reef of gold is found, of course! That is a fair enough premise for a punt or a hedge, but over time this is unlikely to compound your income and wealth in the same way that property and shares can.

Property investing is a slightly different proposition. As funds are usually borrowed to invest in property, after interest costs an investment often generates a negative or neutral cash flow in the early years, leading many to suggest that therefore property investing is also pure price speculation. There is an element of truth in that, but any negative cash flow on a property is purely a result of the way the deal is financed, although repairs and maintenance costs can play their part too.

Quality investments should provide compounding income and capital growth.

What successful long-term real estate investors have learned though is that a property which is owned for the long term, perhaps 15 years or more, can begin to generate very healthy income as the mortgage debt is paid down or inflated away. The rental income from a well located property continues to grow and compound, with prices also driven higher by the increasing demand for real estate in that region or city, provided that you have selected the property well. I will explain to you later in the book what research you need to carry out in order to find the right properties too.

Time should be your greatest ally, not an enemy

I often hear people say that they do not have the time or money to invest, but is this really true? Sometimes, perhaps, but often people who say that cannot afford to invest simply do not want to experience any short term pain in cutting back on what they consider to be necessities such as long overseas holidays or expensive cars. That may be fine, but it is not the same thing as being unable to invest, merely a different priority.

'You have exactly the same number of hours per day that were given to Helen Keller, Pasteur, Michelangelo, Mother Teresa, Leonardo da Vinci, Thomas Jefferson and Albert Einstein. Don't say you don't have enough time.' – H. Jackson Brown, Jnr.

Similarly, when news headlines periodically pop up promoting the notion of an entire generation of youngsters being priced out of the property markets, you have to look beyond the hype. Quite apart from the fact that this is a baseless observation, it also overlooks that any young person can get onto the property ladder if they want it badly enough. It is not easy, however, and they will need to work hard, spend less than they earn and save as if their life depended on it. And I say that as someone who started out my adult life with absolutely nothing to my name financially, so yes I do know exactly how difficult it can be!

Ultimately the pleasure of long-term success in investing can be achieved by anyone, but in life very little that is worth having comes easily. It is likely that you will need to make short term sacrifices in order to achieve long-term goals and take pleasure in achieving them. The way in which this becomes possible is to link directly pain to frivolous expenditure and pleasure towards thrift in the knowledge that your investments will continue to work for you forever.

While your peers will need to work harder and harder just to keep up, you can take pleasure in your investments working harder and harder for you. You will need to make some time to dedicate to investing, and it is also time which can be your greatest ally as an investor. The longer you hold a quality investment for, the more time it has to grow, compound and create wealth for you.

The Pleasure-Pain Principle - transition from dependence on a full time job

In centuries past it was perfectly normal for the average person to be self-employed. In agrarian societies peasants farmed their smallholdings, retained food for the family to eat and sold on the remainder of their produce for a small profit. In the modern world, we are increasingly trained to be employees of corporations, while setting up a business is perceived to be risky.

Often the very hardest step to take in career terms is to set up your own business or become self-employed after you have been an employee. It is hard for many to even imagine a life which is not totally dependent on a pay cheque. Why is this so? Generally, this is due to employees receiving pay rises over time and becoming accustomed to living a standard of living in keeping with the new rate of pay. Each pay rise is subsequently met by a rise in expenditure and employees increase their liabilities and expenditure to match the new level of income - just like any addict they become totally hooked and dependent upon the pay cheque.

Employees often have a mortgage to pay on a house and therefore the prospect of even two months without a pay cheque is pure anathema, and a short period without income would send a high proportion of employees broke. For most employees, therefore, even the very concept of financial freedom, setting up a business or transitioning towards self-employment quickly becomes seen as far too risky a prospect. After all, in the early days of business income may be haphazard or even non-existent.

> For most employees the pain of being without a pay cheque exceeds the potential pleasure of being their own boss.

It becomes seen as too risky to take the chance of experiencing the pain of failure in investing or in business instead of taking the apparently easier option of working up the employment career ladder. I know more than a little about this, because I went through the process myself. As an employee I received a pay rise and a bonus each year, and when I was in my twenties even the idea that I might escape to become financially free or self-employed forever seemed to remain tantalisingly remote. I was simply far too reliant on my pay cheque at that time to even consider that I could achieve the goal.

However, through hard work and sheer persistence I kept building and snowballing my assets until suddenly I had built a considerable net worth. Large enough, in fact, that it became increasingly clear that I was financially free from the dependence on a career job to sustain me. Patiently building and compounding your net worth tends to work like that. When you start out the gains and your progress appear to be relatively moderate and yet often people find that they wake up one day and have achieved more than they could possibly have imagined.

Although I took a couple of years out to travel the world and do some volunteer work, ultimately a fulfilling life does need vision and a purpose, so I then set about building a business. I have always been relatively conservative in my approach and so waited until my wife and I had built a significant net worth before quitting my job. Whether you are able to take such a step sooner depends upon your tolerance for risk, your passion for building a business and your confidence in doing so.

To become financially free, acquire more assets, not liabilities.

Instead of taking out the largest mortgage you can afford on a house and hocking yourself up to the eyeballs on car loans and other liabilities, it is worth considering whether your only debt should be mortgages for investment property. This way you can build up a sizeable portfolio of assets relatively quickly which you can hold for the long term in order to increase your wealth in perpetuity. Once you have established this you can begin to turn your focus away from chasing a salary and towards other income streams from investment and business. Of course, you can still buy a house to live in, but may choose to do it later in life when you have considerably more capital behind you to do so.

It is also worth noting here that by no means must you lurch instantly from working 50 or more hours a week straight down to nil in order to start up a company. That could be a dramatic, challenging and perhaps stressful approach to transitioning out of the corporate or employment rat race. You might elect to work on a part-time or contract basis in the intervening period while you begin to establish your new business or seek employment in a field which you are passionate about.

Rather than seeing financial freedom versus running your own business - or employment versus retirement - as something which must be black and white, try instead to picture a see-saw or counter-balance. Over time you can steadily move from a life which is perhaps nearly 100 percent reliant upon a job or salary, to building a substantial portfolio of investments, to scaling back your paid employment and establishing a business. You can gradually shift from a life which is dictated to you by your career job and your boss towards one within which you call the shots and you choose how you spend your time.

What if money were no object?

Let us stop for a moment and consider this poignant question:

What would you do if money were no object?

If you are in any way like me you will not undertake too many written exercises in books. Rather you will simply observe the above question and muse to yourself internally 'mmm, that's interesting' before moving blithely on to the next paragraph. I am not going to allow you to do that! I will just keep coming back with this question if you do not consider it...

What would you really do if money were no object?

This is an absolutely key consideration, because it must surely form the basis of the life you should be trying to design for yourself. Therefore, it is well worth considering this question for a few moments, for it is the person that asks themselves the right questions in life that finds the right answers and experiences the greatest successes. So consider for a moment. What gets you excited? What gets you out of bed in the morning raring to go? Travel? Sport? Dance? History? Golf? Investing? Surfing? Making money? Reading? Alternative therapies? Fashion? Or something completely different again?

What is it that you are passionate enough about that it would make your life exciting and fulfilling if your work and business revolved around it? I believe that it is a reasonable enough assumption that if you are passionate about something then you will outperform in any business or paid role in that area because you will bring a knowledge and application to that field that few others can hold a torch to. The British philosopher Alan Watts once posed a very similar series of questions when musing upon the question 'what do you desire?' If you have three minutes to spare you can listen to a recording of him speak on the internet, but here is a short transcript:[4]

'What makes you itch? What sort of situation would you like? I do this often in vocational guidance for students. Students come to me and they say 'well we're getting out of college and we haven't the faintest what we want to do'. So I always ask the question, 'what would you like to do if money were no object?' How would you really enjoy spending your life?'

As a result of our kind of educational system, crowds of students say 'well we'd like to be painters, we'd like to be poets, we'd like to be writers, but as everybody knows you can't earn any money that way.' Another person says 'I'd like to live a normal life and ride horses.' I say 'you want to teach in a riding school?'

Let's go through with it. What do you want to do? When we finally got down to something which the individual really wanted to do, I will say to him, 'you do that!' Forget the money because if you say that getting the money is the most important thing you will spend your life completely wasting your time. You'll be doing things you don't like doing in order to go on living, to go on doing things you don't like doing. Which is stupid! Better to have a short life that is full of what you like doing than a long life spent in a miserable way.'

Amen. Do what you are passionate about because you will genuinely enjoy your life, and what is more, your passion for that career will mean that you perform better too. Why do people not follow this advice? Well, some do! Some choose to travel and find work while doing so. Others become sports coaches or do indeed choose to work in a riding school.

I look back on the time that I left school, and later University, and while my main interests at that time were cricket and drinking beer, I felt that ultimately the earning potential for someone of my limited talents (in both fields) would be quite meagre. I knew that I enjoyed working with numbers, I wanted to travel the world as widely as possible and to earn good money, and therefore I trained as a Chartered Accountant. I went to work for Deloitte, being one of the largest accounting firms with offices all over the globe.

I think it would be fair to say that relatively few people grow up with a passion for being an accountant, though I suppose that some must. Now don't get me wrong, accountancy is a fantastic career and a profession with very strong earning potential. A Chartered Accountancy qualification can open a great many doors. When you look at the Managing Directors and CEOs of listed companies they are very often from an accounting background. And being an accountant offers the opportunity to travel more than most careers as I was fortunate to experience myself.

I remember making a clear and conscious choice to train as an accountant because I felt that the career earnings could be quite high, and that is true. However, it would also be true to say that accounting was not what I was truly passionate about, and in particular I was not at all well-suited to advisory roles in professional practice. Fairly quickly I realised that my personality type is far more inclined towards the creative and entrepreneurial.

It is also true that I have earned much, much more money from investing than I ever did from my salary income, thanks to the power of snowballing or compounding growth. That said, it would be fair to acknowledge that earning a good salary, which both my wife and I did as Chartered Accountants, definitely helped to kick-start our investment portfolio. Earning a good income can certainly accelerate the investment process.

Build a portfolio of assets first, then follow your passion.

I have thus far been building my case to encourage you to consider a plan of building a portfolio of quality assets that can continue to appreciate and pay you an increasing income *forever*, and then when you have done so, you may transition towards making a business income from your passion or alternatively take a paid job in that field. Philosopher Alan Watts went on to conclude:[5]

'After all, if you do really like what you doing, it doesn't matter what it is, you can eventually become a master of it. The only way to become a master of something is sticking with it. And then you will be able to get a good fee for whatever it is. So, don't worry so much. Somebody is interested in everything. Anything you can be interested in, you'll find others will. It is absolutely stupid to spend your time doing things you don't like in order to go on spending time doing things you don't like and teaching your children to follow in the same track.

What we are doing is we are bringing up children and educating them to live the same sort of lives we are living. So they may justify themselves and find satisfaction in life by bringing up their children to bring up their children to do the same thing. So it's all wretch and no vomit, and so it never gets there, and so therefore it is so important to consider this question…what do I desire?'

Chapter 4 summary

» Despite appearances, human behaviour is seldom random

» Linking pleasure and pain to the right behaviours in life can determine your success or failure

» Most people focus on avoiding pain in the short term

» Personal finance and investment success requires short term sacrifices to be made

» To achieve long-term success and pleasure in life, you must first link pleasure to the sacrifices needed to reach your goals, and pain to any behaviours which limit your potential to reach your goals

» First build a portfolio of assets, then be guided by your passion

5
Mind-Set
Reprogramming

5

'We will either find a way, or we will make one.' – Hannibal.

Rewiring your brain - challenge preconceptions

Our belief systems and preconceptions are crucial to achieving lasting success. In this chapter will take a look at how and why this is the case, and how it applies to success in investing and business.

Although I have mostly lived in Australia since the 1990s, I was born to British parents, and in fact I had never even been to the Antipodes until I was an adult. That was not unusual for British kids of my generation – a few of my school friends with well-off parents occasionally went to islands in Spain on holiday, but generally people like us rarely travelled overseas. In fact, for most summer holidays we went camping in Wales in the rain!

When he turned 60 my old man came to visit me in Australia for the first time. He had told me before that when he was at school in the 1950s they had been taught that the remote outpost of Australia was a vast, unforgiving and arid desert. So when he came to visit, I deliberately took him down to visit the south coast of New South Wales which has some of the lushest green plains in Australia. He was more than a little surprised at the breathtaking views from the top of Saddleback Mountain, from which you can see endless swathes of green.

The interesting thing to me is that my Dad's preconception of Australia as a huge red desert was not necessarily wrong – in fact a great deal of Australia is precisely that. If you have ever been up to the iron country in the Pilbara you will know just how barren and brutal parts of the country really are. One of the problems with preconceptions, however, is that folk tend to seek confirmation of their beliefs. I see this in business and in the financial and investment markets every single day. Some people only ever see bad economic news, property bubbles, share market crashes, job losses, insolvencies, rising unemployment, spiralling government debt, unsustainable growth, problems, catastrophes, risks and more problems. Always, always. Bad news is all that they can see and thus they never invest in anything.

> 'Begin challenging your own assumptions. Your assumptions
> are your windows on the world. Scrub them off every
> once in a while, or the light won't come in.' – Alan Alda.

Some people will always see the world that way throughout their entire lives. The whole world is a bubble and soon it must all come crashing down. It is very hard to reason with people who hold that world view, because the nature of the world is such that if you go looking for bad news there will always be risk, fraud, corporate failures, market corrections and endless other gloomy news which can be used as *foundations* to support these gloomy beliefs. Somewhere in the financial and business world there always will be something bad happening or someone doing something stupid. Such is life.

> 'Belief gets in the way of learning.' – Robert. A. Heinlein.

What is interesting is that I heard all of the same things when I started out my own journey two decades ago as I do today. The specifics differ a little, but for some people the underlying theme continues unabated. Everything is unfair, investing is too risky, you cannot make money that way anymore, it is all doom and gloom and we are heading for a recession or depression. The fact of the matter is if you believe that the world is ending then you will be able to find evidence which apparently confirms your belief.

Yet there are great investors like Warren Buffett and countless others who prove that it is entirely possible to continue compounding their wealth year in and year out, even throughout the greatest of financial crises. Remember that economies and markets are cyclical so in that sense we actually *are* always headed for a recession or a crash eventually, because these are recurring phenomena. Smart, proactive investors understand this and will always finish ahead over the long term because they take action and understand that market corrections also offer the greatest opportunities.

We see the world not as it is, but as we are

There was an amazing tale doing the rounds on the internet a few years ago about a parking attendant at Bristol Zoo in the United Kingdom who spent 23 years collecting cash from zoo visitors. One day he did not turn up for work, so the story went, and it came to light that both the Bristol Zoo management and the Bristol Council had each assumed that the car park attendant was the responsibility of the other party. However, it turned out he was a fraud and had absconded with the cash.

What does this story tell us about what we as humans see, hear and believe? That we believe what we want to? Well, in fact the story demonstrates quite a lot for those of us who were suckered by the story, because it later transpired that the tale was an urban myth, completely invented by a prankster for a light-hearted April Fools' joke!

We see the world not as it is, but as we are. The great challenge in business and finance is not to go seeking for confirmation of your limiting beliefs, but to expand your beliefs so that you can achieve what others continue to prove is possible.

Humble pie

In his autobiographical book *Humble Pie*, Michelin-starred chef and hugely successful businessman Gordon Ramsay described in detail his troubled early life.[1] Ramsay explained that his father was an alcoholic who was unable to hold down a regular job, was frequently angry, violent and involved in repeated instances of domestic abuse. It is a terribly sad tale and eventually Gordon Ramsay lost his father to his illness and associated ill health.

Over the years Gordon Ramsay's motivation to succeed and keep expanding his business empire appears to have known no bounds. Ramsay himself stated he will never be satisfied and will always keep on going, motivated to move as far away as he possibly can from the poor council house boy with scruffy clothes and the free school lunches.[2]

> Goals and motivations are shaped by past experiences.

Ramsay also described his difficult relationship with his brother - similar such unhappy stories are surprisingly common[3]. While one man sees the sad self-destruction of his father as a motivation to embark upon the most driven mission imaginable to build a global business empire, another follows in his father's footsteps to substance abuse, addiction and the inevitable destruction of his family relationships.

In many such cases when psychologists question the participants as to why they have taken the path in life that they have followed, often both will give essentially the same response: 'With a father like mine, how could my life have turned out any different?' This represents compelling evidence that in life it is how we interpret and then respond to events that determines our destiny, rather than the events themselves.

How we interpret events determines results

In early 2014 I looked on as Brisbane's Jacqueline Freney was crowned *Young Australian of the Year* having already been crowned *Paralympian of the Year* in 2012. Being born with cerebral palsy has not stopped Freney from achieving outstanding sporting success. During the London 2012 Games she won a remarkable eight gold medals which was the finest haul by any athlete in the Australian team. She won every event which she competed in and set multiple world records in the process, before musing:

'Please understand that I'm just a country girl who was born with extra life challenges. I'm an example of how a child with special needs can develop and achieve with support, guidance, encouragement and opportunity.'

Freney went on to explain that she never thought to see cerebral palsy as a disadvantage. Rather she saw it as a challenge to be faced down and an opportunity to excel in the face of adversity. It is precisely this attitude – how we interpret and respond to the cards we are dealt in life – which determines our fate or destiny. Whether we become a criminal or a crook, an inspirational person, a hero or a villain, a person to be admired or a person to be pitied.

In life it is nearly always less important what happens to us than how we *interpret* what happens to us and choose to respond. Some things will not run according to plan in our lives – that much is a given. It therefore follows that we need to learn how to respond appropriately to what plays out and to the cards we are dealt.

Belief systems

While we may not spend too much time considering what our belief systems are actually comprised of, we all surely have them buried deep in our subconscious. And our deep-rooted preconceptions or general viewpoints tend to direct us to consider and question whether events in our lives will bring us pleasure or pain. The answers are to be found in our beliefs, which are often formed in a general or haphazard manner and may not always be accurate or founded upon fact.

Our beliefs are fundamentally very useful to us as humans, since they help us to interpret situations based upon our previous experiences, and to quickly simplify our responses. However, what you must also be wary of is that your beliefs can also be very general in nature and can unconsciously act as severe limitations upon what you are able to achieve.

What about the example of someone who says 'I just can't save. I can sometimes manage it for a couple of months but whenever I manage to save up a little, something comes along like a car mechanic bill and wipes me out again. Money just always seems to disappear from my bank account'? The dangers of such limiting beliefs is that while they may be based upon one or two past experiences, they can quickly become self-fulfilling prophecies. That person will regularly be able to save some money but then will receive an invite to a buck's weekend or an overseas wedding which 'cannot be missed' and then the savings are again lost or spent. And they have once again been proven to be right, thus only re-confirming their belief.

Beliefs have a tendency to become self-fulfilling prophecies.

The trouble is that beliefs can become so entrenched that you do not commit to overcoming challenges, and once you do not commit to something, you will almost certainly fail. Do you see how dangerous the power of beliefs can be when they are limiting in their nature? The scary thing is that our beliefs are often formed based upon only a few experiences, or sometimes even only one fleeting experience! Our beliefs in some situations may be completely false or baseless.

What can we do about this? If a lack of ability to save money is a major hurdle for you then you need to design a plan of action in order to overcome it. As the old adage goes, if you keep doing what you have always done, then you can expect to get more of what you have already got. Perhaps you need to work overtime or a second job. If the idea of budgeting for your personal finances makes you break out in a cold sweat, why not transform your vocabulary in a positive way and write yourself a *spending plan*?

Most importantly of all if you can choose to use the Pleasure-Pain Principle to associate pleasure to thrift and investing by thinking of the wonderful life you will be able to design for yourself, while associating equivalent pain to frivolous expenditure on luxuries, you can begin to win the battle and start the snowball rolling in your favour.

A special case...

After my brother Christopher and I had graduated from junior to comprehensive secondary school, I recall that Chris was classified as a remedial learner and streamed into the 'special' class for 'slow' individuals. He had previously suffered from quite a serious case of glandular fever and this had hindered his schooling. The world has moved on a little since those days, but imagine the psychological damage using such labels had on a generation of youngsters and their self-belief!

While Chris was (and still is, in many ways!) a special individual, there was more than a strong suspicion from me at that time that he was not necessarily a remedial case in educational terms or even particularly 'slow', rather that he was just worked in a different way to some others. What we all need to remember is that people are not inherently lazy or, for that matter, industrious, often they simply lack potent or inspiring goals. If you are not duly motivated to perform in a given field or area, then the inevitable outcome is that eventually you will not be industrious.

> People are not inherently lazy or industrious – what truly determines motivation levels is the potency of your goals.

I have had more than one job where I have been thought of as lazy. The truth is that I am not at all a lazy person - I like to start work at 5am if I can most days. However, like most people I can adopt a take-it-or-leave it attitude towards matters that I cannot see the value in. If during my accountancy career someone called a meeting which was due to begin at 6.30pm, it was a fair bet that I would find an excuse to be somewhere else. Well, life is too short for late night office meetings! What a frightful bore and an unbelievable waste of everybody's valuable time.

Back to my brother Chris. After his glandular fever, the education system believed that Chris was not of an appropriate ability level to mix with the rest of the class, and thus he was classified accordingly. Upon being streamed in the 'remedial' set, Chris matched his performance to expectations and began to score marks in line with a middle of the class result. Note here the power of the self-fulfilling prophecy – the youngster who is labelled as being 'slow' often begins to perform according to the new label. Interestingly after some time the teacher of this class noted that he felt that Chris could do better and he was promoted back into the main classroom with the rest of his mates, where again he adjusted his performance over time to meet expectations.

What is fascinating to me about this short story is that when later in our youth my Dad got a new job as a probation officer in another part of the country, my precocious older brother Nick and the significantly less precocious me were put forward to sit entrance exams for a selective grammar school. Grammar schools in that local area siphoned off the top two percent of candidates and were well known for producing excellent exam results and a great many Oxford and Cambridge University students.

As it transpired the grammar school elected to take all three of us brothers on as a job lot, perhaps inferring a concern that if all of us lads were not admitted they might not benefit from Nick's inevitable straight 'A' grades. Nick got his top grades, and upon transitioning to grammar school the one-time 'remedial' case Chris again lifted his performance to match that of his new grammar school peers - the top two percent of the academic stream. Later still, Chris gained entry to a top University and finished with a much better than average degree - way better than my moderate result, for example.

Beliefs can dictate results.

This is only an isolated case, but think of the impact of beliefs and how they play such an important role in our educational systems, as they do in all parts of our lives. Chris has always been comfortable in educational terms to sit in the middle of the class, but interestingly he proved equally able to perform at the middle of the class in the top two percent of the education system by academic ability as he did in the bottom two percent. In fact, the further up the higher education system he moved, the better he seemed to get.

The academic credibility behind this concept was researched and codified by Howard Saul Becker who coined the term *labelling theory*, which holds that the self-identity and therefore behaviour of people can be heavily influenced by how they are described or classified.[4] Criminals who are sent to prison, for example, may increasingly identify with their new label as a criminal and repeat offences can become more likely upon their release.[5]

In particular, labels and beliefs which are negative in their nature can change a person's conception of themselves and identity.

This is an important concept and we should all consider how this might impact our investing and life success. The problem with beliefs is that we can oversimplify complex areas of our lives and come to believe that if we have failed to excel at something previously then it must always be thus. This is absolutely not the case! If you make a bad investment, have a bad relationship which does not work out, or perform poorly in a job and get demoted, these events should be treated as learning experiences from which to seek better future results. They should not be viewed as failures or as cast iron evidence that you will not experience great successes in the future.

If you want to change the results that you are getting then you need to be able to recognise and then change the beliefs that are limiting your progress. How this becomes possible is to begin to find reference points to support new and more empowering beliefs. If you want to become a great investor, you do not need to believe that you are a great investor immediately. But if you want this belief to become a part of your reality over time then you need to start small, get some wins under your belt and collect a pool of reference points for success.

I have found that in life people who overestimate what they can achieve frequently end up with results far and away in excess of those who underestimate the sum of their capabilities. Even if the optimists are too gung-ho and make costly mistakes, the fact that they are able to see the bigger picture and set larger and more exciting goals compels them to take action, and ultimately action does lead to results.

This goes deeper still. We are often labelled in terms of our choice of career and employment status. Traditional wisdom suggests we should study hard, go to University, get good qualifications, apply for a job, work the way up the career ladder, find a partner, get married, use our salary income to pay for the biggest house we can afford, two cars and to pay for a family.

Challenge your preconceptions and your limiting beliefs.

None of this is necessarily bad advice, but it does not follow that it must necessarily be right for you. Learn to challenge the expectations. Do you really need to own two cars? Do you need to own a large house? Why not own two properties as investments (and, for that matter, why not own ten?). Is a career job for life right for you? Or could you be a business owner? Can you become financially independent sooner rather than later?

Again, these suggestions might not be the answers for you. What I am saying, however, is that you should challenge the labels and expectations which you have been saddled with, because they may not be the right path. Remember that the subconscious is very powerful and even if you are not explicitly told to follow a certain path, implicit suggestions are frequently made and find their way into our belief systems. You should begin by questioning them!

No failures, only results

Whether we like it or not, life continually throws up great challenges and success will rarely be achieved in a straight line. Therefore what often determines success in life is actually how folk respond to adversity. The best way to overcome failures is to not consider them to be failures at all, and instead to look at adverse outcomes as *experiences* to be learned from. Make a decision to thank the results for what they have taught you and resolve to not make the same mistakes in the future. Your past does not equal your future, so resolve to look forward...onwards and upwards.

Indeed, it is often the case that those who are seemingly 'fortunate' enough to experience great success are those who have actually achieved the most failures. Note the intentional use of wording there. Failures can sometimes even be a pre-requisite for greater success and as such can be viewed as an achievement. The more times you fail, the more you can learn.

Never say 'oh dear'. Instead say 'ah, interesting!'

Of course, I am not suggesting that you should deliberately go out and make mistakes in investing and in business, because errors can be costly and painful. But it is nevertheless true that successful business owners and investors often include those who have made many crass mistakes and genuine errors, but learned to treat them as learning experiences or motivation to achieve further success in the future.

I talk a lot about the importance of snowballing investments, and particularly the power of patience and compounding. I have been 'fortunate' in that when I have bought investment properties I have always looked to buy in quality locations which has meant that I have never needed to sell a single property. Of all of the properties that I have bought over the years, I have never needed to sell one. That does not mean I got everything right – far from it, in fact - I have made more than my fair share of mistakes but have resolved to learn from them over time. However, through buying quality assets for the long term I have continued to experience success.

In the share markets, my wife and I have index funds which we have been contributing to every month since the late 1990s without ever having sold a single holding. Notably when we have tried to be clever by making fast returns from speculative ventures we have lost some money too, but this only made us more determined to learn the power of patience and to focus on quality long-term investments instead of being tempted by penny stocks or turnaround stories.

'There are no failures – only your experiences and reactions to them.' – Tom Krause.

One of the most concerning aspects of failure is how remarkably few times people need to fail at something for them to form a belief that they can never succeed. The only thing that many people achieve is learned helplessness. They try buying shares in a company and see the price go down and lose money, and then almost instantly believe forever that shares are a risky investment. Or, they try a business venture but because it is not wildly successful in the first month become convinced that they can only ever be an employee.

Successful people do not see failures or problems as permanent or pervasive, and nor do they believe that simply because they failed at something once that this diminishes what they have achieved in other areas of their lives.

Never-ending improvement

Back in the 1980s, it was common for business leaders in the west to look to Japan for clues as to how success could be achieved. Largely thanks to catastrophic policy errors Japan has been through some tough times in recent decades and has become something of a template for what not to do with respect to central bank monetary policy and intervention against deflation. Despite these major macroeconomic challenges Japan has nevertheless been an industrial powerhouse and a country which has long prided itself on excellence in business.

In Japan there is a fascinating word that is often used in industry which has no direct equivalent in English – *kaizen*.[6] In English, the word is probably best described as a process of consistent and never-ending improvement. What a powerful concept that is for the way we live our lives!

How often do we feel or say that we are 'stuck in a rut', as though we are 'taking two steps forward and three steps back' or we are 'going around in circles'? These are powerful metaphors, and we should be careful with the language which we use to feed to our brains because on an unconscious level we may begin to act in a congruent manner with the metaphor. Be mindful of the vocabulary and the metaphors which you use in your life and to describe it. Successful people tend to use positive vocabulary and empowering metaphors.

> 'Every day, in every way, I am getting better and better'
> - Émile Coué, French psychologist.

A far more powerful way to think of our lives is to think of the concept of *kaizen*. Each and every day make a commitment to learn and improve in any way you can. One of the reasons this is such an effective manner in which to approach life is that people tend to *believe* that they can successfully make small improvements and therefore they are achievable. In chapter 7 we will look at choosing your own adventure through the setting of big and inspiring goals. Although setting big goals may appear a daunting task, it is vitally important, for if you set yourself goals which truly inspire you, for then you will have the motivation in order to take the consistent action necessary to move towards them.

Another worthy analogy is to think of a large sailing ship progressing towards its destination. The sailor does not simply point the ship in the general direction of the target and then simply hope for the best as the ship progresses along its voyage. There will be unpredictable winds and weather and there may be setbacks along the way, but the experienced sailor will not fret. Instead, the sailor will continually make small adjustments to the ship's course as the voyage continues, constantly updating and reacting to movements in currents and the prevailing wind. The most important thing is to make sure you leave the port in the first place!

Do the 'one percenters'.

When Steve Waugh was the captain of the Australian cricket team, he often spoke about the team 'doing the one percenters', by which I believe he meant each and every member of the squad being committed to doing every last thing possible to improve performance.[7] Again, small improvements are believable and therefore they become achievable. I sometimes look back at where I was ten or even five years ago and am amazed at how far I have come. How about you? Are you progressing at the speed you want to? Are some areas of your life going better than others? Are there things you would like to achieve in the next five years?

It is difficult to know all of the answers to these questions without sitting down for a moment and reviewing your actual progress. Below is an extremely useful exercise for you to carry out. It asks you to consider how each part of your life was a decade ago to assess in which areas you have made progress (often we don't give ourselves enough credit!) and in which areas of your life you appear to have stalled, as this may be a signal that you need to take corrective action. Let us take a look.

Five years ago versus today

Do you give yourself credit for your progress in life or do you feel that it is a constant uphill battle with your goals frustratingly always seeming out of reach? I noted previously that if you are anything like me, you do not complete exercises in books. Well, I have some good news for you and I will cut you a deal – there are only three exercises to do in this book, and this is the second of them! Let's complete a short exercise to see how far you have really come in the past five years. Rate your life out of ten in each of these categories as you see it today.

Quality of life exercise

Firstly, rate your life out of ten for how it is today in each of the below areas. It can be very helpful as a point of reference to make a few notes too.

Life today

Physical vitality and health	....
Mental health and personal happiness	....
Personal relationships	....
Friendships and family	....
Home and living environment	....
Social life, skills and confidence	....
Attractiveness and self-confidence	....

Career progression, opportunities and outlook ....

Work and business ....

Financial base and investment ....

Spiritual and charitable contribution ....

How did you get on? Are there some areas for improvement there? Are you doing well in some areas of your life but struggling a bit in others? It is likely that you are because life is a journey, and we are rarely close to meeting all of our ultimate goals in most areas of our life at the same time. The interesting thing is how rarely we benchmark our progress (or in some instances lack of progress) and therefore we have little idea of whether our lives are moving in the right direction or not. For this reason, repeat the exercise for how your life was five years ago.

Life 5 years ago

Now repeat the exercise by rating your life out of ten for how it was five years ago below. It is probable that you have made progress in some areas of your life and perhaps less so in others.

Physical vitality and health ....

Mental health and personal happiness ....

Personal relationships ....

Friendships and family ....

Home and living environment ....

Social life, skills and confidence ....

Attractiveness and self-confidence ....

Career progression, opportunities and outlook ....

Work and business ....

Financial base and investment ....

Spiritual and charitable contribution ....

All done? This is an interesting exercise to perform, isn't it? It is very informative to note how far you have progressed in some areas of your life yet perhaps less so in others. Progression is rarely linear. How did you fare? Have you improved the quality of your life a little? Or a lot? If so, then that is great news! You are making progress, and you should give yourself a pat on the back.

Perhaps on the other hand you are progressing a little less quickly than you imagine or in a less smooth manner than you had hoped. If this is the case for you then this also sends a message – and the message is that you need to alter your strategy so that in five years' time you will be scoring higher marks across the board.

What is stopping you from scoring a perfect 10 in every category in five years' time? Recall that the 80/20 Principle holds that if something is working for you this is not a signal to ignore this area of your life to focus on other things. Often it can be as beneficial to double down on your successes to become outstanding in one sphere of your life.

Setting huge and exciting goals

When I look back on my life in my mid-twenties, I sometimes smile just a little at how far I have come from the emotionally fragile mess that I was at that time. Back then, I earned a good salary in my job as a Chartered Accountant but I often found the work to be boring or stressful, I commuted more than *four hours* a day to work and back, I drank way too much lager, my personal relationships were unbalanced to say the least, my diet was unhealthy...I could go on, but I sense you have the general picture.

I did achieve successes, particularly in investment where I continued to progress in spite of the weaknesses in other areas of my life. However, overall my results were sporadic, and just when one area of my life seemed to progressing nicely I would have fires to fight in another. We know that the universe is out of balance, and my life was indeed to some extent out of balance in some areas, but not always in a healthy or the most productive way. What changed? Well, a lot of things, but many of the changes stemmed from one factor – simply, I made a *decision*. Remember, what a decision means - to *cut off* any other alternatives. And my decision was to live a more abundant life.

Interestingly, I started out simply by reading as many books as I possibly could on investing, just as you are doing now. And once I started, I simply never stopped! I steadily became obsessed with learning about finance, economics and investment (my career was also in finance with the accounting firm Deloitte, which naturally helped), and then over time I began to broaden my interests into discovering how I could improve all areas of my life.

The 80/20 Principle is the secret to achieving more with less.

The 80/20 Principle holds that the universe is out of balance and we should look to get the big decisions right. In particular if you want to achieve exceptional results, I argue that the best course of action is likely to be doing more of the things you are best at and enjoy doing the most. Further, you should consider looking to the areas of your life where you are achieving great results and double down on them in order to achieve excellence in one or two fields rather than mediocrity in many.

Of course, I am not saying that you should focus on your financial and career health and ignore your physical health – I am not saying that at all! What I am saying is that by following your passion and learning from your successes you can experience more and more success in a constant and never-ending quest for improvement. Today is the day to start setting some big and inspiring goals. And as this is the exciting part, that is exactly what we are going to do shortly in chapter 7.

Procrastination and self-sabotage?

I have been putting off writing this section of the book for two days now, since I keep getting distracted by online media. Procrastination! It is one of the most common of all forms of self-sabotage, and particularly for investors or for those of us who go on to be small business owners.

Procrastination kills results.

Other popular means of self-sabotage include comfort eating, self-medication or a selection of self-defeating behaviour patterns such as worrying constantly, a restrictive or even debilitating fear of failure, perfectionism, an inability to take risks or being unable to say 'no!' to people. Getting started on your quest for success can be the hardest part. Once you are underway you will get some wins under your belt which you can use as reference points for your self-belief and ultimately achieving your goals. But you do have to get started, and that's why this short section is important. The time to take action is today!

How is self-sabotage defined?

The practice of self-sabotage, derived from the French word *saboter* – to wilfully destroy - is likely to stem from a combination of negative thoughts and feelings, and manifests itself in behaviours which disrupt your ability to achieve longer term goals. If you consciously set yourself desires and targets, but subconsciously continue to ensure that you cannot attain or meet them, then here is likely to be your inner-saboteur at work.

The reason self-sabotage can be so damaging is that it's often unconscious and those engaging in it may not be aware that they are repeating self-defeating behaviour. The good news is that it is more than possible to overcome self-sabotage, so let's take a look at how to recognise it, and how to take corrective action.

1 - Understand - why do people self-sabotage?

Psychologists tell us that people in business, sport and life self-sabotage when they have reached a level of income, wealth or success which, consciously or otherwise, they do not feel worthy of. Therefore, the root cause is likely to be a lack of self-worth, and a lack of self-confidence or belief. Think of the footballer who elects to skip a training session, or the business person who overanalyses and refuses to delegate or outsource. Armed with this knowledge, it becomes possible to identify the risks of self-sabotage and begin to address them, through...

2 - Raising self-esteem and confidence

If self-sabotage is caused by low self-worth or a diminished lack of confidence, then we must learn how to raise and improve them. The best way I know of is to surround yourself with supportive and positive people, and, correspondingly avoid those negative types who make you feel worse about yourself, your business, or your life.

Another frequently effective action is to commit to achieving a task which you have been deferring, such as making an awkward phone call, arranging a key business meeting or invoicing your clients. All of us have necessarily experienced past successes, so resolve to recount those wins instead of dwelling morosely upon past failures - the past need not equal the future. This step is vitally important. If you do not feel worthy of the fees you charge this is likely to be communicated to your clients, and ultimately there will be an impact on the bottom line of your business.

3 – Recognise why self-sabotage exists

Self-sabotage is a safety mechanism which exists to keep humans within their comfort zones. A comfort zone can be useful - up to a point - if it stops us from taking undue risks or diving headlong into unfamiliar or dangerous territories. However, a comfort zone also introduces an effective glass ceiling to the level of your business and investing success. Acknowledge that glass ceiling, thank it for its kind interest in your well-being…and then resolve to push past it!

The one thing that all self-sabotaging behaviours have in common is that they appear to offer us comfort by short-circuiting the emotional rollercoaster of day-to-day living. But ultimately such behaviours are false friends. That is, they may appear to be helpful in offering us short term relief, but in fact remain harmful, and the negative consequences of the behaviour persist.

4 – Acknowledge negative thoughts

We all have dozens of negative thoughts every day and sometimes, they can seem overwhelming.

- 'I can't do this…'
- 'I am simply way too busy…'
- 'I am not ready to take that risk…'

Acknowledge negative thoughts, notice their fear-mongering, and consider what you can learn from them. Think carefully about this: could your negative thoughts simply be saying 'you don't deserve this'? If they are, refuse to wallow in those thoughts, interrupt the pattern!

5 - Reconnect with your goals

It is well known that we all have up days and down days, so at a time when you are in your peak state, reconnect with your goals. Look for answers not problems, and aim to view fears as a positive – perhaps you even need to do the opposite of your fears to reach your desired targets? Implement a healthier new behaviour pattern which is commensurate with achieving your goals and recognise its advantages.

6 - Control the controllables

Most people never consider to define what success is to themselves, and thus may be chasing objectives which remain forever elusive. To be in control of your life, and to be happy, ensure that you have defined for yourself how you will be successful, in a way which is not reliant upon external circumstances which are beyond your control.

Onward to success!

Self-sabotage is an interesting subject because it affects everyone to a greater or lesser extent. Inevitably, we will all continue to engage in some damaging behaviours some of the time, but what can make self-sabotage problematic and damaging is repetition. What ultimately separates the successful from those who continue to under-achieve?

Successful investors and small business owners tend to be enthusiastic, ambitious, focused and motivated to achieve their dreams. Just as importantly, successful people who achieve results take decisions regularly, and they have the courage to acknowledge their mistakes and resolve to learn from them.

Well, this section of the book is finally written. And, you know what? I do feel more energised for having stopped procrastinating. Taking action works!

Don't listen to the wrong people on your financial health

All the way along your journey to financial freedom you will have people say to you that 'you can't do that' or 'you're doing the wrong thing, because…', and similar such comments and observations. For both my wife and I this has been a recurring theme almost throughout our adult lives. It could be your friends, your family, the press or your work colleagues, but you can rest assured that there will always be someone on hand to tell you that you are doing the wrong thing.

The global financial crisis saw global stock markets fall to incredibly and irrationally cheap levels. There were bargains to be had everywhere for experienced investors. But most people simply didn't want to know. The world was ending, apparently capitalism as we knew it was finished and shares were too risky. The fact is that some people continue to say that it is a bad time to invest for year after year after year – they never invest in anything and therefore they never achieve anything in financial terms.

It is always a bad time to invest…for some people.

Looking back my wife bought her first house immediately after graduating for a price which seems almost ridiculously cheap today. Not that it seemed so at the time, of course. Indeed, there was no shortage of friendly advice from colleagues and friends saying that taking on such a heavy debt burden at a young age was a remarkably foolish thing to do and that the property simply wasn't worth the price tag. Yet that one simple investment decision set her up financially in the years to come and she was able to progress on to bigger and more exciting investments in both real estate and shares.

This is a theme which repeats itself over and over again in investment. Markets move in cycles and the crowd is always a day late. In fact, the crowd is often not only a day late, they are weeks, months or several years too late as the market runs upwards due to a fear of missing out on what skilful counter-cyclical investors have been profiting handsomely from. The crowd often buys at the peak of the market just as the experienced investors who have lived through more than one market cycle are getting ready to sell or scale back on buying.

You will often find through your investing life that if you choose to invest in property there will be folk on hand to advise you that now is the worst possible time to invest in real estate and there is bound to be a sharp correction or re-setting of prices. What is amazing is how often the same people who tell you that are the same folk who wait and wait and wait before finally capitulating and buying a property right at the true peak of the market cycle.

Market cycles repeat.

Timing is not everything in investment, but it is still important. In chapter 15 we will look at how to recognise market cycles. It is partly this fear of missing out which causes and exacerbates market cycles in the first place. It becomes self-fulfilling. Even the hardiest of souls become softened as they see friends and colleagues making handsome profits year after year, and eventually feel compelled to join the crowd, often at the least opportune moment. The saddest thing about this is that they then become convinced forever that investing is risky and a bad idea because they buy their first investment right at the market's peak.

How much might you earn in your lifetime (and how leaky is your bucket)?

'There's a hole in my bucket, dear Liza' – traditional.

One of the jobs we used to earn pocket money for as kids was from car washing. That might not sound too bad if you grew up on the Sunshine Coast or by a tropical beach, but if like me you grew up in an industrial city in Yorkshire in northern Britain you would know that for most of the year it is not a particularly pleasant task! The general goal was to get the job done as quickly as possible before your hands froze.

We had an old bucket at my parents' house with a couple of small holes in it which only re-emphasised the need for demonstrating great speed between the tap at the side of the house and the car - you had to get to the car before all of the water leaked from the bucket. Naturally, a huge amount of water was wasted and by the time you reached the car you'd only have a small amount of water left. The net result was making many more trips back and forth than should strictly have been necessary. Deep down, I guess it was pretty obvious that if just a little time and effort had been spent at the outset plugging the gaps, then the whole enterprise would have been far more efficient and the entire car could have been washed spick and span with the use of only a few buckets of water.

How much do you think you might earn in a lifetime?
Thanks to inflation, it's much more than you might think.

I said that I would not include too many numbers in this book, but consider this - if your age today is 21 and you have weekly earnings of, say, $17 an hour or $650 per week, you will find that with a 4.5 percent annual salary increase, your lifetime earnings could be more than $5 million!

Figure 5.1 – Cumulative lifetime earnings

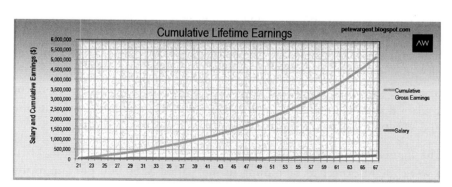

So, when people discuss questions such as 'can anyone be a millionaire?' it is not really so much a question of whether you can earn a couple of million dollars, it is rather a case of whether you can keep a couple of million dollars. The problem in the modern consumer focussed world is that most people have personal finances and an investment plan which resembles a hole-filled bucket. By the time the end of the month comes around, most people do not seem to have enough money left to do anything at all, let alone invest in a portfolio of wealth-producing assets.

If you want to see how productive your investment plan has really been to date, first calculate your net worth, which is the sum of all of your assets (house, car, pension, shares and so on) minus all of your debts and liabilities (mortgage, loans, credit card debts). Then divide your net worth figure by the number of years you have been in the workforce. If the number is substantially less than the annual salary you have earned over your career to date, where did the rest go?

Tax accounts for some of it, of course, and essential living costs. But what about the rest? It is amazing how as employees people are conditioned to spend everything that they earn. The interesting thing is that if you can invest in the right assets you can earn far more from your investments than it is ever possible to earn from a salary in a hundred lifetimes. I have read some fascinating case studies where effective investors have used the power of compound growth to earn more money from investments in only a few years of retirement than they did from their entire working careers. An arresting thought!

Compounding earnings

As a child, on really long and dull car journeys (essentially anything more than about 20 minutes) I would sometimes amuse myself by asking my Dad how much money he earned. The amounts seemed huge to me then and like most children, the real yardstick of money for me was how many sugary treats any such figure could theoretically buy. Yet today those sums represent a salary that would be illegal as they would not even remotely constitute the prescribed minimum wage.

The figures we looked at above show that a 21 year old who earns $650 a week might expect to be pulling in more than $250,000 per annum by retirement age thanks to the compounding effect of the assumed salary increases. The absolute numbers are not all that important here, but the principle definitely is.

It is exactly the same principle which investors use to their advantage. Compounding growth accelerates wealth creation with each increase in value being greater than its preceding equivalent. The great challenge today is to maintain the discipline to invest a healthy portion of your earnings into assets that produce a wealth-producing rate of return before you spend the balance.

The first step is to plug the holes in the bucket. Where is money leaking out of your life? Car loans? Student debts? Takeaway food or restaurant meals? Expensive nights out? Electronic gadgets or i-Phone plans? Exotic overseas holidays? After you have identified the holes and found ways to plug them, you will be ready to invest sooner than you may imagine. And if you get the investing part right, you might even be able to splash out a few bucks for a coffee at the car wash café while someone else does the car washing for you!

The millionaire next door...

I have always felt that how we define success in the modern world is misguided. Too often, people say to themselves: 'I will be successful when I have achieved the following…' and then list a string of goals which they have not yet achieved. That is completely the wrong way to look at the world. Why can you not decide to be a successful person here today? Right now! Success is always relative. If you are reading this book you are most likely already more privileged than most of the people on the planet. Why not decide that, right now, today, you are a successful person and you are going to live like one. Success does not have to be a mountain to be scaled. You can start today!

Most millionaires do not live exceptionally lavish lifestyles.

In their book *The Millionaire Next Door*, the authors Thomas J. Stanley and William D. Danko noted that, far from expectations, most of the millionaires they surveyed in America did not live the lavish lifestyles that people have come to associate with wealth.[8] Instead, most drive moderate cars, live in moderate housing and have relatively modest lifestyles.[9] The authors' findings showed that most millionaires became so precisely because they lived moderate lifestyles and did not spend large amounts of their income on cars, expensive watches and other depreciating assets.[10]

On the flip side, so many people who only appear to have the trappings of wealth live immoderately. They drive expensive cars, take the most expensive holidays and spend far too much of their time and money worrying about 'keeping up with the Joneses' who don't have the good will to stay still. Don't worry about the Joneses – they will be too concerned with what they are doing to notice in any case. The message, then, is quite clear – do not pretend to be wealthy…concentrate on *being* wealthy!

The 4-pronged approach to achieving your goals

Enough of the theory. How, then, can you take practical steps towards achieving your goals? In my experience, there is only one tried and tested approach to achieve exactly what it is that you want. This is the proven four-pronged strategy which must be employed:

- decide *precisely* what it is that you want to achieve

- take committed action towards achieving that goal

- recognise what strategies are working effectively for you and which of them are failing to achieve the desired results

- take corrective action and adjust your strategies accordingly

The analogy I previously used is that your success should be viewed as similar to a ship heading towards its final destination. First, you must choose your destination very carefully and then make decisions today to get started towards it. Of course, it is very difficult when you first leave port to get the bearings exactly right, but that really does not matter – you can make adjustments to your course as you progress along the voyage!

As you progress along your life journey, at various points in time you will veer slightly off the planned track due to headwinds, unforeseen tides and other problems, but you can easily make small adjustments to your direction as you go. The most important thing is that you leave port in the first place and commit yourself completely to reaching the final destination, even if you are scared of the seas or being out of your depth when you first start out.

Perhaps the most important trait of successful investors, and perhaps indeed of all of those who are successful in life, is that they take decisive and committed action and they never, ever give up. Too many fall or fail at the first hurdle because at the first sign of trouble they determine that investing is too hard or too risky and go back to living in ignorant bliss of their personal finances instead. This is vitally important because there will always be setbacks along the way for every investor. You must be aware of this and resolve, no matter how difficult the outlook seems to become, to never, ever be a quitter.

Chapter 5 summary

» Belief systems tend to determine results as over time they become self-fulfilling

» How we interpret and respond to events is often more important than what actually happens to us

» People self-sabotage when they do not feel worthy of their successes

» Lifetime earnings tend to be much higher than you think – spend less than you earn and invest the difference wisely!

» Some people will always say that it is a bad time to invest. They rarely achieve much in financial terms

» Goals are achieved by deciding what you want and taking committed and sustained action towards those goals

6
The Psychology Of
Wealth Creation

6

'For as a man thinketh in his heart, so is he.' – Proverbs 23:7.

The psychology of wealth creation

In order to be truly successful in investment, business and life, you need to have the right mind-set. Before we move on to setting huge and exciting goals in the next chapter, a short but key section on the psychology of wealth creation. When I was younger I felt that the concept of the psychology of wealth creation was mere psycho-babble. My internally held belief was that if you worked harder you would better off. And if you didn't, you wouldn't. And that was that! Now, I am a little older and a little wiser, I know that the psychology of wealth creation is of real importance in achieving success. In fact, it is vital.

Wealth psychology starts early in life...when you are born.

Your internal beliefs concerning money and wealth are ingrained into our subconscious without us ever having realised it. Australia's leading expert in the psychology of wealth creation Michael Yardney asks us to consider what happened to us when we were young.[1] What did our parents teach us about money? You should get a good job? Work hard? Rich people are to be mistrusted?

'Money doesn't grow on trees, you know...'

'We'll never be able to afford that.'

'Share markets are risky'.

'Rich people are greedy and dishonest.'

Whether or not we realise it at the time, these are powerful messages being programmed into our subconscious. And it goes deeper than this too. In my family it was more or less pre-ordained that as lads we should work hard at school, pass our exams, go to University and seek out a professional career. All of which is solid enough advice.

It is also generally accepted in society that you take the best paying job you can find, work hard, get into a relationship, settle down, buy the best house you can afford, buy maybe two or even three cars for the household, perhaps have a couple of children. Nowhere here is any bad advice to be found, but it is important note how many things in life (and there are many more) are taken to be received wisdom.

Certainly in Britain, where the idea of a classless society has never really been believed in, there appears to be a general perception that professional careers (e.g. lawyer, accountant, doctor) or office-based careers (e.g. insurance broker, consultant) may be somehow superior to those worthy careers which involve using your hands (e.g. electrician, plumber or builder). Indeed, plenty of people seem to believe that any job where you wear a tie is somehow inherently better than one where you do not. What tosh!

> Your earnings will increase when you can find more ways
> to add more value to more people, more quickly.

Whether you are employed or self-employed your earnings can increase when you are able to find ways to add more value to more people, especially if you can do so in an efficient manner. This is true whichever field you operate in. A medical specialist tends to earn more than a GP because he or she has learned a niche skill which people need and will pay handsomely for. A plumber who is also a business owner tends to earn a good deal more than one who is employed because he or she can reach more people through leveraging their networks.

There are a number of things I commonly hear people say regularly about building wealth. Here are a few:

- 'Share markets crash regularly'
- 'Property is too expensive – it is a bad investment'
- 'Going into business is a risk'
- 'Get a good, safe career job'

Each of these statements might be true for the person who makes it. Interestingly I recall some of the above statements being made back in the 1990s too, and yet fortunes have continued to be made since in property, shares and business. A notable thing here is I have never once met someone who believes that property is a bad investment succeed in property, since their belief becomes almost inevitably self-fulfilling. Even if they make one successful foray into the market they believe that the success is too good to last and sell out of the market again too soon. Beliefs tend to become self-fulfilling prophecies over time.

The key point here is that it is important to remove limiting beliefs about money if you want to build wealth. If you want to turn your passion into your business you need to think about how you can add more value to people, and also to consider how you can reach more people. We will look more at this in much more detail in Part Four of the book. But now let us consider…

The 6 key rules of the psychology of wealth creation

Here are the six rules of the psychology of wealth creation which you must follow if wealth for the long term is your goal:

1 – Increase your self-esteem

Why is self-esteem relevant to wealth creation? The reason is because if your self-esteem is low and you then achieve a level of success which exceeds what you believe yourself to be worthy of, you will unconsciously sabotage your success. Wealth creation expert Michael Yardney uses the analogy of a thermostat - each of us has a financial thermostat that is programmed to a certain level. The temperature may fluctuate a little from time to time, but eventually we return to the level at which our thermostat is set.[2] A top consultant or specialist is usually comfortable with charging handsomely for his or her time because, in the words of the jarring *L'Oreal* advert, they believe that they are 'worth it'. This would not be sustainable without a commensurate level of self-esteem.

Share trading author and doyen Dr Alexander Elder has stated that 'failure is a curable disease'.[3] He believes that if we can understand and recognise our own potential to self-sabotage then we can retrain our brains to think more positively.[4] We can be cured of our propensity to make suboptimal decisions, he argues. Further, Elder states, we will never be successful until we can remove this subconscious need to sabotage any outperformance of our own expectations.[5]

2 - It pays to invest for the long term

Too many people in life devise plans to make themselves a little better off in the short term, but have no cogent plan for building wealth over the long term. True wealth and fortunes are built slowly but surely. Investing for the long term creates greater wealth because of the awesome power of compounding growth which can use to multiply your earnings.

Consider the following. Historians tell us that the American Indians were dealt a raw deal when they sold the island of Manhattan to the Dutch leader Peter Minuit in 1626 for beads and trinkets worth just $24. It is indeed true that $24 does not sound like a great deal of money, and certainly not for the sale of Manhattan Island! Yet controversially, revisionists have since argued that had the $24 from the beads and trinkets been invested safely at a rate of return of 8 percent per annum, the unhindered compound growth would have ensured that the trinkets could today buy back Manhattan in its entirety with all of its prime-location real estate, leaving a few hundred million dollars over as walking around money.

> Re-invest your gains in order to compound your wealth.

While this is largely a theoretical point, it is nevertheless food for thought! Following the principle and power of compound growth is the key to building wealth. If you can add some leverage, including the use of other people's time and other people's money, it is absolutely possible that you may be able to join the ranks of the super-wealthy over time.

3 - Study and counsel with wise men

If you want to be successful, learn from successful people. Find someone who has achieved what you want to achieve. Resolve to study and follow their methods. The ingenious thing about this is that you may well be able to learn from some of their mistakes and reach your goals even more quickly and completely than they did themselves. This is the powerful tool known as *modelling*. I consciously and actively use this strategy every single day – in some cases it even allowed me to achieve success more quickly and at a younger age than the mentors I learned from!

4 - Pay yourself first

What do most people do in a typical month with regards to their personal finances? Make the mortgage payment, pay the bills, clear the credit cards and shell out for other essentials. Then they look to see what is left over at the end of the month. You need to see things another way. Invest a decent sum of your earnings safely away in quality investments first and then worry about the other payments thereafter. This sounds tremendously arrogant. But guess what? It also works!

5 - Controlling expenditure

In the simplest terms achieving financial freedom is about having passive income, which flows to you regardless of whether your work, that is greater than your outgoings. There are two variables in that equation that can be adjusted to achieve the goal. One is to increase the passive income figure, through successful investment in income-producing assets. The other variable is to reduce your outgoings through the unfashionable deployment of thrift. Where are the holes in your financial foundations? Where do you tend to spend big? Holidaying in Honolulu? Wasting at the Westfield shopping centre? How can you plug the gaps?

6 - Taking action

It is all very well studying and learning from these first five steps, but what really counts is taking concerted and consistent action and simply never, ever giving up. What is holding you back from starting today? A fear of failure? A fear of losing money? Are you 'doing OK' without investing? When will you start to take action? Next month, next year, next decade? You need to dare to be different to achieve wealth. Procrastination is the killer of all opportunity. Take action today!

Self-esteem

'Improve your self-esteem and wealth will follow.' This is one of those seemingly glib statements which people tend to read and think: 'Mmm, yes that is a very good point…but how can I just become wealthier? Now *that* will surely improve my self-esteem!' However, life generally does not really work that way, and it is worth spending a brief moment considering why success books and coaches reference self-esteem so frequently.

It largely comes back to your own self-image - the way in which you view yourself – and therefore how you project yourself. If you have a poor or diminished self-image or if you lack self-esteem then you will find it much harder to promote yourself in terms of how much you believe you should earn (either in terms of your job or how much you feel that you can reasonably bill your clients in business) and in terms of raising your own profile. A key point of note here is that self-esteem not only helps you to achieve success, but it also helps you to maintain it. With low self-esteem even the most deserved of successes can be rapidly reversed through unconscious self-sabotage. You have to truly believe that you are worthy of your successes for it to be sustainable over the long term.

You need to believe you are worthy of success.

This is an issue which impacts people when they first experience exposure in the media. The glare of the spotlight can become uncomfortable when you begin to experience negative feedback, which inevitably goes with the territory. This has become even more pertinent with the high volumes of instant feedback brought via social media and online content. Criticism is so much easier to deal with if you believe in what you are doing, if you are passionate about what you do, and if you believe that you are executing it to the level best of your ability.

Naturally raising your own self-esteem is not something which occurs overnight. The best method to begin improving the way you view yourself and feel about yourself is to set a number of achievable goals and then immediately put into place an action plan to reach those targets. By starting to get a few small wins under your belt you can start to see yourself as someone who is successful and on the route to achieving greater things rather than a person who has not achieved everything in life that they want.

The 5 key steps to making dramatic changes in your life

With the above points in mind, I make the assumption here that there are areas in your life within which you would like to see greater results. If not, there should be! Remember we should think of our lives as the Japanese treat their business efficiency – a masterpiece which is a work in progress for constant and un-ending improvement. In order to achieve greater results, you will need to make changes to your beliefs and strategies accordingly. There are five key steps which you need to take in order to make dramatic changes to your life, and, in order, these are:

1 - Decide what it is that you want

In the next chapter I am going to ask you to consider setting some huge and inspiring goals. This is the first key step to making a dramatic change to any area of your life that being to decide exactly what it is that you want to achieve. After all, to paraphrase *Alice in Wonderland*, if you do not know where it is that you want to go, how will you know when you have arrived?

You must also then consider what exactly it is that is currently preventing you from achieving your goals and consciously remove your limiting beliefs. Let us take the example of Adrian, a client of mine who earned a good income as an IT consultant and wanted to invest in the property market. Adrian's problem was that although he earned a good income and was often able to save reasonable sums of money, he then always seems to find new ways in which to spend his cash.

I am, of course, always a big advocate of thrift and finding ways to save money through looking for trade discounts, using cinema vouchers, or using public transport instead of paying for taxis. In fact, I always try to link pleasure to seeking value for money in whatever it is that I do. That said, in this instance the 80/20 Principle dictated to me that if Adrian wanted to make significant progress quickly what he really needed to ascertain what exactly it was that was causing him to blow his savings so regularly. A self-conducted review of his bank statements showed that the big ticket items outside of his rent and taxes were:

- **Cars** – Adrian had upgraded his car twice in the past five years, and the insurance and running costs in total were crippling

- **Luxury holidays** – Adrian was taking two major holidays each year which were costing the equivalent of two entire months net salary

- **Nights out** – as a work hard and play hard character, Adrian frequently spent the equivalent of two full days of net pay in a weekend on partying

In particular Adrian loved travelling to exotic locations, but he only had four weeks of holiday per year and he felt he needed to maximise those four weeks, which he did by always travelling on a five star budget. Earning a relatively high income he felt that he could justify the expense and so he stayed in some of the most prestigious resorts around the world.

There is nothing particularly unusual about this in the modern consumer economy. Contrary to how it might sometimes feel, people on average today have more disposable income than did any generation in the history of the world. Unfortunately advertisers are very clever types and have tricked us into associating pleasure with using their products and pain with living a life that is apparently inferior in quality to that of our peers. Advertisers send us subliminal messages that the answers to our insecurities, frustrations and inadequacies lie in buying ever more of their products.

If you have ever spent time living in a developing country you would quickly come to realise what a load of utter nonsense this really is. Consumerism is cleverly designed to bring you short term pleasure, but these results and feelings are transient and contribute very little to lasting happiness.

After we had stepped through the thought processes above Adrian understood that he needed to make a change and made a decision to take the first step towards breaking the pattern. He decided that what he wanted to do which was to invest some of his money in the property market in order to build wealth instead of repeatedly frittering away his savings, and through a high level 80/20 style analysis of his bank and credit card statements I quickly helped him to realise that there were three areas in particular through which he was haemorrhaging his personal finances.

2 – Link pleasure and pain to the right behaviours

The next step in making dramatic changes to your life is to change exactly what it is that you link pleasure and pain to. You need to link massive and immediate pain to whatever it is that is stopping you from achieving your longer term goals. In particular, you need to link pain to sabotaging actions which you may be using as a crutch or for short-term comfort. Conversely you also need to link great pleasure to making the changes you need to make in order to create a better outcome over time.

Like many people who work long hours in a professional occupation, my client Adrian had long associated pleasure to instant gratification. He attached status to renting a property in one of the most exclusive areas of town, although living in a prestige location cost him more than one third of his net pay in monthly rent. He also had a more expensive car than any of his friends and took the finest holidays to the extent that his peers and colleagues thought him to be one of the wealthiest and most successful people they knew.

'There are plenty of ways to get ahead. The first is so basic I am almost embarrassed to say it: spend less than you earn.'
- Paul Clitheroe.

Beneath the veneer, though, Adrian had become frustrated because despite the thousands of hours he put in to his professional career, he continually wasted his savings and due to the regular upgrading of his car loans, he actually had a negative net worth; the value of all of his assets less the value of his liabilities was negative.

I helped Adrian to understand that the only way in which he would be able to change this damaging routine would be to make a dramatic change to the way in which he linked pleasure and pain to his personal financial habits. Instead of linking pleasure to always driving a car which was less than two years old,

Adrian began to see the pain it was causing to his financial statements. His luxury beachside rented apartment, once a source of Adrian's greatest comfort and relief, he began to see as a painful monthly liability.

Adrian knew that in theory he was supposed to link pleasure to being thrifty, using car-pooling, going to bring-your-own venues or using discount vouchers instead of frequenting plush restaurants, taking short weekend breaks up the coast instead of fortnight-long jollies in Las Vegas or Hawaii and so on.

But the truth was that Adrian wasn't really feeling it! He missed the so-termed high life and the kudos he had achieved among his peer-group from his happy-go-lucky approach to spending and working hard while simultaneously playing hard. Initially, Adrian found it very hard to link any such pleasures to a more sedate and thrifty way of living. At this point we discussed the third key step to making any significant changes in life, which is to…

3- Break the existing pattern!

At some point if you are going to make a dramatic and sustained change to your life you need to make a decision to break the pattern, to smash the existing routine to pieces! The problem with the way in which we link pleasure and pain to our actions is that often we have been doing things the same way for so long that the linkages we have created are virtually hard-wired into our brains. It can be very difficult to unscramble the existing subconscious process of linking pleasure to short term comforts.

> If you keep doing more of what you have always done,
> you will get more of what you have already got.

The old adage states that if you keep doing what you have always done, you will get more of what you have already got. While this seems an obvious truism, it is absolutely vital to understand that if you want to get different results, eventually you need to make a decision to change your behaviours, and you will need to find a way in which to break or interrupt the existing behaviour pattern.

If you have spent years behaving one way and deriving short term pleasure from an ultimately destructive behaviour, you need to find a way in which to respond when the pattern repeats in order to link pain to that behaviour. In Adrian's case he simply decided one day that he had had enough of the earn-and-spend treadmill and decided to have a weekend at home instead of going out.

While his circle of friends did not comprehend the reasons for him refusing to join them (which was essentially unheard of), he decided to leave work on Friday and head straight to a treadmill of a different kind – the gym treadmill – since his gym membership had been unused for six months. When he got home after the gym on that Friday night Adrian decided to sit down and take a full and fearless inventory of his personal finances. It was not a great deal of fun as Adrian knew that the results would not make for happy reading, but he took a small amount of solace in the knowledge he was now taking positive action.

4 – Create an empowering alternative choice

It is usually possible to break a habit for a while. Smokers quite often manage to stop smoking for a few days, for example. But what can be challenging is putting an absolute stop to behaviour patterns which you formerly turned to for pleasure, comfort or as a crutch, as this can seem to leave a gaping hole in your life. For any dramatic changes you make to your life to be effective and lasting you need to create a *new and empowering alternative* choice.

I recall that one summer I desperately wanted to buy an apartment on the waterfront at the fabulous One Darling Harbour complex in Sydney, though we did not have anything like the deposit money to do so. There was plenty of fear around in the property market at that time and prices were sliding, but we intuitively knew that property prices in such an exclusive location could only sky-rocket once the full regeneration of that part of Sydney was underway and once positive sentiment returned, which one day it surely would.

When we sat down to work out how much money we would need to buy an apartment there I could only let out a quiet but decidedly nervous gulp. The only way in which it would possible, it appeared, would be to spend absolutely no money whatsoever for about six months! While that did not appear to be a realistic goal, we did feel that, in the words of the old saying, if we aimed for the stars we might hit the moon.

Create alternative choices – empowering choices!

I am not sure which of us came up with the hare-brained idea or exactly when, but my missus and I cooked up a scheme to begin training to run the Sydney Marathon instead of socialising for six months. I am absolutely certain that if we had simply come up with a plan to go to the gym on Friday nights instead of going out then the new behaviour pattern would only have lasted a few weeks because the new behaviour pattern would not be inspiring or empowering enough. After all, you can go to the gym any night of the week, so Friday nights would soon enough have reverted to party time, I have no doubt about that.

But now we had a genuine goal to work towards and for six months we trained, ran massive training runs, ate healthy food and didn't spend very much money at all. And you know what, at the end of it all, I will always be proud to say that we ran the Sydney Marathon through nearly five gruelling hours on a roasting hot Sydney day when plenty of other participant runners dropped like flies onto the side-walk. Better still we bought our dream apartment too. And it has indeed sky-rocketed in value over the years, just as we had predicted, doubling in value in only the first seven years we owned the place.

Of course, I am not suggesting for a moment that training for a marathon is the right idea for you, and in fact road running may not be a great idea for your physical health at all! My wife Heather did so much damage to her knees during the training runs that her doctor told her that she should not run the marathon on the day. But she is a stubborn farmer's daughter and ran the course anyway, resulting in some lasting damage to her knee. Nevertheless it was a super day, and we will always remember with wry amusement us runners being heckled in the early morning section of the course by the nightclub stragglers of Kings Cross.

What I am suggesting here is that if you want to break a limiting or destructive behaviour pattern you need to find for yourself a stimulating, exciting and empowering alternative. My client Adrian came up with a plan to spend less and save towards an investment but realised that he was not going to achieve this solely by staying in on Friday nights and watching television. Instead, in Adrian's case he became interested in securing good deals online, and particularly how he could fulfil his passion for luxury travel on a budget. Could he still visit premium locations in Europe and across Asia without busting his bank balance? He wasn't sure, but he decided that would find out!

Be guided by your passion.

Over the coming few years, Adrian became something of an aficionado in international travel on a proverbial shoestring. He began to consider how he could use his technology skills to build a business which found ways in which people could experience five star luxury on a two star budget. Where once he had taken great pleasure from consumerism he began to instead associate pain to paying large sums of money for expensive new consumer brands or holidays, and pleasure to buying second hand goods or getting cheaper deals for his holidays. Eventually he became such an expert at getting value for money he wondered whether he could turn his passion for travel into an online business through using his strong computing skills.

Better still, Adrian was able to combine his passion for travel with a bit of writing and travel journalism. The seeds of some exciting new ideas were only just beginning to form in Adrian's brain. In the meantime, the money he was saving from his new thriftier approach to living meant that the dollars we beginning to pile up in his bank account. For the first time in his life Adrian looked forward to receiving his monthly bank statements because each month he was saving nearly a quarter of his income and was quickly able to consider buying an investment property to begin his portfolio.

5 – Condition the new pattern until it becomes hard-wired

The final step to making dramatic and lasting changes to your life is to fine-tune and condition the new behaviour patterns as regularly as possible until they become your new reality. It appears to be very difficult to change facets of your life dramatically but eventually if you condition the new behaviour in your life regularly your brain will recognise the consistency and the new behaviour pattern will become hard-wired.

Here is a brief example. Until I was thirty years old I ate meat every lunchtime and during every evening meal. On especially good days I scheduled in a full English breakfast with all the trimmings too! I loved eating meat and made sure that I did so at every opportunity. But why? Is eating meat really that important, or even that tasty? Not really. Rather I had built up an association over time with eating protein for strength and eating meat as being a masculine thing to do. I reinforced the message and behaviour at every opportunity through my actions and my words, until the behaviour pattern had become hard-wired - so much so that I openly scoffed at the idea of any meal which did not contain meat.

Condition the new behaviours until they are consistent.

What changed? Well, one thing was when I met my now wife, she introduced me to vegetarian food, and since she did most of the cooking at home (by which, of course, I mean *all* of the cooking) I ate more vegetarian food than I ever had before. Gradually this led me to question my preconceptions about being a meat eater until eventually I gave up eating meat altogether. At first this was a matter of principle more than anything else. Was I the sort of vegetarian who looked at meat eaters with disdain? Hardly. I still thought bacon smelt very tempting. But the interesting thing for me has been how over time the new behaviour pattern of not eating meat has become so conditioned so that now the old alternative seems completely alien and even slightly repulsive to me.

Over a period of some years my actions and words have re-wired my brain to associate pleasure to eating fantastic quality food such as delicious vegetarian curries. On the other hand I look at plates of cheap, watery chicken or hear news stories of British lasagne being infested with horse meat and other unappetising offal, and experience a vague queasy feeling. The new alternative has become hard-wired into my brain as my new reality.

'You can, you should, and if you're brave enough to start, you will.'
- Stephen King.

This book is certainly no forum for jumping on a soap-box about whether or not people should eat meat. For one thing I probably ate more meat in my first thirty years than most people do in a lifetime! Rather it is simply a noteworthy example of how something which I believed to be the only way to live can be changed and reversed where a new empowering alternative is found, and then is conditioned consistently and for long enough. It now seems quite amazing to me that I ever ate meat at all.

Another interesting aspect to this is that these small changes can have knock-on effects that you had not expected or intended. Out of the blue, my old man became a vegetarian having been a meat eater and some-time leather jacket owner for more than sixty years. I find it interesting how these small flow-through effects can have unforeseen consequences, sending ripples out into your world. Remember, condition your new empowering behaviour patterns until they are consistent and become a part of your reality.

The questions you ask yourself

The co-founder of the London School of Economics and great Irish playwright George Bernard Shaw once observed:

> 'Some men see things as they are and say 'why?
> Others dream of things that never were and ask 'why not?'

I believe that this is very important analogy. Too often people are limited in what they can achieve in life because they ask themselves such disempowering questions, such as 'Why does this always happen to me?' instead of asking 'How can I change this? How can I instead find ways in which to achieve everything that I have always wanted?'

This is a subtle yet crucial distinction. Humans are naturally inquisitive creatures and we are designed to ask ourselves internal questions almost all of the time. The process often happens unconsciously, yet we are continually posing questions to ourselves. Never is this more so the case than when it comes to personal finance and investing. Suppose you get an annual bonus. What is the first question which you ask yourself? Consider the following possibility:

• 'What can I spend this money on as a <u>reward</u> for my hard work? What can I treat myself to this year? Perhaps I would <u>enjoy</u> driving a new sports car or a trip to Paris?'

Alternatively, you could ask yourself the following empowering question:

• 'How I can best use this money to secure my <u>long-term</u> financial future and to achieve my financial freedom? What investments can I buy with these funds which will bring me returns forever? How can I make <u>sacrifices</u> today so that my life tomorrow will be filled with abundance?'

When it comes to personal finances and investment success, you very often find that the difference between success and failure is determined by whether or not someone is prepared to make sacrifices today in order to secure their long term future. The alternative approach of looking for short term pleasure or gratification practically guarantees suboptimal results. The same is true of almost any area of your life. If you ask yourself the right questions, you can achieve outstanding results and making sacrifices today can help you to achieve the goals you want.

Chapter 6 summary

» Subconsciously we all have a wealth thermostat which is likely to determine our ongoing financial health

» There is a proven pathway to the creation of wealth – follow it!

» In order to make dramatic changes to your life you need to decide exactly what you do want

» To make changes to your life and results you need to create empowering alternative behaviours and choices

» The level of your results will ultimately be determined by your beliefs

7
Choose Your Own Adventure:
Big Goals...
Inspiring Goals!

7

'People do not fail in life because they aim too high and miss, but because they aim too low and hit.' – Les Brown.

Choose your own adventure

When I was growing up there was a great series of books around under the aforementioned title which allowed children to engage in fighting fantasy adventures. They were superb! The basic premise was that after the first page of the book you were given a choice of what to do next and the book would signal to you to turn to a new page based upon your choices - and thus you were to some extent in control of how the story progressed next. Sometimes there were dice rolls to be carried out in order to determine your fortunes, such as whether or not you could successfully swim across a river, climb a snow-capped mountain or slay a goblin (or whatever else it was that took place in fighting fantasy tales).

I loved those books. They were genuinely exciting for kids because they allowed you to take control of what happened in the story and you really could choose the path of your own adventure. Admittedly it was quite common for us to cheat, by having fingers and thumbs in half a dozen different pages in case a poor decision was made and we wanted to retrace our steps. Of course what we should really have done was to learn from poor choices and resolve not to make them again!

> Is the world your oyster or the future your clam?
> Your beliefs will determine the answer.

Sometime around our teenage years too many folk give up on believing that they can choose their own path in life, dismissing the idea that we can do what we are passionate about as just another type of fantasy. We are told that we must be realistic or limit our expectations. Small defeats knock our confidence and cumulative knock-backs amend our reality. We begin to see the world differently. Well, you made a great step forward when you picked up this book and now I am going to ask you to choose your own adventure. Now is the time to restore your dreams and make *them* your new reality.

Aiming high

Do you know someone who set their sights low and then reached them, but never progressed much further? I am sure that you do, because sadly it is all too common. If you want to achieve more you must set your sights higher.

I grew up in chilly England where my childhood passion, like many English lads, was playing cricket. One of my team-mates up until I was around 25 years of age or so was a lovely young lad named Alastair Cook. He's still a great friend today. When we were playing club cricket it was quite evident that Ali was a class apart from the rest of us. He represented England schoolboys at every age group from the age of 11 upwards and always seemed to have the happy knack of scoring heavily, even when he was not playing at his best (which, by the way, was very good!).

When I look back at what set him apart from his peers, it seems to me that much of Ali's greatest advantage was his mind-set and unshakeable self-belief. While most of us lesser mortals were focussed on grinding out scores week in week out, even from the very youngest age Ali had it in mind that he wanted to be the number one batsman for the full England side and one day go on to captain his country. He was always able to visualise a much bigger picture.

Not only did he go on to represent England by the time he was just 20 years old scoring a brilliant century in his very first Test Match, within six years he became the England captain and he has gone to become England's greatest ever scoring Test match batsman. And the thing is, he achieved all of this before he was even 30 years of age! That level of success simply would not have been possible without him having set his sights so high. Note that he did not set the goal of making a living as a professional cricketer or making the county side – his goal was to go right the way to the very top and captain his country, and he set his milestones and targets accordingly.

Aim for the stars and you might reach the moon...
set big and exciting goals!

Subconsciously a great many people set themselves each month a target of making their pay packet last until the end of the month. Sometimes they achieve their goal. In other months the money runs dry and they need to dip into their credit card. But they never really seem to get ahead, because their goal is so limited…and *limiting*.

When I started out in investing years ago I set myself a target of reaching a portfolio of $10 million in assets by the age of 40. My thinking was that even if I fell short by some way, I would still be in far better shape than if I set myself a smaller but more achievable target of increasing my bonus by ten percent or being promoted to become a Chief Financial Officer of a listed company. Consider how you can set your targets much higher, because once you understand compounding or snowballing, you can achieve them.

'Think big!' – Donald Trump.

This seems to happen again and again in investment – people who set small and realistically achievable goals often achieve less than those who set unrealistically high ones. This does not mean that you should be tempted to gamble or take mindless risks, rather you should resolve to understand the power of compound growth and to keep on using it and using it to your ongoing advantage. As Donald Trump used to say before he thought he would become a TV star and started telling people they were fired: 'Think big!'

The 5am club

Have you ever noticed how some people wake up enthusiastic and seem to be on the go from morning until night, kicking goals and remaining incredibly active throughout the day? Yet others appear to slope out of bed at the last possible minute having re-set their alarm clock four times in order to maximise their time in bed. How is this so? I do not believe that it is all down to inherent energy levels, though in some cases this may of course be a factor.

No, instead the difference is down to some people having huge, exciting and inspiring goals which get them up each morning raring to go! If you only have a target in life of 'just getting by' or 'making ends meet', is this likely to empower you to over-achieve in every aspect of your life? Hardly! Without inspiring goals, you will lack the energy and power to achieve. I see this on social media pages all the time: 'Thank God it's Friday – what a crappy week!'

A friend of mine who has proven himself time and again as one of Australia's most successful share market traders once said:

'Weekends are two days of the week that get in the way of the thing I love doing – trading and making money for me and my clients!' – Assad Tannous, *Asenna Wealth*.

Of course Assad loves his weekends and this comment was a little tongue in cheek, as that is his way. But I also detect more than a grain of truth in his quip. Assad loves what he does – he is absolutely passionate about trading for a living and could scarcely picture himself doing anything else. And that is why he is among the elite few, because his passion drives him to make constant and never-ending improvements to his skills and techniques.

When I was working in professional practice I can remember all too well that dismal sinking feeling associated with resetting the alarm clock for just an extra ten minutes in bed, delaying the inevitable moment when I would have to get up to face the onslaught of tedious meetings and stressful phone calls. If this sounds familiar to you, here is a heads up - it is no way to live life! This does not mean you should phone your boss and quit tomorrow. What it does mean is that you should consider how you can get yourself into a position where you can choose to design the day that you want, doing what you are genuinely passionate about.

These days I cannot wait for the day to start, so much so that my ideal day starts at 5am when I get up raring to go. One of the truly great things about getting up at this time is that without the distractions which dog most people you can have a *full day*'s worth of work completed before most people have even contemplated their cornflakes! Carry out some research into this subject and you will find that successful people are very often early risers. Is this the reason that they are successful? Not quite. More likely the reason that they are successful is that they love and are passionate about what they do and they cannot wait to get started each morning! That is why they are early risers.

Creating a thrilling future

We have already looked at how your life was five years ago compared to how your life is today. But what about five years from now? Is there any reason that you cannot take yourself up to great heights in every area of your life? I do not believe so. There is no reason that you can't be scoring at least an 8 or a 9 in every category. Heck, why can't you even be scoring a 10? Set yourself some targets. Instead of just writing a number here, add in a short sentence or bullet point next to each category to explain your goal in a little more detail.

Life in 5 years' time!

Physical vitality and health	....
Mental health and personal happiness	....
Personal relationships	....
Friendships and family	....
Home and living environment	....
Social life, skills and confidence	....
Attractiveness and self-confidence	....
Career progression, opportunities and outlook	....
Work and business	....
Financial base and investment	....
Spiritual and charitable contribution	....

Now this is all well and good, but if it were that easy then surely everyone would simply set a few goals of high achievement in all areas of their lives, and we would all be heroes. Life would be so simple! In practice, life does not work quite in that way. It is important above all else to ensure that you keep things moving in the right direction.

Success does not happen immediately and nor does it happen in a straight line, but provided that you can learn to accept failure, mistakes and adversity and see these as learning opportunities – and crucially, resolve to continue working towards your targets – eventually you will get to where you want to be. The power of compounding also means that successes in one area of your life can have exciting and important flow-through effects into other parts of your life.

The first rule of achieving goals is to never, ever give up. Most people never get there because they decide on a goal but then somewhere along the line they experience a setback and then they give up trying. I can tell you before you even begin that you will experience setbacks, so what actually determines whether you will reach your goals or not is how you respond to the failures.

Another important factor in the ability to achieve targets is to break down the bigger goals into smaller milestones and more achievable targets. It is great to set a goal of owning 25 investment properties or a share portfolio worth millions, but these goals might appear to be so large for beginners that the appear to be impossible. Instead you need to be able to make constant small improvements and achieve regular, smaller targets. What you really need are some more specific action points.

Setting goals in four key areas of your life

And now for the last written exercise in the book, after which you are permitted to breathe a sigh of relief. Below I am going to ask you to set some goals in just four areas of your life. I have been doing this exercise myself for well over a decade now. I come back to the exercise and set myself new goals every couple of years, and it is always fascinating to look back and see how I have fared against my goals.

What is notable that sometimes I do not achieve a goal that I have set and frequently my goals shift a little as time passes. But often I also find that in other areas I have achieved things that I did not even believe that I could. What is inarguably the case is that by setting specific goals and then putting in place an action plan to reach them my results in life have improved beyond all recognition, and they can for you too. Let us start with setting some…

1 - Personal development goals

Many years ago, I set myself the following goals which I still have jotted down on a slightly yellow looking and faded piece of paper:

- Become a great public speaker

- Learn how to build a business

- Developer the following character traits – open, honest, trusted, cheerful, happy, confident, successful, respected

- Exercise for one hour daily and be in great shape

- Become vegetarian, eat a healthy diet

- Develop outstanding writing skills

- Publish my first book

- Become Australia's leading real estate analyst

- Cement important friendships, drop negative or toxic friendships

- Cut down on caffeine

- Stop becoming anxious!

It is interesting to look back at these goals to see how I have fared. I have been successful in most areas simply because I set myself these specific goals and took immediate action towards them, but I still have a bit of a way to go in others. I love coffee and still sometimes glug too much caffeine (which doesn't help my anxiety levels either, in truth!). Meanwhile my public speaking has improved in leaps and bounds, though I could hardly be described as a great in this area. I have resolved to keep practising, however, and eventually I will reach my goal.

My circle of friends now comprises positive people who help to improve the quality of my life rather than those who drag me back or are toxic, and I have made great strides in other areas, including publishing several books and being widely featured in the media. In fact in some areas I have achieved much more than I thought was ever possible when I started out. The key to this entire exercise is to set yourself big, exciting and inspirational goals and work towards them, and then to review and recalibrate them again every year or two years.

Your personal development goals

....

....

....

....

....

....

....

....

Well done for completing the exercise. In the section below I will explain how the key to reaching these goals is to take immediate action today in each area to kick things off. But first while you are on a roll and brainstorming these ideas, let us next consider…

2 - Career, business and financial goals

Moving onto career and business goals, here are a few of the goals I set for myself years ago on that same crusty old piece of paper:

- Add more investment properties to my portfolio in London and also in Sydney
- Publish and sell 10,000 copies of my investment books
- Continue to invest every month into index funds
- Improve share trading discipline and money management skills
- Replace salary income with business income
- Open business offices in the London and Sydney

Interestingly I surpassed my investment goals relatively easily and compounding growth allowed me to achieve more than I had expected sooner. I set my sights high and achieved them in this area, with my business now established in two countries. Now it is your turn – remember to think big!

Your career, business and financial goals

....
....
....
....
....
....
....

Excellent. You are getting the hang of it now, so while you are still fresh let us cover off the penultimate category of goals, being…

3 – Adventures, experiences, travel and toys goals

In my experience it is important to set yourself some exciting adventure and toys goals because these can really give you the drive. Is this selfish? To some extent, perhaps. But humans respond well to exciting targets and we will consider your contribution goals further in the fourth and final section. Here are a few of the goals that I set myself for adventures and pleasure:

- Buy a country house in the United Kingdom
- Purchase an apartment on Darling Harbour and live in it for a couple of years
- Take a round-the-world cruise on the *Queen Elizabeth*

- Buy a 4x4 car
- Drive the Big Lap of Australia in a camper van for 12 months
- Visit 30 countries of the world
- Live in a developing country for two years

Toys and adventure goals can tend to vary wildly from person to person. I loved doing that world cruise so much that I desperately want to do it again. Yet for another person being cooped up on a boat with hundreds of (mainly older) people could be a version of their living hell! Similarly, 'slumming it' in a camper van may not be everyone's idea of fun, but I cannot think of any better way to appreciate the wonders of Australia than to take a year seeing all of this wonderful land. In fact, I cannot recommend it highly enough.

Ultimately you will need to pick out some adventure and toys and goals which suit and excite you. It is fine to have some material goals as well as adventure goals, particularly if these excite and inspire you enough to get out there and begin achieving, but as I will explore in a little more detail below, you do need to give yourself a higher purpose than this too. Your turn again:

Your adventures, experiences, travel and toys goals

....

....

....

....

....

....

....

4 - Giving it back or contribution goals

When people are beginning to make their way in life the concept of contribution or giving back tends to be lower down on their list of priorities, but the notion is very important and here I will explain why. If you set yourself purely financial goals or targets which involve acquiring toys or taking adventurous trips, one day you might reach those goals, and then what? Your success might never be enough and you will never achieve the sense of fulfilment and happiness which you believed your goals would give you when you started out.

There can be no satisfaction in life greater than that of making a difference to the lives of others, and that is why it is important to have a higher purpose for your personal goals than simply building success and wealth for yourself. If building wealth and success for you is your solitary goal and purpose then your journey will ultimately be an unfulfilling one because you can be certain that there will always be someone who has more than you do. This is why I say that it is important to find a cause which has meaning to you and to set yourself a higher purpose goal of being able to contribute to that cause. Here are some of the contribution goals I set myself some years ago:

- Donate 10 percent of book sales to a breast cancer charity
- Return to East Timor and work as a volunteer
- Work as a volunteer for *BlazeAid* in Australia
- Work at the homeless shelter in Sydney
- Donate annual school fees to friends with children in East Timor
- Set up my own charitable foundation

I still have not set up my own charitable foundation, so this is a big goal with a tough administrative hurdle which I will need to keep working towards in the future. Again the goals you set here should be personal to you, and importantly, they should have a genuine meaning to you. If you can find a higher purpose for your success, then your success is far more likely to be maintained and sustainable.

Your charitable and contribution goals

Next we will consider how the key to achieving goals and making them a part of your reality is to take some immediate action towards reaching those goals. Before we do so, let us first briefly consider…

Finding your higher purpose

Last year I met for coffee with Peter Thornhill, an excitable character at the best of times, and I noted that he became particularly animated when we began to discuss some charitable work that he had initiated in Africa. Among other deliverables the project had involved building a well to provide clean drinking water for disadvantaged communities. I clearly recognised the sheer sense of satisfaction which he had clearly gained from the ventures, and he had become passionate about doing much more.

There is truly no sense of fulfilment in life quite like that which can be gained from helping others. In particular, this is the case when we can see the direct results of our contributions. It is the same reason that I take so much pleasure in paying school fees directly rather than only donating to a large charity which incurs administrative costs – it is thrilling to see direct outcomes.

Humans tend to look for instant feedback and link instant results to actions, which is why volunteering is also such a satisfying experience, since we can see with our own eyes when we are making a difference. Charitable giving and contribution is necessarily a personal matter and what feels right for one person may not be so for another. I urge you here to consider your higher purpose and to find a cause with meaning to you.

Getting started towards your goals

The real key to beginning to achieve your goals is to take some real and immediate positive action in order to get you on your way. If one of your goals is to build a large business from scratch, then why not start researching someone who has achieved that exact goal? And do so today!

If your goal is to own a huge portfolio of investment properties or build a massive share market portfolio, find someone who has done that and learn from them. If, for example, you have a goal of owning a Ferrari or travelling around the world, get out there and find some travel brochures or book yourself in for a test drive. The important point here is not so much about what your specific goals are, it is about taking some *immediate action* towards that goal in order to get you started.

What are you really worth? Seeing the bigger picture

One of the most limiting human character traits is that people become mired in unimportant matters or they major in minor decisions. People can get bogged down in the day-to-day challenges that they face and lose sight of the bigger picture, become mired in the detail. This is why setting targets is such an important part of achieving success.

'What gets measured, gets done.' – Peter Drucker.

Humans respond well to targets. If you can set yourself specific, measurable and achievable targets then a plan can be put in place to achieve them. As we looked at in the sections above, targets should be not only financial, but also emotional, spiritual, reflect meaningful relationships, good health, happiness, and so on. After all, financial wealth without happiness is a fairly impotent goal.

There is an old law of business known as the *Peter Principle* which states that folk are promoted to one level above the level of their competence.[1] In other words employees progress through the system performing jobs and roles that they are capable of performing until they reach a position which they are less well equipped to handle.[2] The implication of this is that when analysing a big business you might expect to find a surprisingly significant percentage of employees in roles which see them struggling or out of their depth. By and large, there is probably an element of truth in this.

I believe we should look at this another way. It is likely that we rise to the level we are comfortable with then self-unconsciously sabotage the level of our performance thus ensuring that we progress no further. For my money, this is a convincing explanation of why some employees can walk into Managing Director or CEO roles as if to the manner born, while others are paralysed with fear by change of any kind and remain in the same role or same organisation for decades, until change is forced upon them.

Beliefs will ultimately determine the level of success you achieve.

Whether we like it or not, change is inevitable – it will eventually happen, even to those who take positions or roles at the age of 16 and stay in them for decades. Technology changes and the world changes, so it is likely to be better for you to learn to embrace shifting trends and adapt with them than it is to cling to old ideas and resist all change.

Another inescapable conclusion is that the level of our success is indelibly linked to the level of our self-worth and confidence in our ability to deliver value. There is simply no getting away from this. If you do not believe you are adding value to your clients or to your employer, then you will not be comfortable drawing your pay cheque or invoicing your customers for your time and service and you will convey this lack of self-worth in your actions.

> If you become a true expert in your field,
> you can add value to others.

There are two variables which need to be worked on here. Firstly, there is the level of your self-esteem, which can be built up through achieving small successes and making constant improvements to the way you live. And secondly, you need to feel comfortable in the level of value you are providing. I believe that this is best achieved though focusing on your passion and becoming an expert in your field to the extent that you can add more value than anyone else in your chosen specialist area.

The power of this becomes self-fulfilling. Not only will you be working in your area of passion and automatically be driven more than ever before to become the best that you can be, you will feel ever more confident of your ability to deliver value through your expertise for which you can charge more fees and use to reach more people.

Thinking bigger still

In the classic self-help book *The Magic of Thinking Big*, the author David Schwartz opines that what holds people back in life is often that they think small and do not expect to achieve great things.[3] Argues Schwartz, humans view things as they are, not as they might be. Schwartz identifies three 'failure diseases', these being:[4]

1 – 'Excuse-itis'

How many times have you heard someone say: 'Oh, I can't do that because…'? All too often! Once you close off your mind to the idea of achieving a goal, then it is all but a certainty that you will not achieve it. You must not make excuses for failing to achieve your goals!

2 - Detail-itis

Remember, we need to see the big picture. Set big and exciting goals, but do not get too bogged down in small and ultimately immaterial short term goals. It is said that the wealthy see the big picture, the poor get bogged down in the details. There is more than a good deal of truth in that and I see it in my business every day with clients. It is as clear as daylight that my wealthier clients, while they manage risk carefully, do not let small details prevent them from taking the action needed for success. Beginner investors often fret over irrelevant details and become paralysed by fear and unable to invest. They panic over what are ultimately insignificant matters to the investment decision.

More experienced investors tend to understand that, for example, paying for a lawyer to proofread a contract is a part of the cost of doing business and use of a lawyer's expertise could potentially save many thousands of dollars down the track. Thus they do not balk at the prospect of paying legal fees and understand that payment for an expert is an important step in de-risking the investment process.

3 - Procrastination

For the procrastinator, there are always reasons why you cannot do something today. You do not have time, you cannot take that risk right now, or you are doing fine without taking action. There are plenty of common excuses. Success comes from decisive and committed action, so you need to be able to move past the procrastination and get to work!

Time horizons – short term to long term

What would you consider to be a long-term investment? If you ask people what they might consider to be a short, medium and long-term investment, they will probably give you an answer something like the following:

- **Short term** – one month to 12 months

- **Medium term** - more than 12 months

- **Long term** – five years or longer

In this book, I want to get you to rethink these preconceptions, and instead consider a much bigger picture, where a long-term investment could mean the duration of your lifetime. Better than that, I want to think of your investments as vehicles which can generate wealth through your lifetime and even way *beyond* your own lifetime. That is the type of bigger picture I am talking about!

Humans cannot predict the future accurately.

Am I being too outrageous if I say that humans cannot predict the future accurately? I do not believe so. There are more than enough examples to prove my point. Yet what do you see when you turn on the news or the internet every day?

- 'Stock prices will moderate due to the fiscal cliff.'

- 'Property prices are going to ease in December due to household debt stress.'

- 'Interest rates will be cut twice by July 2016.'

- 'We should definitely be short the dollar this week but we are going long on gold.'

Humans love to make predictions but it is absolutely crystal clear and beyond the shadow of any doubt that as a race we are generally quite hopeless at them. So therefore could it follow that any investment which relies upon an asset price moving in our favour over any time period under at the very least a decade is to some extent something of a guess? Or worse, a gamble?

Longer term predictions can often be more reliable.

Over the longer term some things are reasonably predictable. Company earnings will move higher and the dollar value of dividends from the share markets will rise. Property prices in the inner suburbs of capital cities with strong population growth will increase. The currency in our pocket or stashed in our bank accounts will depreciate and be worth less. In developed countries with inflationary economies, it has always been thus.

Although even these outcomes are sometimes not 100 percent certain, they are nevertheless extremely likely in part because central banks actually plan for it to be so. Central banks and governments today are well aware of the dangers of deflation such as was experienced in Japan and will therefore fight tooth and nail to maintain a steadily inflationary economy. If required their interest rates will be cut to near zero, central banks will effectively print money through asset purchasing programmes and in truly desperate times, they sometimes may even just give us money to spend.

Deflation can be staved off by 'dropping money from helicopters'.

The concept of dropping money from helicopters was conceived by Milton Friedman and later quoted by the Chairman of the US Federal Reserve, Ben Bernanke, who became known colloquially as 'helicopter Ben'. While not to be taken literally, the notion is important. The key point is that central banks have powerful tools at their disposal to ensure that prolonged deflation does not take hold of the economy, and they will use them to ensure that it never happens.

Think back to direction of the Dow Jones chart we considered in Figure 4.1. That, right there, is the direction of asset prices - up. Not risky, and not flat. And they certainly are not heading down over the long term. Just up. However, over the short term not you, I, or anyone else knows exactly what share indices and property prices will do exactly. No, not even those aggressive-sounding, tiresome, know-it-all commentators who insist so adamantly that they must be right. Not even them! I will discuss further in chapter 10 how share prices in some cases may have become materially over-valued in recent years, but for now let is consider this question:

What really is investing?

Here are some more realistic time horizons for investment:

- **Short term** – one decade
- **Medium term** – 10 years to your lifetime
- **Long term** – your lifetime and beyond your own lifetime

We have already established that we cannot predict the future, and therefore the length of our life is unknown. But we can certainly take a reasonable guess and work with that. True investing does not focus upon the immediate price action of a security or asset. Instead, investors focus on the fact that over the long term – yes that means a lifetime – quality assets that they hold will generate them both strong recurring income and dependable capital growth.

Think beyond your own lifetime.

Although the concept of continuing to steadily build an asset base over time is simple to grasp, the mind-set is not easy for many people to accept. In fact, for most it seems to be a totally alien, almost abstract concept. Think of how often you hear people with an opposite view:

- 'You can't take it with you'

- 'You're only young once…'

- 'Don't be so tight!'

- 'I plan to spend the last dollar on the day I die'

- 'I'll take the lump sum on a long holiday and then live off the government pension!'

Unfortunately, the average pension balances at retirement ensure that for most, drawing the meagre government pension is the only option that remains. If you are not sure how much the state pension is (or, more accurately, is not) likely to pay for, take a quick look. The government pension doesn't go a long way in the modern world.

You need to able to move beyond the idea that money is simply something that you earn and then spend. Instead, a portion of what is earned should be donated to charity, some should be spent on moderate living costs, a reasonable buffer saved for emergencies and the remainder invested for the future. Better still make the charitable donations and investments first and then spend or save the remainder.

Through first grasping and then embracing these very simple concepts, over a lifetime of application perfectly ordinary individuals achieve results that are staggering. Spend less than you earn and buy quality, appreciating assets with the difference. And as for what will happen to stock markets and property markets over the next few months or years? Rhett Butler said it best in *Gone with the Wind*:

> 'Frankly my dear, I don't give a damn.'
> – Rhett Butler.

Chapter 7 summary

» Setting yourself inspiring goals is what gives you the energy and excitement to take committed and decisive action

» Do not limit yourself...think big

» You can only genuinely believe in bigger goals by raising the level of your self-worth

» See the bigger picture and plan for longer term success

» Taking a longer term view of investment, business and your life can afford you the scope to achieve massive goals

Part Two
Snowball Your Way To Wealth

8
A New Attitude
To Debt

8

'Blessed are the young, for they shall inherit the national debt.'
– Herbert Hoover.

The modern way

When my accountancy career took me to London, I worked with a high-earning couple who always had two brand new sports cars. Always. Every year they had the latest model and each subsequent year they upgraded to the newest design. And they had a brand new house too, and always had the most expensive and exotic holidays.

This is only one small example, but it is a neat microcosm of modern society and attitudes to consumerism where people tend to believe that what they have is a better measurement of worth than who they actually are. Silly though it may sound when written down, people take on debt to pay for expensive cars in order to impress others with how 'wealthy' and successful they are! They do the same with their houses, holidays, furniture, golf clubs, watches and any other status symbols that you may care to mention.

The problem with always financing depreciating assets such as cars and continually upgrading them is that you get clobbered on each new deal and the interest charges continue to compound against you. If you want to generate wealth you need to get compounding interest working for you by owning assets which continue to pay you income and appreciate in value.

Consumer debt

Karl worked in banking and earned a good salary but also enjoyed the finer things in life. He liked to live in a prime location suburb close to the city and the beach and so he paid out a fair proportion of his salary in rent each month. Karl actually always seemed to have a reasonable balance of cash sitting in his bank account, more than $30,000 on average at the end of each month. The problem was that he also had a painful loan on a new sports car to service each year and he wanted to take an expensive holiday. After all, he worked pretty hard.

The unusual thing about Karl's finances was that he often paid for holidays and luxury items on credit. Sometimes he put them on a Visa card and on other occasions he took advantage of 'Buy now, pay in two years' time' deals advertised in stores. These store offers incurred very high effective rates of interest of up to 20 percent per annum, but they did buy Karl some time to earn more money and receive the next year's bonus.

For this reason while Karl usually had a sum of money in credit in his bank account which was topped up by his salary each month, he also always had balances due on his credit cards which were incurring interest at between 10 percent and 20 percent. Intuitively, Karl knew that it did not make a lot of sense to have cash in the bank and loans outstanding which attracted high interest charges, but it made him feel a bit better off. He always kept several hundred dollars of cash in his wallet too, for similar reasons.

Carrying cash makes people feel wealthier, but building assets is what makes people wealthier.

Karl was a chap who in his own words liked to work hard and spend hard, and his employer was generally pleased with the long hours that Karl put in at the office, although he did on occasions seem prone to having a short temper or become stressed easily. When the financial crisis hit, the bank that Karl worked for was forced to make some cutbacks and several of his colleagues were made redundant. Fortunately for Karl, this did not impact him directly as his role was safe, but his employers did announce that there would be no bonuses this year, and as the firm had made net losses there may be no bonuses for some time going forward.

This was a problem for Karl because he had come to rely upon his annual bonus to pay down the credit card balance a little, especially as the balance (while fluctuating from month to month) generally seemed to get larger with each passing year. The problem he now faced was that he had become accustomed to driving a sports car which had become a little older and no longer impressed his mates, and he wanted to upgrade it.

Bad debt causes compound interest to work against you – eliminate it as quickly as you can.

Further, Karl had also become used to the idea of an expensive fortnight's holiday each summer as compensation for the thousands of hours per year he was putting in at the office, which had become increasingly stressful. Even more annoyingly, the credit card balances just seemed to be getting larger. He rarely read the statements because they were too painful to look at, but if he had taken the time to read them more closely he would have seen that the credit balances in total added up to more than $50,000 and were incurring nearly $10,000 every year in compounding interest charges.

Being a banker by profession Karl was good with numbers, but he did not pay a lot of attention to his credit card bills because they made for unhappy reading. Interestingly, he still maintained his $30,000 cash balance and by this stage had taken to carrying around as a matter of course around one thousand dollars in cash. He had become a little more ostentatious with his cash, always being the first to offer to buy a round of drinks, pay for taxis or meals out.

When the next annual holiday rolled around, Karl had a problem because his credit card balances had reached his maximum allowable balance of $60,000 and the bank would not extend him any more credit. He found this to be quite stressful, but had been heartened to receive a pay rise in the financial year, despite the lack of bonus. Karl now earned a good deal more than most of his mates, and was generally considered to be quite successful.

Compound interest can work for you, or against you.

Karl resolved the holiday issue by taking out a payday loan for the maximum amount he could source of $10,000, which he had seen advertised on the television. Had he read the small print he would have been astonished by the rate of effective interest charge, which ran into the thousands of percent per annum. Karl understood numbers pretty well though, and knew that these figures were essentially meaningless, or at least, not that important to him. After all, the whole point of a payday loan is that you pay it back at the end of the month when you get paid.

Unfortunately, while the holiday was riotous fun - even more so than it usually was - when Karl got back to the grind of work he stumbled upon a problem. His car needed urgent repairs and since he needed the car to get to and from work he had to stump up the cash for the mechanical maintenance work to be carried out. Since Karl had only one form of income from his job, it was out of the question that he could sell his car, and despite now earning a significantly higher than average salary, Karl was running into financial difficulties. Unable to repay the payday loan on time, penalty and interest charges began to add up at an alarming rate and Karl knew that he had to do something about it.

Seeing an advert for consolidating his debt he took out one loan to cover all of his debts and incurred interest of a more manageable 9 percent per annum. The total of the consolidation loan was $100,000 with interest accruing at $9000 each year. Including the repayment of the principal of the loan, Karl made annual payments of $18,000 which was the equivalent of pre-tax earnings from his salary of well over $30,000. The first quarter of Karl's salary was used to pay down the loan, which, he calculated sombrely, he should be able to clear by the time he was in his late thirties.

What is your net worth?

How many hours have you worked for that net worth?

Unfortunately, by the time Karl turns 40 all he is likely to show for his thousands of hours in the workforce is a head of grey hair and some great experiences. We looked earlier in the book at the power of compound interest. It is important to understand that compounding works its magic on debt when it used in the wrong way, and if compound interest is not working for you then it is likely to be working against you.

It is likely that you know of someone a bit like Karl or recognise some of these behaviour patterns. It is potentially an insidious trap but not a difficult one to fall into because society almost trains us to some extent to be like Karl. We are taught that a professional career is a sign of success, which may be true but this does not always lead to financial wealth, and running high levels of consumer debt is not considered to be unusual.

Farming for the future

My wife, Heather, comes from a farming family. I have always felt that farming is an excellent analogy for how people should invest because farmers always have to prepare for the future by sowing the crop and feeding the herd. Farmers also tend to be excellent at avoiding waste. They take a make do and mend attitude and tend to think carefully before parting with money unnecessarily. Farmers tend to be asset rich and, increasingly farmers have effectively needed to become skilful derivative traders too – locking in crop prices ahead of actual sales as a form of hedging risk.

Heather was lucky when she went to buy her first car because her father offered to help her buy it. They went along to the local car dealership where they found a car that seemed to fit the bill (in short, it was blue, and she really wanted a blue car) and the dealer offered to finance the deal at a seemingly attractive rate of interest.

Farmers often have to buy secondhand machinery so tend to be wise to the ways of financing deals, so they asked for the details of how much the total repayment would come to over the life of the loan. The dealer became coy and said he could only offer to tell them what the monthly payments would be together with some complex calculations around how the interest rate charged would shift over time.

Car loan companies have become very adept at these manoeuvres. Some of the large US car manufacturers in recent decades at times made greater profits from financing car deals than they did from the vehicle sales themselves, effectively becoming financiers who happened to also manufacture cars.[1] The reason for this is that car dealerships understand how compounding interest works, so they use it to work for themselves…and against you.

In the end, Heather had to walk away from the desirable blue car because there was no transparency on the finance. Eventually they bought a red car, and paid cash for it. Farmers, as I said, tend to be very smart with their money.

The dangers of credit

Credit cards are a modern curse. When I was a child, the idea of credit cards for average households was a relatively new one. I remember the adverts for the new *Access* cards…'your flexible friend!' They certainly seemed like friendly little characters on the commercials. They would give you money whenever and wherever you needed it to buy white goods or a holiday, and would always be there when you needed them most.

Make no mistake, however, credit cards are a blight on personal finances. You see, compound growth, as we have already established is one of the most powerful forces that any investor can use. Growth upon growth can make even a modest income earner seriously wealthy if you can understand which assets to invest in. However, it needs to be remembered that compound growth also works in reverse, and if compound growth isn't working for you, then be assured that it is working against you. Credit cards charge interest at hefty rates, sometimes at rates of up to 20 percent per annum or even more. The seemingly innocuous charges can start to grow and compound against you, especially if you have near-permanent balance outstanding. The effects may not seem too damaging, but they are most certainly there.

When inflation devalues a currency, as tends to happen in modern economies in line with central bank policy, this can represent a transfer of wealth from creditors to borrowers. This is why investors use debt to invest in appreciating assets like real estate and why companies often use debt themselves to create further wealth through their own particular line of business. Unfortunately, credit card companies understand this all too well – usually better than the unfortunate borrower – and as such often charge cripplingly high rates of interest on outstanding balances, which continue to accrue each month if the balance is not repaid in full.

> 'Neither a borrower nor a lender be; for a loan
> oft loses both itself and friend' - Polonius, *Hamlet*.

This famous quote is from the character Polonius in Shakespeare's play *Hamlet*, and it is still as relevant hundreds of years later. I can relate to this all too well, for in my younger life on two occasions I made material loans to friends in need. Both times the loans remained unpaid, and on both occasions the friendships were damaged almost irreparably.

So why do people and companies use debt at all then? Without getting too bogged down in economic theory, there has been a long-held view that because companies could borrow funds to invest in projects which generated a positive return, and because the interest on debt allows a tax deduction, then theoretically a company which takes on as much debt as possible becomes more valuable.

Clearly, as we saw through the financial crisis, there is a flaw in this theory. A company which takes on too much debt risks not being able to service the repayments and could become insolvent. For this reason, most large companies use a moderate amount of leverage in order to boost returns, but do not maximise their leverage to the absolute hilt. Even risk-averse companies such as Warren Buffett's company and investment vehicle Berkshire Hathaway, use a moderate amount of leverage.

> 'When you combine ignorance and leverage, you get some
> pretty interesting results.' – Warren Buffett.

Very similar principles apply to individuals. Some debt can be taken on for the purposes of investment, particularly in relation to investment property. Debt should not, however, be carried for the payment of luxury items or living expenses for this is unproductive debt. In some jurisdictions debt for investment can also attract a tax deduction when used to invest in income-generating assets.

However, the use of debt should always be respected and not abused. Borrowers for investment purposes should keep a reasonable buffer in order to stay well away from the risks of financial duress. Leveraged investors must never become forced or distressed sellers into weak markets, as this is likely to be the time when asset prices are close to the nadir of their cycle.

Neither a borrower nor a lender be (except when investing!)

As referenced previously, for their best-selling book *The Millionaire Next Door* the authors carried out extensive research into the characteristics and habits of millionaires in the USA.[2] The findings and results of these authors came as a surprise for many people. Sure there are some mega-rich people, but the research showed that the majority of millionaires drive average cars, do not wear Rolexes, drink wine that is of a moderate price and live in reasonably affordable housing.[3]

Most crucially of all, millionaires, it was shown, live below their means. It matters not whether your income is $30,000, $300,000 or $3 million, if you spend more than you earn on luxuries and depreciating assets you will never become wealthy. Think again of the words of wisdom:

> 'Neither a borrower nor a lender be.'

Ideally, the only time you should take out a loan is to invest in property. It is possible to take out loans to invest in other assets such as shares, but, unless you are securing the loan at a very low rate of interest I am not an advocate of that for most average investors. What you should definitely not do is take out consumer credit to pay for luxury items, because then compound interest will begin to work its magic, but this time it will be working against you and pushing your finances towards a life of struggle.

What is bad debt?

So we have established that some debt can be acceptable for investment purposes, but what is bad debt? I include under the heading of bad debt loans for items such as cars, holidays, televisions, furniture and white goods. Although some of these items often give the appearance of being 'assets', in that that have some value to you and could in theory be resold, the reality is that over the long term they become worth steadily less or depreciate.

As for boats, well, they may even be the worst of the depreciating assets. Strangely, boats often actually hold their value reasonably well in general – frequently much more than is the case for cars – but the holding costs can be diabolical. As the old saying goes, the second best day of a man's life is they day he buys a boat. The best day of his life, of course, is the day that he sells it!

How to get out of bad debt

All bad debts are not created equal. There is proven formula and method to getting out of bad debt, and I will explain it briefly here. First, you need to find a way to save a couple of hundred dollars a month, either through earning more or spending less. Then start paying down the debt with the highest cost attached to it first.

How to save the couple of hundred dollars? Thinking the 80/20 way, run down a quick budget on where most of your money is leaking out of the door. Travel? Car ownership? At the pub? Holidays? This should give you a good clue as to where the most money can be saved quickly. Alternatively you might choose to work an evening shift or a second job to add a couple of hundred dollars to your monthly income.

When I say here that you should pay off the debt with the highest cost attached to it first, it may sound as though as I am referring implicitly to the debt with the highest rate of interest. While this may be the case, certain types of debt can have an even higher cost attached them. For example, debt to family and friends should normally be paid off before all else. Other types of debt may risk you scoring demerit marks against your credit record or even incur the threat of legal action. It likely makes sense to tackle these first, even if other debt incurs higher interest rate charges.

'Bad debt is debt that makes you poorer. I count the mortgage on my home as bad debt, because I'm the one paying on it. Other forms of bad debt are car payments, credit card balances or other consumer loans.' – Robert Kiyosaki.

Then you should move to pay off debts at the highest rate of interest first by applying the couple of hundred dollars to the credit card or loan with the highest interest rate charge. When each tier of debt is paid off, move funds down to the next highest interest level, paying against it both the money you were previously paying on the last tier of debt plus a bit extra for the interest you have now saved yourself by paying off the previous tier of debt.

To give yourself some breathing space, consider trying to transfer credit card debts which are attracting a high rate of interest to a credit card with no interest charges for the first six months – and then aim to have the balance paid off before the new card begins to attract interest charges. This is not always possible but at some stages in the lending cycle it may be an option.

Using debt to invest

The 80/20 Principle is based upon the idea of achieving more with less. Another way in which this can be done is through the use of leverage. In fact real estate investment very much lends itself to the 80/20 Principle, since very often investors use a 20 percent deposit and an 80 percent mortgage in order to leverage their returns.

Leverage has many meanings, and one definition of leverage is to achieve greater results with less input. Setting up a business, for example, can be one powerful form of leverage. Using other people's time (sometimes known as OPT) to enable you to achieve more with less. I will consider this in Part Four of the book. Another form of leverage is using debt or other people's money (known as OPM) to invest.

'Give me a lever long enough and a fulcrum on which to place it, and I shall move the world.' – Archimedes.

Used sensibly to invest in real estate and sometimes stocks, debt can be a very powerful tool allowing you to magnify returns by investing with more capital. However, leverage is necessarily a double-edged sword. If you get it wrong, your losses will also be magnified. Therefore, if you are going to use leverage to invest, it is absolutely imperative that you get it right.

Chapter 8 summary

» There are two types of debt – good debt (used for investment only) and bad debt

» If compound interest is not working for you, it is likely to be working against you

» Get out of bad debt, especially credit cards and consumer loans, as soon as possible

» Debt can be a powerful tool either to create wealth or destroy it

» Debt should be respected and only used with great care

9
Automated
Investing

9

'What we do regularly, we become.' – Aristotle.

Ron's story

Ron was as an insurance broker in London, a bullish extrovert and a larger than life character who took life by the horns and enjoyed working hard and socialising. He was known to be a bit of a 'wheeler dealer' and had experienced some success in a number of side-line business ventures. He had variously been involved in some venture capital projects as well as some property developments in Spain.

Ron enjoyed playing the share markets and often talked about his latest tips and inside market information with mates and work colleagues in the city. It was quite well accepted by Ron's mates that he was a success in the share markets game and that he had made good money over the years. He was often quite vociferous about his successes.

'To be outspoken is easy when you do not wait to speak the complete truth.' – Radindranath Tagore.

The problem was that Ron had no real investment plan, and he approached his share trading ventures in a haphazard manner. He switched regularly from trading to investing to short-selling. While he had experienced some fast returns from a small percentage of his investments, the majority of them tended to at best tread water, and most paid no dividend income being speculative in nature. Ron also had a couple of howlers in his portfolio but he had not realised these paper losses in the hope that one day they might come back to their break-even point.

Ron was quite quick to tell his friends and colleagues about his successes but invariably failed to mention the paper losses. When he ran his share trading transaction history to pass on to his accountant at year-end Ron's broking package showed that after netting out the unrealised losses on his loss making investments he had made only a small net profit. Indeed after deducting all transaction costs, he had made a small net loss for the year, as indeed he had in the prior year too.

It pays to be very wary about people who only ever seem to discuss successful investments or trades with you. Most experienced investors will be able to share with you just as many stories of mistakes! Moreover the overwhelming majority of share portfolios I have seen are fundamentally quite boring and involve a number of quality investments being held for the long term. Some experts do make a success of trading the market, but most average investors and amateurs who fail to commit to applying maximum discipline to their trading make a complete hash of it over the long term.

Mike's story

Mike had always been quite successful in the property market. He married at a young age and had bought a small terraced house at around the same time. Within a few years the bank he worked for paid him out some share options and he was able to pay down the majority of his mortgage by the age of 25.

Over the next five years, Mike expanded his property portfolio, first by trading up to a larger house close to where he worked in the city (which later he rented out as an investment property) and then later by purchasing three rental apartments close to the train station for the city. Mike's friends often joked with him that they thought he must be playing *Monopoly* in real life, and he was widely acknowledged as being a smart cookie when it came to knowing what to do with his money. When he was 38, Mike decided that he wanted to cash in his investment properties so that he and his wife could move into a mansion.

They did not have children and they did not really need the space but Mike quite liked the idea of an ostentatious home in order to impress his friends and family with his great success. In order to maximise the bang for his buck Mike bought a huge six bedroom house which was located in a remote area a long way from the city.

Instead of trying to *appear* wealthy, focus on being truly wealthy.

In the coming years, Mike's relationship fell upon hard times, not helped by the four hour round trip commute to work and back each day which meant he spent little time at home, and unfortunately Mike ended up getting divorced. As part of the divorce settlement Mike paid out his wife an amount equivalent to half of the equity in his large house, which was painful, although he was relieved that he could keep the trophy home. Subsequently the property market hit quite a severe downturn, which Mike had never experienced in nearly 20 years as a homeowner – he had only ever seen property prices going up at close to 10 percent per annum.

Being located in quite a remote area the property market close to where Mike lived was illiquid and there were very few sales of equivalent properties. Unfortunately due to the downturn, Mike's neighbour Joe lost his job as a lawyer and was forced to sell his home and received a few percent less than he had paid for the house some seven years previously. Mike calculated that the equity he had left in his house at this stage was far less than he had previously expected.

At around this time, Mike met a new partner named Laura who he subsequently married. Laura had also recently been through a divorce but had received a divorce settlement from the sale of her city house which she and her first husband had owned for 15 years. Mike was surprised to learn that Laura received more from her divorce settlement than the level of his own equity, in spite of all of the various property successes he had experienced over more than two decades in the market.

In fact, by the time he reached his early forties a number of Mike's friends had built more equity in their own homes simply by owning a home and paying down their mortgages than Mike had in all his years of successful property market investing and trading, which somehow did not feel quite right to him.

Lessons from the experiences of Ron and Mike

The above stories illustrate that while capital gains which are allowed to grow and compound unhindered by transaction costs and capital gains taxes can be phenomenally powerful, if you trade too often or try to be too cute by timing the market, your results are likely, on average, to be far less successful.

From time to time stories spring up in the financial press of elderly ladies – and it nearly always does seem to be ladies, which I do not believe to be a coincidence – who have invested a few thousand dollars in the share markets many decades ago, and have been found to be millionaires many times over. The reason is simply that they have allowed capital gains and dividend income to grow and compound for decade after decade completely unhindered by transaction costs and taxes.

Studies show that women are frequently far better investors than men simply because they demonstrate these two key principles of discipline and patience.

Men on the other hand are frequently far too confident in their own abilities to beat the market with clever timing, and they inadvertently become action junkies who feel the need to trade incessantly.

Just like Ron in the story above, on average frenetic traders score some wins (which they are often quick to inform their mates about) but these are usually offset by losses, while the transaction costs and taxes take care of the rest. This haphazard approach fails to see them get ahead, while a patient investor who simply resolves to buy quality assets and hold onto them for as long as possible can achieve a surprisingly high level of wealth. When gains are re-invested in order to multiply earnings, they can achieve a level of results even beyond the wildest of their own expectations.

6 places you might invest your money (and 4 rules for doing so).

In economics, interest rates act a little like gravity. Any changes in interest rates, anywhere in the world, changes the value of financial assets. Of course, this is blindingly obvious when you are looking at bond prices shifting, but the rule also applies to all other classes of financial assets, including equities, farmland, commercial and residential real estate or commodities. Simply put, if interest rates are at 10 percent then the present value of each dollar you receive on any investment is much lower than when interest rates are at 3 percent.

> Interest rates impact financial markets – always.

Famously, Warren Buffett, who knows a thing or two about investment markets, provided the empirical evidence for this in a key note speech in 2001.[1] He noted that in the 17 years between December 1964 and December 1981, the US Gross National Product (GNP) increased by a whopping 373 percent, yet the Dow Jones share market index essentially went absolutely nowhere, increasing by one solitary point.[2] A major driver for this was that long term bond rates ran from 4.2 percent in 1964 to an eye-watering 13.6 percent by 1981.[3]

In the next 17 years from December 1981 to December 1998, GNP in the US only increased by less than half as much at 177 percent, yet the Dow Jones index went on a bonanza run from 875 to 9,181, a truly staggering increase.[4] Why so? Largely because interest rates altered the landscape for financial assets by falling from above 13 percent to only 5 percent and this changed the way people invested their money.[5]

We have seen this happen again from 2009 to 2014, with rock bottom interest rates in the US firing the Dow from below 7,000 to well above 18,000 since the financial crisis. Given that investors must contend with inflation, and with interest rates at rock bottom, bonds and fixed interest investments have about-faced as an investment choice from offering 'risk free return' to practically guaranteeing 'return free risk'.

We appear set for a decade of low interest rates.

You did not have to be a genius to work out that very low interest rates across the globe since 2008 would cause a shift in the way people invest their money. The thing about money is that there is an awful lot of it around the world and all of it has to find a home, so low interest rates are pushing asset prices higher. Here are the six main places you might choose to put your money.

1 - Cash/fixed interest (lending investments)

Lending investments range all the way from cash in your bank account, to term deposits, government bonds, inflation-linked bonds, corporate bonds, notes, debentures, or hybrid investments, subordinated debt, and a stack of other stuff. The basic principle is that the lending of money is exchanged for interest payments. Clearly with interest rates at historic lows, fixed interest returns are presently weak. High yields are generally only obtained from low grade or perceived riskier investments. As a result, lending investments are far less popular than they have been and this has seen a huge shift of global capital towards other asset classes, in particular...

2 - Equities

When my book *Get a Financial Grip* was published, I put forward the opinion that if financial freedom is your goal, then the best means of achieving it for the average investor could be (1) to get broad exposure to certain suburbs of Sydney and London real estate for the long term, (2) to continue building a diversified portfolio of dividend-paying equities, and (3) keep a very healthy cash buffer.[6]

For long term investors, assets which bring income and the potential for capital growth tend to beat the cash/fixed interest investments. Buffett stated that only certain asset classes fulfil these criteria from his perspective: profitable businesses, equities and real estate. I noted that my suggestions were particularly so given the low interest rate environment which would likely see funds flowing away from cash and fixed interest and into share markets.

Low interest rates were indeed very kind to share markets as I expected – perhaps too kind, in fact! - whilst investors continue to derive annual benefit from tax-favoured dividends which come with franking credits attached. However, after huge gains it now seems likely that some share markets are overdue for a correction in the years ahead and investors need to be ready and prepared for this as I will discuss in chapter 10.

3 - Real estate

Remember that all financial assets are in some way sensitive to interest rates. Questioning of the effectiveness of monetary policy tends to be a part of every economic cycle, but monetary policy generally does work and, like all financial assets, housing markets are ultimately responsive to changes in the cost of capital. There tends to be a lag in effect, with the full impact of interest rate cuts on occasion taking up to 18 months to be seen in full. Since 2012 a dramatic turnaround in the tenor of online commentary from *schadenfreude* to snarky eventually proved to be a fairly reliable indicator of the property markets having moved into a new upturn phase, and so the cycles continue. I will discuss in detail in chapters 11 to 13 exactly how you can profit from this new low interest rate era in real estate.

4 - Commodities

The most popular for average investors are gold and silver, which do not pay an income or yield but can represent a hedge with a portion of a portfolio. It has been a rollercoaster ride for the precious metals over the last year or two with the gold price falling to four year lows in 2014 and the silver price faring little better. Who knows where to next?

Warren Buffett sees gold as a barren asset, since it pays no income or yield. In 2011 he drew the analogy that the world's gold stock of 170,000 tons or about 68 square feet had a total valuation of an incredible $9.6 trillion, equal to the value of all the cropland in the US, plus 16 Exxon Mobils (the world's most profitable company in 2011, generating net profits of $40 billion annually) and around one trillion dollars of walking around money.[7]

When put in those terms, of course, Buffett explains that the choice of assets is a no-brainer and he steers clear of gold and silver. Profitable companies, real estate and farmland will continue to produce income and growth over the decades as they always have.[8] The price of gold tends to peak at times of fear and so can represent a worthwhile hedge for some investors with part of their portfolio. Buffett's main gripe is that if you hold a bar of gold for 50 years, at the end of the process you still have that same gold bar, and it still pays you no income.[9] Thus, he argues you are hoping for more speculators to push up the price in times of fear.

5 - Collectables

Investing in collectables such as art or antique coins tends to generate a handy income, but only for experts.

6 - Get rich quick schemes

There have been a lot of these over the years, from pyramid schemes to exotic new diamond mines and emu farms. Get rich quick schemes tend to be suitable for people who have some money and want to rid themselves of it quickly.

...and 4 rules for investing

Having considered where you might invest your money, now let us look briefly at four rules for doing so.

Rule 1 - Diversify

Do not put all your eggs in one basket. A diversified portfolio should include your business, property, shares and cash. It is easy enough to attain diversification in the share markets through using low-cost products hold a range of companies or trusts or index funds. One of the challenges related to real estate is that the leverage involved sees you quickly gain exposure to only a handful of correlated assets in one asset class. For this reason, I invest heavily in property in Australia and the UK, since I do not want to be fully exposed to one market only.

Rule 2 - Investment is not about luck

Successful investment is not about luck. It is about patience, research and discipline.

Rule 3 - Markets are cyclical

In every cycle, people argue that this time will be different. But corrections follow booms and markets slump before recovering and then eventually booming again. Cycles will continue as they always do. Investors need to have an awareness of whether asset prices are near their peak or nadir and plan accordingly.

Rule 4 - No free lunches

Very high returns tend to be achieved only through riskier ventures. If something sounds too good to be true, it probably is. This is true in bonds where high yields often come with a high risk. In equities, the opportunity for doubling your money quickly tends to come with an equivalent chance of halving it or worse. And high yields in residential real estate are frequently found in areas of lower demand or in riskier or illiquid property types.

When it comes to property, my view has always been while you may certainly start small, you ultimately need to play in a big pond. Just like Buffett's point on barren assets like gold, if you invest in a cheap property in a cheap location, then at the end of the process you will still have a cheap property in a cheap location, and the returns adjusted for inflation will likely be lacklustre or possibly negative.

On the flip side those who invested in markets like London and Sydney over the years have achieved returns that are consistently outstanding - both in terms of capital growth and in terms of income. Cheap regional properties can perform reasonably well over short periods of time, but over the long term well-located capital city properties outperform for reasons discussed in more detail later.

Other ways to invest in shares

In the coming chapter, I am going to cover briefly the principles of successful long-term investing, and I am going to explain the simplest form of investing: averaging. The reason I will do this is because in an inflationary economy it is the approach for the average investor with the lowest level of risk, and thus the approach which will afford the greatest number of people the greatest likelihood of success.

Of course, there are other forms of share market investing such as value investing or attempting to time the market through a combination of fundamental and technical analysis. It is also possible to learn how to trade shares in the market in order to earn additional income. If you are interested in more advanced explanations of these strategies, I recommend reading my book *Get a Financial Grip*. When I wrote my first book there was a great deal of deep value to be found in the market, so hearty congratulations if you followed that value investing plan! Share markets have been booming for some years now and any sensible strategy should have seen you generate outstanding returns.

*The simplest investment strategies are
often the most effective.*

However, valuations are generally not nearly so favourable for investors today, with stock markets having outperformed for years in the prevailing low interest rate environment. In this book I am going to keep it simple and stick to the tried and tested approach which works for most people of investing small amounts regularly.

In keeping, with the spirit of the 80/20 Principle and doing the important things well, the automated or averaging approach to investing means that you will see the great majority of your results from a relatively small amount of effort. But it is also more than that. You will also find over time that the overwhelming majority of your returns come from snowballing of your existing investments – you will enjoy most of your gains from compounding growth rather than your initial investment capital.

5 practical tips on compounding

There are a few things to note about compounding that don't appear at first glance to make any logical sense. One is that is where you build a portfolio which doubles in value fairly consistently over time, the increase in value of the portfolio at each interval totals more than *all* of the previous gains. For example, in the example below where the portfolio doubles in value every seven years through recording gains of 10 percent per annum, in the seven year period between year 35 and year 42 the portfolio gain of $3.2 million exceeds the gains of *all* of the previous 35 years of $3.1 million.

Figure 9.1 – Portfolio growth

Year	Portfolio ($)
0	100,000
7	200,000
14	400,000
21	800,000
28	1,600,000
35	3,200,000
42	6,400,000

Watching how the gains can accelerate when left to grow unimpeded by capital gains taxes and transaction costs should draw investors to two logical conclusions:

- it is best to start investing now; and

- investing in assets which you never have to sell can be very appealing.

Examples of such assets might include:

- an index fund; or

- a Listed Investment Company (LIC) with a low management expense ratio which invests in more than 100 profitable and dividend-paying industrial companies; or

- a well-located house in a capital city that has rapid and sustainable population growth.

I am not sure there is much value in adding another numerical example here, only to re-iterate that often an investor who starts earlier achieves a far better end result than one who starts later. Even if the late-starter invests more capital per annum, it is very difficult to play catch-up simply because of the accelerating power of compounding growth. As you can see, therefore, building wealth is ultimately only reliant upon three things:

- having some **capital** to invest;

- the ability to command satisfactory **returns** consistently; and

- **time,** to allow the portfolio to compound.

It is this simple realisation that allows apparently ordinary folk to build massive, multi-million dollar investment portfolios. Note that it is not necessarily really down to exceptional asset selection – quality well-located properties, shares in a handful of great companies and a few low-cost industrial Listed Investment Companies (LICs) might easily do the trick. It is much more about patience, time and understanding how wealth is created through compounding returns. Let us take a look at five practical tips for using compound growth to your benefit.

Five practical tips

Here are five practical pieces of advice on how using compound interest in your favour might work in practice.

1 - Starting small is OK

If there is one thing that the above concepts tell us is that's it is better to invest something rather than nothing. Investing small amounts regularly works over time because of the compounding effect. However, if you are going to start small do be aware of the impact of transaction costs, such as brokerage or fund management fees, and invest efficiently wherever possible.

2 - Forced saving is good

Have you ever heard anyone say: 'Money in my pocket or in my bank account just seems to disappear?' - I have! It is a truism of personal finance that simply attempting to pile money up in a bank account does not often work very effectively over the long term. Partly this is because you must pay tax on the interest and price inflation eats away at the value of the balance. Moreover, it is also because sooner or later that balance of money tends to get spent. How can you set up a means of forced saving? A standing order or a direct debit into a specified investment account?

3 - You do not miss what you have never had

You do not miss what you have never had - another truism, and one which suggests to me that the more automated your system is for investing (for example, a standing order from your pay cheque) the greater the likelihood of your success. This also leads to the logical conclusion that it can be a great idea to...

4 - Re-invest your gains

Sometimes you might hear the bean-counters, of which I am one myself by profession, say that you should not re-invest dividends because this can lead to an accounting headache when capital gains taxes fall due some period of time down the track. I have heard similar arguments in favour of not using a line of credit against your home to reinvest in further investments because the accounting entries can 'get a bit tricky'.

In fact, from a value investor's perspective there actually are some sound logical arguments in favour of not re-investing dividends at certain points in the share market cycle, particularly when share market indices are significantly over-valued.[10] However, believe it or not, engaging a lazy professional who cannot be bothered to run a simple spreadsheet to keep track of a few accounting entries is not a solid argument against re-investment.

Re-investing gains can snowball your portfolio efficiently.

As a general rule, re-investment during the growth phase of your investment portfolio can be an efficient way to grow and compound your wealth. Just as importantly, re-investment of your gains makes use of the underlying principles of all of the first three tips listed above: small amounts make a big difference, re-investment is another form of forced saving and you don't miss what you've never had.

5 - Most people are not very good at saving

Unfortunate, but true. Most of us begrudgingly pay our electricity bills more or less when they fall due, but equally, most people are simply not very good at saving dollars every month (at least, not over the long term). Some might be able to build up a decent cash balance over the course of a financial year through spending less than they earn, but it is also deceptively easy to spend the balance on a car or a holiday when that time of year rolls around again. This is really just another point in favour of setting up an automated investment strategy.

Real world personal finances

The cornerstone of personal finances for most people in economies where home ownership rates are high such as Australia or the United Kingdom is the family home or place of residence. In other words, the majority of people are in one of these categories:

- living mortgage-free in a home;

- paying down the mortgage on a home; or

- saving a deposit for a home.

The practical tips detailed above suggest that regardless of which category you are in, having a forced saving or investment strategy is a sound idea.

1 - Mortgage free

If you are in the fortunate position of being in this category it might be useful to continue making payments as though you still do have a mortgage into a separately allocated investment account. After all, you have already proven that you can spare that amount per month! You might also consider using some of the equity in your home to borrow to invest in a sensible manner. Using gearing to invest is a powerful means of accelerating returns, but should only ever be done moderately and sensibly, and obviously individual circumstances and risk appetites differ so consult a financial advisor where appropriate.

2 - Paying off a mortgage

Think back again to the practical points listed above. Can you accelerate repayments on your mortgage debt? Can you make repayments fortnightly instead of monthly? Mortgage debt does not get treated so favourably for tax purposes in Australia or the UK, so paying down the mortgage more quickly is a strategy that works well for many.

3 - Not a homeowner

If you live in a big capital city, it is likely that we will see more people over time in this category, which leads to a decision to be made as to whether you even aim for home ownership at all in the first instance. Although admittedly my wife and I have lived in some of our properties over the years, we have often been renters because we could accelerate returns much faster by renting a smaller property and hammering the investments while we were younger. This strategy can definitely work miracles if you are able to adhere to the principles of forced saving, patience, discipline and re-investing gains.

On the other hand you should caution against listening too much to those advising you to sit back casually and wait for an inevitable property correction. In capital city markets like London or Sydney, that has generally over time turned out to be poor advice. It is far better to be proactive rather than reactive, whether your goal is home ownership or not. There is no one size fits all when it comes to personal finance, but obviously if you are not planning to be a homeowner soon, you should avoid spending the remainder of your income and so implementing an automated saving and investment strategy is likely to be a great idea.

Buy low, sell high?

You will often hear in the financial press the phrase 'buy low, sell high'. It makes perfect sense, of course. Have you considered, though, that if it were really that simple, then everyone would do it? Remember that even the most experienced and professional of investors have not been able to consistently time the market well, so what chance for amateurs to time their entry and exit to the market accurately?

Rather than building an investment plan around constantly trying to dip in and out of the market, why not buy, hold and focus on the growing income or dividend stream? When the market crashes or corrects – as it will periodically – why not aim to buy more when the market is on sale? I discuss how you can recognise when the market is cheap or on sale more in Chapter 16.

By following this approach your investment plan will be much more efficient. You will not attract regular capital gains tax liabilities in the manner of a trader. Meanwhile, dividend streams can be tax-advantaged in some circumstances when they are received with franking credits attached under prevailing dividend imputation rules. Alternatively, you can reinvest the dividends via what is known as a DRP (Dividend Re-investment Plan) and not incur tax until you choose to sell.

Averaging in practice

My wife has an index fund which she set up nearly two decades ago with a direct debit which directed funds to buy new units every month. This investment principle is founded in great common sense and the strategy is known variously as averaging or dollar cost averaging. It works because by spreading the entry times into the market the investor buys more units when the share market is low and fewer units when the market is high, thus spreading the risk and 'averaging' out the entry cost. Meanwhile the investor enjoys income from the investment which typically grows each year, ideally ahead of the rate of inflation.

In his classic investment book *The Intelligent Investor* Ben Graham talks of such a strategy as being one of the most sensible and straightforward approaches for the averaging income-earning investor to employ.[11] And I wholeheartedly agree. While in hindsight timing the market always seems to be very easy and obvious, in real time when you are reading the share price chart from left to right it definitely is not. Even professional fund managers have shown themselves to be poor on average at exploiting a market-timing strategy so what hope is there for the everyday investor?

> Spreading your entry into the market can reduce risk.

The concept of dollar cost averaging earned something of a bad name because the personal finance author Robert Kiyosaki criticised it in his *Rich Dad* fable series.[12] He said that investors should time the market rather than riding markets down to the bottom. In theory, this is fine, but in reality what happens is that investors sell in anticipation of a forthcoming market fall and then the market roars upwards – and the same happens at the bottom of the stock market cycle too, but in reverse.

The simplest way to create wealth through shares is to choose an appropriate investment product or products – suggestions I make include index funds or Listed Investment Companies (LICs), as I will explain later – and to write yourself a contract such as the one below, agreeing with yourself to continue to buy at regular intervals. This key concept is elaborated upon further in *The Intelligent Investor* by Warren Buffett's mentor Ben Graham, which I recommend highly:[13]

Dollar cost averaging – Contract

I (name) ....

Hereby commit to investing the following amount: $ ....

Every month/quarter (delete as applicable)

I will invest the amount noted at the interval stated above in the following equities products:

....

....

....

....

Signed ....

Date ....

Why does this work?

Why does this simple approach work so effectively? Firstly, it is due to the averaging effect and a natural smoothing out your entry price which helps to make up for a lack of market timing. When the market is depressed and prices are cheap your dollars automatically buy more shares helping you to buy more units when the market is on sale. On the other hand, when the market is expensive, exuberant or over-priced, your dollars do not go as far and purchase fewer shares.

The simple genius of averaging is that the automatic stabilising effect of smoothing your entry price helps to eliminate risk to a large extent. The share market can be risky if you engage an approach of pushing large sums of money at the market too quickly since you are then reliant upon the market moving in your favour at any given point in time.

Buy quality assets for the long term.

By instead committing to investing an affordable amount of money regularly into the market, in doing so you can give yourself peace of mind that over the long term you will prosper regardless of short term gyrations in the market provided that you buy quality, well-diversified investment products. In an inflationary economy, a basket of quality, profitable companies will continue to generate larger profits and pay greater dividends to you over time, which you may elect to receive as income or simply reinvest into the market in order to continue snowballing your portfolio.

In the next chapter of the book, we will consider whether you might reinvest dividends or take them as income, but for now, it is only important here to recognise what a powerful tool dollar cost averaging can be if it is used smartly. The world is not Japan – most economies do not suffer from decades of deflation -- and therefore a long-term approach of investing regularly into quality companies is an effective means of building wealth.

Why most people only have two successful investments

I estimate that in most developed countries the majority of people only have two genuinely successful investments which account for more than 80 percent of their wealth – their house and their pension. Why is that? Generally it is because they see them both as long-term investments which they can 'set and forget' for many years or even decades. Like shares, real estate can be an excellent investment if you buy well and hold for the long term – long enough for household incomes to increase, dwelling construction costs and labour costs to increase and resultantly for dwelling prices to do the same.

Residential property tends to be an effective long-term inflation hedge if you buy in a capital city with a growing population. This is because new dwellings must be built to house the growing population and the new dwellings will always be built at today's prices and with today's labour, construction and materials costs.

However, capital growth in real estate never occurs exactly in a straight line. In the simplest terms as the population grows this puts upwards pressure on the housing market - vacancy rates fall and property prices start to rise as more people compete for the existing stock of dwellings. As prices rise, developers see the potential for profit and begin to develop some of their land-banked holdings with new dwellings which they can sell for a reasonable profit margin at the prevailing higher prices.

Nobody rings a bell at the top of the market.

Unfortunately nobody rings a bell at the top of the market and the rate of construction tends to overshoot. Construction continues beyond the point which it is desperately needed and an oversupply of properties ultimately eventuates. As the population is now competing for more properties on the market vacancy rates rise, rents tend to ease and prices begin to soften or decline. This in turn leads to a slowing of construction until vacancy rates tighten once more and upwards pressure on the market eventually returns.

Of course, the real world property market cycle is far more complex than this and engaging an expert can help you to recognise how different sectors of the market behave in markedly different manners regardless of the stage of the cycle, but the basic principles described above are absolutely correct. If you can begin to recognise how safe and profitable an investment property can be if you understand the market, you can begin to turn this to your advantage to generate very substantial wealth.

Property does not tend to be a great short term investment, unless you happen to be a highly skilled renovator, because of the material transaction costs involved when buying and selling property such as taxes and legal fees. However, over the long term, by which I mean 15 to 20 years or more, very substantial gains can be made if you can learn the appropriate skills to significantly outperform the averages.

Set and forget

Experience shows that most average investors experience the greatest success when they can adopt an automated approach to their investing and adopt a set-and-forget attitude. One of the key themes of this book is to consider how you can buy assets which you can hold onto forever – it is the most efficient way to build wealth there is.

Chapter 9 summary

» Most people only have a couple of successful investments which account for most of their wealth

» The best chance average investors have of creating wealth is to have a strategy which is automated or repeatable

» Invest regularly in quality assets for the long term

» Trading too frequently incurs transaction costs and capital gains taxes

10

Shares
– Get Rich Slow

10

'The broker said the market was poised to move. Silly me,
I thought he meant move up!' – Randy Thurman.

Keep it simple

Analysing companies and share market investment is not everyone's cup of tea. Yet you should have some exposure to share markets over the long term since the productive enterprise of profitable companies generates wealth and returns which everyone can and should aim to participate in.

Now I have seen what happens to some people when I talk about share market investing in public speaking events. For plenty of people, their eyes glaze over and they practically drift off to sleep! If that means you, I urge you to skip on to the next chapter rather than abandon your quest for financial freedom. However, before you do so, if you take away only three points from this very short chapter, they should be these:

• Share markets should be your friend, not your enemy!

• Investing small amounts regularly is a low-risk approach to building wealth

• You do not need to be an expert in picking individual stocks

If you are interested in more advanced share investment strategies, I recommend reading my 2012 book *Get a Financial Grip: a simple plan for financial freedom.*[1]

Are stocks risky?

Have you ever heard it said that successful people have views which are opposite to those of the crowd? It is often true. Popular consensus would have you believe that share markets are risky, and this may be true if you do not know what you are doing. If your approach is to pile large sums of money into shares in a handful of companies in the hope that you have guessed the direction of the market correctly, then indeed engaging in the share market is likely to be a risky venture for you.

What people seem to have forgotten is that the point of buying shares is to buy a *share* in great businesses and a claim on the future earnings and distributed profits.[2] These days, largely thanks to media commentary, too many investors (or, should one say, speculators) are instead buying a number on a chart without carrying out any due diligence worthy of the name into the company that they are buying shares in.

When I began writing my first book some years ago I devoted a full chapter to the concept of value investing – buying shares in high quality businesses when prices are cheap - partly for the simple reason that there was a good deal of deep value to be in the market back at that time. And what a successful strategy that has proved to be for anyone who followed those simple principles of buying quality companies at a value price! Since that time we have lived through a roaring bull market across global share market indices with half a decade of stonking gains being recorded in the US, the United Kingdom, Australia and elsewhere.

Consequently as I write this there is generally far less value to be found in stock markets at this time with low interest rates having pushed market valuations higher, with US indices having hit unprecedented heights. In short, depending upon when you are reading this book, it is probably not such a good time to be pouring a huge amount of your net worth into the stock market while valuations are so stretched.

If you are interested in the Warren Buffett approach to investing of buying value stocks, then you need to be able to carry out detailed analysis of financial statements, including ratio analysis and profitability forecasts, as well as understanding the industry outlook for the companies you are investing in and how each company will fare within its own field.

> 'Price is what you pay. Value is what you get.'
> – Warren Buffett.

I have come to appreciate the conclusion that the great majority of investors who claim to be value investors are in truth no such thing because they do not carry out any genuinely detailed research at all into the companies that they are buying. Researching a company's financials can be painstaking work and at times quite dull, which is why, one supposes, most people do not bother to do it. Others do not have the financial education or the expertise.

It is no secret that one of my favourite books is *The Intelligent Investor* by Ben Graham. If you want to understand the principles of value investing this might be a great place to start. The trouble is today that too many people want to ask 'what do you think of XYZ stock?' instead of taking the time to analyse and understand the criteria for understanding what makes for a sound investment and what denotes a good value proposition.

The beautiful thing about the share market is that this does not necessarily matter provided you can adopt a sensible alternative approach for the long term of diversifying and dollar cost averaging. If you genuinely want to learn the skills of value investing read my book *Get a Financial Grip*, but if you do not have the time or inclination, please do not kid yourself about what you are doing, adopt a sensible averaging approach using diversified products which give you peace of mind, and instead apply your efforts to other more productive pursuits...like setting big and exciting goals for the future!

The index

When my wife Heather went to work at Deloitte after graduating from University, in one of her early training courses the facilitator asked the new graduates a simple question: 'At what level is the stock market index approximately today?' only to be met with blank stares all round. Not only did no-one in the room know the answer, none of the new trainees knew the answer to within hundreds of points. So much for accountants having their finger on the pulse!

The thing about averaging is that you do not actually need to know what the index is doing on a day to day basis, or even a week to week basis. It is not important because of the natural smoothing effect of buying a set dollar amount of shares regularly. When shares are cheap you naturally purchase more, and when shares are expensive you acquire less.

However, that said, it might be worth me explaining here what an index actually is! A market index is a measurement of the market value of a cross-section of the stock market which is calculated using the weighted average of last traded prices. It is essentially a way to ascertain the sentiment across a section of the wider stock market but it can easily disguise the price of individual components or stocks acting a markedly different manner from others within the index.

'The best way is just buy a low-cost index fund and keep buying it regularly over time, because you'll be buying into a wonderful industry, which in effect is all of American industry. People ought to sit back and relax and keep accumulating over time.' – Warren Buffett.

Investing in an index fund can be an efficient way to invest because instead of you paying a percentage of your money to a fund manager to churn over stocks for you (which creates further transaction costs and taxes) you simply hold the top companies by market capitalisation and liquidity – it is the ultimate form of simple buy and hold investing for share market participants. Later in this chapter I will go on to look at whether you should invest in an index fund or whether you might consider a similar low-cost product which performs a similar function.

Most people overestimate what they can achieve in a year, but hugely underestimate what they can potentially achieve in a decade or a lifetime. If you truly understand how compounding works then your potential can be almost limitless over the long haul, but you do need some time to allow compounding to work its magic.

'When dumb money acknowledges its limitations, paradoxically it ceases to be dumb.' – Warren Buffett.

The long-term trend in most stock markets tends to be upwards for a number of reasons. Generally over time, successful companies tend to increase their profits which is reflected in higher share prices, while unsuccessful companies eventually disappear off the bottom of the index or becoming completely insolvent and are wound up – thus there can be an element of survivorship bias in some indices. Inflation plays a role too, as profits in dollar terms are pushed up by the depreciating currency. The thing to remember for long-term investors is that market crashes, far from being something to be feared or panicked about, can represent great opportunities to load up on more quality stocks at an attractive price.

DIY investing

The advent of internet brokerage sites has seen a huge increase in individual share traders selecting their own stocks in which to invest or speculate. Unfortunately, most average investors do not take the time to learn the laborious process of how to analyse financial statements and nor do they have strong market-timing skills. Therefore, for most, the process is largely one of forlorn guesswork which is thus inevitably reflected in sub-optimal results.

What hope is there then for average investors who do not want to be slugged with expensive fund management fees? The answer is to promote an investment plan that is both repeatable and spreads your risk through averaging. That is, to contribute a regular dollar amount into a well-diversified product on a regular basis. When the market is low, you will effectively buy more stock, and vice-versa. But what product to buy? Here are five reasons why you might elect for a low-cost Listed Investment Company (LIC).

1 – Diversification

Through buying into an LIC which holds up to 100 or more stocks and trusts, you can be instantly diversified. The approach of not having all of your eggs in one basket is a tried and tested approach to reducing risk over time.

2 – Low costs

Net returns can be improved substantially over time if you select a LIC with low administrative costs. What would represent a low administrative cost? This means that the LIC does not charge you a cripplingly expensive performance or management fee, and the costs charged for remuneration, office rent and other administrative expenses such as for the company's IT and stationery represent lower than perhaps 0.2 percent of the average assets of the fund at market value.

> Look for products with low fees and
> low management expense ratios.

Compare this with the fees charged on your pension fund and you will begin to see why LICs can be a superior choice. While pension fund management fees of 1 to 2 percent may not sound dramatic, if you consider how much of your expected annual return this might represent the effect on your ability to create wealth over time can be overwhelming. A well-selected LIC does not trade hyperactively. Instead, it will aim to identify quality companies to invest in for the long term and will only rarely look to sell. This reduces unnecessary brokerage costs and taxes.

3 – Outperformance over time

By choosing an LIC which is heavily weighted towards profitable industrial stocks and financials you may be able to outperform the index over time. Why do industrial companies tend to outperform the resources index?

Because the performance of resources stocks can be cyclical and dividends can be substantially weakened in the downturn phase. Resources companies also tend to retain vast amounts of capital to source and reinvest in new projects which can hamper shareholder returns.

Overall, industrial companies have tended to be more sustainable and more self-perpetuating, in contrast with resources companies with their necessarily diminishing reserves. Further, at the time of writing, commodity prices are declining after a huge bubble in certain commodity valuations in the decade leading up to the global financial crisis.

4 – Dividend reinvestment

You may have the choice in an LIC to receive dividends or to reinvest them to grow your portfolio in an efficient manner. A Dividend Re-investment Plan (DRP) should not attract brokerage, stamp duty or other transaction costs and thus can be an effective method of allowing your portfolio to grow and compound your wealth.

5 – Control over investment

As you can buy an LIC on the securities exchange it is remarkably easy to buy and sell, provided you select an appropriately liquid investment, that being one within which it is easy to buy and sell parcels of shares when you need to. This gives the investor great control, and while selling may be inefficient, the liquidity of such an investment can allow funds to be accessed easily in an emergency.

Summary

By choosing an LIC with a reasonably conservative and appropriately experienced management, you can take comfort in your investment approach. Through holding shares in all of Australia's major, profitable industrial companies, even in times of recession you know that the LIC will retain value and your averaging approach will ensure that you pick up more holdings when prices are lower.

Better still, if you can buy more heavily when the market has experienced a major correction, you can begin to move further ahead of the pack in an efficient manner which does not generate excessive brokerage and capital gains taxes through trading. The more repeatable a strategy is, the greater the likelihood of its enduring success for the investor.

3 additional considerations about LICs

Above I have noted some great reasons for considering investment in a LIC. However, before doing so there are a handful of risks to consider.

1 – Track record

When investing in a LIC you want to know that the company has a proven track record of success that has been delivered over a period of decades. I like LICs which have proven themselves over 50 or 60 years! At the very least, you probably want to look at investment companies which have a proven track record of increasing their dividend payments consistently over a period of three decades or so. Why so? Because this period of time should outlive the working lifespan of an individual CEO or portfolio manager, and thus you know you have found a LIC with the right philosophy. The company should not be reliant on the skills of any one individual because then there is a risk that the company could deteriorate when that individual departs!

2 – Liquidity

When you start out investing most of the LICs of a decent size will have sufficient liquidity for you. What do I mean by liquidity? The ability for the market to absorb your buy and sell orders easily. The way to check this out is to look at the volume of shares traded in a normal day on the stock exchange for the LIC you are looking at. When you are investing relatively small amounts this may not be an issue, but it can be a problem as the size of your investments gets bigger.

If your shareholding is huge but only a relatively small number of shares are traded each day then it may be difficult for you to exit the investment should you ever need to. Even those of us with a strong bias towards buy and hold never know when we might need to liquidate an investment for other purposes.

3 - Leverage

As we have considered in other sections of the book leverage in the form of debt can be a useful tool for maximising returns. If you look at the balance sheets of most successful companies you will find that they tend to employ a moderate amount of debt, and this can be true of LICs too.

The key word in the above paragraph is moderate. There is no problem with buying shares in a company which is using an easily serviceable amount of debt, but you should be very wary of investing in an entity which is heavily reliant on debt or might struggle with servicing interest charges. Moreover, a sensible investment in the share market should be able to return you a comfortable 8 percent per annum over the long haul, and there is no need to invest in heavily leveraged companies in order to take on undue risk.

What about when the market crashes?

But what about stock market crashes? Stocks markets are liquid and thus they can and will crash from time to time. It is a natural part of the cycle. Remember, though, that crashes are not permanent and the long-term trend in stock market indices is up. I asked my friend Peter Thornhill about the impact of share market crashes. He discussed with me the emotional impact of investing through the financial crisis and said:

> 'When the market crashes, you would have
> to be dead not to feel it.'

I am certain that this is particularly so for someone such as Thornhill who has invested in the market for decades and thus commands a large portfolio of assets. It is interesting to note that even the most experienced investors felt the psychological impact of share market movements. Incidentally, Thornhill is also a strong advocate of the principles of investment described above. Why? Because he worked for years in the fund management industry and he fully understands the folly of fund managers attempting to churn stocks over all the time in order to chase instant returns.

What is important about market corrections is not only how you feel but how you react. I have noted elsewhere that success in life is frequently far more attributable to how you interpret and respond to events than what actually happens to you. Perhaps most inexperienced market participants panic when the stock market falls and sell their assets at the most inopportune moment to the professional investors.

Experienced investors know that sizeable stock market corrections which bring price-earnings ratios down to single digit territory are actually great buying opportunities rather than a reason to panic. They will continue to acquire shares in the normal fashion, but the true and experienced experts will have set some money aside to buy even more when the market falls to irrationally low levels, because they understand that markets are cyclical.

Stock markets are liquid and therefore can be volatile.

Remember my key principle of investment is to buy a quality investment that will pay you income forever and offer you growth potential. Also recall the Pleasure-Pain Principle - investment is something which you should associate with the pleasure of knowing that you are building a nest egg for your future. If you associate investing with pleasure you will do more of it and do it better.

Too many people associate investing with pain, stress and loss, and as a result they do less of it and do it badly. If you have adhered to this rule then stock market corrections are something to be embraced rather than to be feared – they offer you the chance to buy more of a wonderful thing at a mouth-watering price!

The yield trap

People often tell me they have found a good investment because of its high yield or income. However, yield can be a very misleading indicator of the quality of an investment. We need to understand the dimensions of yield and growth and how they interact with each other. This is neatly illustrated by Thornhill himself in his share investment book *Motivated Money*.[3]

Back in 1980, he notes, term deposits were paying around 10 percent interest, so on the face of it were far more attractive investments than, for example, a portfolio of industrial shares, which were yielding only around half of this percentage.[4] High yield (and supposedly low risk) investments tend to attract retirees who seek certainty of income. There is a hidden trap, however, and it is this: a high yield is not the same thing as a high income.[5]

High yield does not mean high income

A yield is simply a spot figure calculated at a point in time. Income of $100 on an investment of $1000 gives a yield of 10 percent, which is superficially attractive. Income is the dollar figure that the investment pays you over time. Suppose a retiree invested $100,000 in term deposits in 1980. Income of $10,000 in the first year may have seemed more attractive than the lower percentage dividend yield of shares.

Yield and income are not the same thing.

By 1993, however, an initial $100,000 portfolio of industrial shares, whilst still paying a 'weaker' dividend yield of around 5 percent, was paying income of closer to $20,000, and by 2006 a huge dividend income of around $75,000 on a portfolio value of a massive $1.75 million.[6] What happens to the capital value and income of a term deposit over that time? Oh dear. So much for the high yield!

Investing in investments upon retirement such as term deposits might only be a good investment if you plan on dying quickly. What we actually want, rather than high yield, is high income over time. The percentage yields on shares over the long-term tends to fluctuate with prevailing sentiment and prices, so yields do become comparatively higher when share prices crash and lower when prices boom. Thus a stock market meltdown is a great time to buy both for yield and future capital growth.

Concentrate on potential future cash flows for financial freedom

In the simplest terms when you have income which flows to you which is greater than the sum of your financial commitments then you are financially free. Therefore if you can learn to focus on continuing to invest in shares and equities products which pay you a strong and increasing dividend stream, then eventually you will become financially free. This can take a long time which is why young investors often look to property and leverage in order to accelerate the process, but it's important to note the key lesson here. Just as the true value of a company is ultimately the discounted present value of its future cash flows so it is with the value of an investment.

Share prices gyrate around from day to day and from month to month, but an investment which increases its income streams in perpetuity will also see its price increase over the long term. When investing in the share markets learn to take a longer term view and watch the ever growing income streams rather than fussing over haphazard movements in the share price. What is remarkable about this approach is that when done successfully share investors can see more income from their dividend streams in retirement than they ever earned from their salary incomes during their entire working career.

Chapter 10 summary

» Share markets provide strong returns over the long term

» Investing small amounts regularly spreads your risk

» You do not have to be an expert in picking individual stocks (and most people aren't)

» Learn to think of shares as an income asset

11

Real Wealth
Through Real Estate

11

'The best investment on earth...is earth.' – Louis J. Glickman.

The long term trend in capital city property prices

I recall that when I was but a nipper my parents sold our family home in sunny Sheffield in northern England for £27,500, a house they had bought for less than £5000 not too many years before. They traded up to a house which they bought for £30,000 which they later sold for more than £100,000, and then they traded up again. I am sure other families can recount similar stories from around that time. There were certainly many days of high interest rates and elevated levels of unemployment to navigate through, but most families that were home owners built reasonable levels of equity over time.

Even as a youngster I was struck by two things. Firstly, I could not help but notice the sheer size of these numbers as compared to my Dad's relatively moderate probation officer salary. And secondly I observed how the numbers involved always seemed to get much bigger over time, and not only because my parents were trading up or renovating. Perhaps prices did not ever seem to rise that much in any individual year, but the cumulative effect of the increases over time is staggering.

> A house is the biggest investment in financial terms that most people will ever make.

Even as a child I can remember finding it difficult to reconcile these big house price numbers with a domestic household budget which was genuinely stretched. Additional unexpected expenditure of just a few extra pounds could put genuine stress on the purse strings for my parents - being a Catholic family, there were seven of us in total including us five sons and only my father's salary to support us. Yet when it came to negotiating purchase and sale prices for the family home the numbers involved could be measured in tens of thousands. I was inadvertently learning my first lessons about the power of leverage and compound growth, and in particular how those who get it *right* in property can potentially make a lot of money.

My wife Heather recounts the story of when she bought a townhouse back in the mid-1990s at the age of 21, paying £72,000 for mortgage repossession close to the centre of Cambridge in the United Kingdom, within walking distance of the train station to London. She used a 10 percent deposit of £7200 and had to tip in some extra funds to pay for repairs. She also endured years of lodgers to help her meet the mortgage payments.

The prevailing viewpoint at that time was that Heather was crazy to pay so much for a townhouse, property prices were in a bubble and were certain to return to three times incomes. Heather's grandmother who lived in a small single storey home in the much cheaper north of England was mortified that anyone could spend ever so much on a townhouse! The mortgage rate was fixed at one percent above the Bank of England's base rate. The interesting thing about this to me is that whatever Heather does in the future she will find it very hard to improve upon that first property investment she made, because having held it for two decades the gains have compounded for so long that she has recouped her initial investment more than 30 times over.

In fact, if you take account of the additional returns she has made from pulling out some of the equity to invest in further properties then the real return on the initial investment goes through the roof. Interestingly, precisely the same views are aired today as was the case at that time: prices are too high, the economy is likely to slow, there is sure to be crash and new entrants to the market could be making a grave mistake.

There is nothing new under the sun, of course. Global capital city property markets will continue to move in cycles as they always have and always will. Those who are prepared to take the time and effort to study the markets and demographic trends in detail as I will discuss in the coming chapters will continue to generate healthy returns and multiply their earnings for decades to come. And those who do not, preferring to learn from popular consensus, un-researched hype in the media or unending doom predictions from 'perma-bear' websites, will not.

The 6 basic characteristics of property as an investment

Before drilling into some analysis of how and where you need to acquire property in the future in order to secure strong capital growth which can multiply your earnings, let us first take the concept of property ownership right back to basics and consider the simplest aspects of what investing in property actually means.

1 – Property is immobile

Most, though not all, properties are immobile. If you like your house but not your suburb, the chances are that you will have to move suburb and leave your house behind. Lenders like this! You cannot easily default on your mortgage and disappear while taking your house with you, and even if you could somehow manage this, the land will still be there. This tends to make lenders more comfortable and as a result they can offer very long mortgage terms, at low interest rates and often require only relatively small percentage deposits.

This is a unique triumvirate of lending conditions and as such it makes residential real estate unique as an investment. Everyday Mum and Dad investors can use significantly more leverage to invest – they can borrow more capital – than is the case in any other asset class. Leverage is a double-edged sword, however, for it magnifies both capital gains and losses so it must only ever be used wisely.

2 – Property is durable

It is often said that because buildings can stand for centuries then real estate is durable. While this may be true to a point, one disadvantage of property as compared to, say, a parcel of shares in a self-sustaining, dividend-paying industrial company, is that if you do not re-invest money in repairs and maintenance, your property will tend to deteriorate, and eventually it could even fall down.

This may not always be a problem. Some investors buy property for its land value and as noted above, for the land itself is virtually indestructible – it will always be there, and if it is in a prime location land tends to appreciate in value. Nevertheless, property which is rented out to tenants usually requires some maintenance expenditure. Because real estate can be durable, in most market sales tend to consist primarily of existing stock rather than new builds.

3 – Property markets can be illiquid

It can take a long time to buy or sell a property. This makes it extremely important where real estate is bought as an investment that there is a continual high demand for the type of property that you buy. The worst case scenario in an illiquid market is owning an asset which is sliding in value with no buyers available.

Illiquidity in a market may be both a good and bad thing depending on how you look at it. In most years only a very small percentage of capital city housing stock is transacted, which tends to keep property markets relatively stable. However, where a market is illiquid it can be very difficult to sell a property quickly if you need to, and in a declining market there may be no buyers at all of your depreciating asset. This is why I recommend only owning good quality properties in capital cities for which there is a strong and growing demand, and strongly suggest that you do not buy junk properties that nobody wants or needs out in the sticks.

4 – Property incurs high transaction costs

Buying a parcel of shares is simple. You might pay a few dollars as a brokerage fee but there is presently no stamp duty to pay in Australia (although this is not true in all countries). Not so in property. In Australia, transaction costs when buying property can be hefty: stamp duty, legal fees, lenders mortgage insurance, mortgage transfer fees and more. There can be other costs when selling too: agents' fees and capital gains taxes, for example. The inescapable implication of this is that property as an asset class is nearly always better suited to long-term ownership than short term flipping or trading.

5 – Residential housing - both a consumption and an investment good

Residential property is a truly unique investment proposition, for it serves both as an investment and as a consumption good. Sometimes people buy property as an investment, others buy it purely to have a roof over their head. Others still buy property for both purposes. People will always need somewhere to live, so a well-located property investment which is in strong demand should generate a growing income stream in the form of rental income.

6 – Property is heterogeneous

Each individual property is different, so ascertaining the exact fair market value of an asset can be difficult and thus some level of experience and access to the full suite of sales data is very important. Market values can be somewhat easier to determine where there is a block of similar apartments with recent sales which can be used as a guideline. At the top end of the market in the premium sector a fair market value can be very subjective and much more difficult to determine. Consequently the property market is imperfect and smart investors with access to all of the available data are able to profit from this.

What makes dwelling prices move?

Of course there are many things which can shift the market value of real estate, such as the availability of mortgage financing, the prevailing level of interest rates and so on. In the very simplest terms, prices are dictated by supply (the properties available) and demand (how many people are willing and able to buy those available properties).

So who buys residential property? There are a number of categories of buyer, including owner-occupiers, investors, developers and renovators. Demand is driven by demographics, the size and location of the population, and also its ability and willingness to pay for real estate. Consequently, investors in property should invest where the population is growing in wealth - generally, quality suburbs of the capital cities are the best bet - and in capital cities where the population is growing in size.

Where demand exceeds supply, prices rise...and vice-versa.

Investors only have limited control over the new supply that comes to market. The cost of new property is determined by land prices as well as the costs of building materials and construction. If prices are to move higher as investors hope, then it makes sense to invest only in areas with a growing population but a limited supply of new land available for development. In the case of medium density dwellings such as apartments, oversupply can be a risk, so look towards areas where huge new tower blocks cannot be built due to planning restrictions. City centres, central business districts and sometimes transport hubs can have relatively few restrictions on the height of residential buildings and therefore oversupply in these areas can be a risk.

Leverage

To recap, what does leverage actually mean? Leverage means *being able to do more with less*. What do you do when you have a tin of paint with the lid stuck on it? Answer: employ leverage. If you are anything like me you find a spoon or a fork (though not from the kitchen draw, of course) to use as a lever in order to generate the extra power to force the lid open.

In the financial world, leverage often refers to borrowing. A company which is highly leveraged is one with a lot of debt on its balance sheet. When it is used sensibly, leverage can be beneficial to the borrower who uses the extra capital to fund profitable projects. Sometimes, however, companies may overuse leverage and get themselves into financial dire straits. We saw this during the global financial crisis where companies that were over-stretched, could not afford to service their debt and became insolvent. So we can see that leverage is a double-edged sword, and so it is for property investors.

Leverage is a powerful tool, but only when used wisely.

Leverage has the potential to be the greatest advantage that a property investor has over investors in other asset classes. The principle is simple enough. Let us say you have a pool of capital of $50,000 and decide to invest in shares which then appreciate in value over the forthcoming years by 25 percent. You have done very nicely and made an unrealised gain of $12,500. If you have chosen a profitable company you will receive dividend income of perhaps $2500 each year too.

Alternatively, you might choose to use your $50,000 to invest in a $500,000 investment property. If you can achieve 25 percent capital growth on the property it would result in an unrealised gain of $125,000. It is possible that you may take some time to see the 25 percent capital gain and in some cases there may be holding costs, of course, but take a look at the difference in the absolute size of the gain!

Leverage magnifies both gains and losses.

In an ideal world, we would never have to borrow money for anything, including investing in property, and borrowing money does introduce some risk into our investing. In our hypothetical but non-existent ideal world, we would simply take funds out of our hugely healthy bank balances and invest in a diversified portfolio of shares, commercial properties, farmland, commodities, bonds and other fixed-interest investments which would pay us a healthy and increasing income from now until the end of time.

Naturally if we all started out our financial life with a vast pool of capital available to invest, you would not be reading this book and I would not be writing it! This is why leverage is potentially so important for the average investor. It presents the opportunity to invest with some of our money and much more of the bank's money in order to super-charge returns. In plain English you have a better chance of generating significant wealth with millions of the bank's dollars than a few of our own. The leverage offered by residential investment property is the number one reason that property offers the average investor the best chance of not being average.

Compound growth and real estate investment

You have already heard the Albert Einstein quote on compound interest. It is a neat quote but what does it actually mean for property investors? Another way of describing what compounding is might be *growth upon growth*. In nature, water lilies only cover a small part of a pond for some years but in subsequent years they begin to run rampant and suddenly cover the entire surface of the water. Think back to the incredible spread of the rabbit population in Australia - from just a handful of bunnies shipped over from England – to there being millions of them in a relatively short space of time.

Let us delve into how this might relate to investment by looking at an asset worth $100,000 which appreciates at 8 percent per annum.

Figure 11.1 – Compounding growth

Year	Value at 8 percent capital growth per annum ($)	Growth in year ($)
0	100,000	-
1	108,000	8,000
2	116,640	8,640
3	125,971	9,331
4	136,049	10,078
5	146,933	10,884
6	158,687	11,754
7	171,382	12,695
8	185,093	13,711
9	200,000	14,907
10	216,000	16,000
11	233,280	17,280
12	251,942	18,662
13	272,098	20,156
14	293,866	21,768
15	317,375	23,509
16	342,765	25,390
17	370,186	27,421
18	400,000	29,814

Intuitively, you might expect an asset that is growing at 8 percent each year to take nearly 13 years to double in value. It would seem to make sense, wouldn't it? Yet in fact, as you can see above, in only nine years the asset has doubled in value and in 18 years it has doubled twice. The reason for this is the compounding growth. As you can see, in the first year the property has grown in value by $8000, but in the eighteenth year the property has grown in value by nearly $30,000. Each increase is greater than its preceding equivalent. That is, to say, there is growth upon growth which is what investors use to multiply their earnings.

The reason that investors who get it right can achieve financial freedom is that instead of investing with only $100,000, they can potentially use those funds as a deposit to invest in property worth $750,000. If they achieve 8 percent capital growth per annum they can generate equity of more than $1.7 million over 15 years, *more than 20 times* the initial deposit. And if they do not achieve 8 percent capital growth? Well, they can still comfortably outperform the returns from every other asset class provided that they can achieve reasonable capital growth, due to the leverage involved.

Of course, property prices will never appreciate in such a linear fashion, and you might not achieve 8 percent per annum growth if you invest in the wrong asset. What tends to happen in reality is that values remain flat or slightly falling for a number of years, before surging upwards in value. However, the principle remains the same - over time, compounding growth can work in your favour to help you build very significant wealth if you choose the right asset to invest in.

Meanwhile, inflation makes the real value of any mortgage debt effectively worth less with each passing year. The implications of the chart above are quite clear, and this is something which my wife and I have found having owned properties and shares for more than 15 years – with each passing year, an appreciating asset can begin to make the associated mortgage debt look very small, while rental incomes can easily rise to double or even more than triple of the mortgage repayments over the long haul.

Of course, there are no free lunches in investing, and the cost here is that the use of leverage introduces risk and you cannot afford to get it wrong. For this reason I advise using an expert such as a property buyer's agent to buy your investment properties for you. While there is a cost attached to this too, it is a relatively inexpensive price to pay in order to avoid making potentially very costly errors.

The rule of 72 revisited

Remember that the *rule of 72* can help you to calculate how long an asset such as a property will take to double in value. Just to remind you, here is how it works: take the number 72 and divide it by the growth rate per annum of the property, and the answer you get is the number of years the property will take to double in value. In the table above an asset appreciating at 9 percent per annum doubles in 8 years (72/9 = 8).

Using an expert

I have changed my views on the use of experts over the years. When I started out in investing all those years ago I thought that the smart thing to do would be to try to do everything myself and learn as I went. This approach does have the benefit of helping you to learn, but it can also slow down your progress, as lessons do tend to be learned the hard way.

Through a combination of good fortune and what I liked to think of as common sense I did not make too many genuine howlers. My strategy was to buy houses and apartments close to key transport hubs and near to the centre of capital cities like Sydney and London that I would like to live in myself. Indeed, my wife and I did live in several of our investment properties over the years when we were in full time paid employment. Our basic strategy was to continue accumulating and holding properties that people like us - being young professionals - would also choose to live in.

However, looking back we did make some mistakes. We didn't always time the market perfectly, although we sometimes did through blind luck! We bought some apartments with swimming pools, a gymnasium or a 24 hour concierge – all things which are nice to have when you are living in an apartment block yourself, but can incur annoying ongoing holding costs and commitments as a landlord.

In hindsight I feel now that we may have paid a little too much for some of our investment properties (although, over time, property tends to be a very forgiving asset class if you have bought well in a great location) and more than once we have been hit by unforeseen repairs or special levies. This tends to go with the territory for the inexperienced investor.

I now believe that investors should use a professional and licensed buyer's agent when they start investing – and I do not only say that because my company provides such a service. The reason I say that is that due to the leverage employed buying property is too big a transaction to get wrong.

Crucially, particularly in this era of lower inflation, if you do not buy the right investment property or make a mistake you will not get the capital growth which you need to leverage into new investments, and therefore your investment plan will stall before it has ever really gotten going. The worst case is that you could buy an illiquid, depreciating asset using leverage which continues to slide in value, a potentially devastating outcome, which I have seen happen to investors in the Irish property market.

> Make a few great investment decisions rather than many average decisions.

I also advise that when investing in property you should consider using a team of experts to make sure that you get it right. You should use an accountant with expertise in property to ensure that you maximise tax deductions in the most efficient manner possible, and you should use a solicitor or conveyancer to make sure that the contract of sale is fully understood.

Where applicable it is best practice to consider engaging building and pest inspection experts, and to pay for strata reports to ensure that there are no issues with the strata scheme which could result in painful levies in the years of ownership ahead. In most cases it makes sense to engage a property manager to help you to ensure that the investment property is well maintained and is always tenanted at the right market rates.

What buyer's agents can do to de-risk property investment?

Just as you can engage a fund manager to buy and sell investments for you in the stock market, you can enlist a buyer's agent to oversee the process of buying an investment property or a place of residence for you. Some of the processes that can be delegated to a professional buyer's agent include:

- Arranging a meeting with a financial planner/accountant
- Helping the buyer to obtain mortgage finance
- Locating a property or shortlist of properties for purchase which meets the buyer's criteria

- Researching properties with scarcity value which will outperform the market
- Finding off-market property opportunities or 'silent sales' that are never listed
- Engaging a solicitor to review contracts and to oversee the acquisition and settlement process
- Arranging pest and/or building inspections where appropriate
- Obtaining and arranging review of strata reports for issues within the strata scheme
- Engaging an independent valuer or analysing a comprehensive database of comparable sales to ensure you do not overpay for a property
- Attend the auction process on your behalf or negotiating the purchase price
- Engaging a property manager and ensuring that the property is tenanted
- Some experienced buyer's agents will also project manage a renovation for you if that is your plan

There are costs associated with using a buyer's agent.

Sometimes buyer's agents will used a fixed fee structure and on other occasions they may charge a percentage of the purchased property's value as a fee. It is vitally important that you are absolutely clear on the terms and conditions of the contract and how the proposed fee structure works before you sign anything.

While buyer's agents fees can sometimes appear to be expensive, the idea is that if the agent can buy you a property for a better price that performs better than one you could have chosen yourself even by, say, one percent per annum in capital growth terms, then they will have saved you more than the value of their fees very quickly. As buyer's agents are in the market every day, they also should have a good chance of securing you a great property at a value-for-money price. Experienced buyer's agents should be great negotiators too.

Buyer's agents can give you peace of mind.

Perhaps even more importantly than this, the expertise a professional buyer's agent should give you the peace of mind that you have not purchased a poor property which results in financial loss. Very often, individual property purchases are the most material acquisitions individuals make in their lifetime – these are not transactions you want to get wrong.

Be aware though, that, as in most fields, all buyer's agents are not created equal. If you are planning to use a buyer's agent, look for one with a proven track record of buying quality properties at a fair price for satisfied clients and for themselves. Using a team of expert advisors, informed information and qualified professionals to make your life easier and to create wealth is exactly what successful investing should be all about!

Strategies - buy, renovate and sell?

Buying properties to renovate them and sell on for a profit is sometimes known as *flipping*. This is a strategy used by very experienced renovators to generate profits purely by adding value to the property. The renovator will generally be aiming to complete the transaction in a relatively short space of time, and therefore cannot place reliance on the property market increasing in value for their gains.

Experienced renovators may take on significant projects that might involve subdivisions, knocking down old houses to replace with blocks of apartments or adding extra bedrooms to existing properties. These can be lucrative strategies for the experienced investor. However, I do not recommend that you start out with a major renovation.

There is of course no problem at all with a beginner investor buying a run-down property with the idea of giving it a rejuvenation or adding some value through hard graft or sweat equity. Simple cosmetic renovations such as repainting or replacing carpets or even upgrading kitchens and bathrooms can be very effective strategies even for the inexperienced. One of the biggest traps to avoid is paying too much for the property in the first instance, for if you do this then the benefit of any cosmetic renovation will be negated.

> To create wealth for yourself, first add value to others.

One rule of thumb that is sometimes used for investors doing smaller scale renovations is that they should try to add $1500 of value to the property for every $1000 spent. On a larger scale renovation the desired return might be higher to compensate for the additional risks being managed and longer timescale of the project.

The problem with selling property for a profit is that it costs money. There are agent fees and legal fees to pay, and then there are capital gains tax liabilities to pay on profits. And if you elect to re-invest whatever profits you have left over in another property then you incur more fees and stamp duty charges. Buying and selling assets too frequently creates transaction costs, tax charges and erodes profits. The most efficient strategy is to buy a quality asset and hold it for as long as possible, ideally forever.

Buy and hold

The idea of a buy and hold approach to property investment is very simple. If carried out successfully, the investor will buy a desirable property in high demand for a great price at somewhere close to the bottom of the property market cycle. He or she will then aim to hold the property for as long as possible – hopefully forever – in order to allow the power of compounding to work its magic on the value of the property, while the relative value of the mortgage in present value terms falls as inflation devalues the currency over time.

The benefits of not selling

What the numerical examples looked at above showed is that often the greatest value for investors can be in not selling their properties. Rather than constantly buying and selling properties in the hope of a quick profit and getting stung for transaction fees, the investor who identifies a great asset and holds on to it indefinitely can continue to reap the benefits of multiplying growth for years and decades to come.

So many times we hear of investors bemoaning having sold a great property to lock in a profit only for the value of the property in question to continue appreciating substantially for many years to come after the sale. Wouldn't it be great if that never happened to you? Like most people I have made some ordinary decisions in my life and some really great ones too – certainly one of the best choices I have ever made is not selling a single one of any of the properties I have ever bought! Buy in quality locations and hold for the long term.

Buy, renovate and hold

Many experienced investors come to the conclusion that the superior strategy for them to use is to buy, renovate and hold onto property. This way the investor obtains the benefit of adding value to the property through a renovation or cosmetic rejuvenation, can add perhaps 10 percent or even 20 percent to the amount of rental charged and can also benefit from the compounding growth of the property for many years into the future. Alternatively some investors buy a property with 'equity on ice', being one which can be let in its current state but renovated for capital gain some time in the future.

Timing the market or time in the market?

What the numbers in Figure 11.1 above show is that time in the market can be the greatest friend of the small percentage of property investors who buy well. The longer a property is held for the more it has the opportunity to compound and grow, and the longer time horizon should compensate the investor for the lean times, of which there are sure to be some.

However, it is certainly the case that by timing your entry to the property market to the best of your ability, you can super-charge your returns. If you invest in a property at the peak of the market for your state it is perfectly possible that you will see falling values and perhaps see no capital growth at all for years, possible even more than a decade. So while time in the market is vital, one should have an appreciation of the property market cycle and timing the market too.

Figure 11.2 – Property market cycle

A property cycle is relatively easy to identify in retrospect. There will be a period of flat or falling values followed by a significant upturn in values, before flat prices again become the order of the day. The specifics may change to some extent, but the general principle stands. Different states and locations tend to be at different stages of the property cycle at any given point in time. Therefore, if your home state has recently seen a boom in values then it can definitely make sense to invest in another state.

While there is a tendency for property investors to favour their home state and often even their home suburb, you should appreciate that where you choose to live often does not represent the smartest investment. In a similar vein, where you like to go on holiday is often not the best place to invest either! We will look at the best areas in which to invest in the next chapter. For now, be aware of the existence of property cycles and resolve to use them to your advantage.

Invest through two market cycles to become wealthy

In the last section I discussed how there are property cycles that we should be aware of. What I also want to introduce here is that if you can stay invested in quality assets throughout two boom periods of property cycles then you should have generated significant wealth. Here is how that might work in practice using some very over-simplified numbers. Let us go back once again to our investor who has invested in a $750,000 property at a low point in the property cycle. Having timed the market successfully the investor is delighted when perhaps a decade down the track the property has nearly doubled in value to close to $1,500,000.

What the investor then might be able to do is borrow an extra $400,000 from the bank on the basis that his property has increased in value. The new funds are then used to invest in three further properties each worth, say, $675,000. Again, the investor looks to invest at the bottom of the market cycle, but this time in a different state and capital city which has not had a boom in values for some period in time.

> Remain fully invested through two full property
> cycles to become wealthy.

When the three newly-acquired properties subsequently increase in value from their combined purchase cost of around $2 million the investor will have generated a very significant pool of equity. The neat thing about this approach is that all of this wealth or equity has been created from that initial deposit on the first investment property and funds borrowed from the bank.

Now, let us cut to the chase and be frank about this - firstly, is an extremely over-simplified example, and the leverage involved in making property purchases in such a manner introduces risk if the investor gets it wrong. It should also be acknowledged in this era of lower inflation, it could take quite some time to generate the equity from the first investment in order to re-invest in further assets.

However the basic principles the above example introduces are exactly those which experienced property investors use, and this is the way in which investing through two property cycles can work to the investor's great benefit. Compare the simplicity and effectiveness of this approach to that of the 'flipper' who is constantly buying, renovating and selling, and trying to overcome the substantial hurdles of stamp duty, transaction costs and capital gains taxes.

In this example, the money is working harder so the investor does not have to. The other thing to point out about this pyramiding approach using personal debt is that if the investor gets it wrong they may bankrupt themselves. Leverage can either be the most powerfully effective or the most lethally dangerous tool in investing depending upon how it is used.

Living off equity

Living off equity is a controversial strategy that is often advocated by property clubs and may possibly have been more suitable to more profligate times, but perhaps less so today.[1] Let me up take the example of the investor in the previous section who upon buying his three new investment properties, now has a total of four properties worth $3.5 million. The idea of living off equity promotes the idea that as the value of the properties increases, the investor borrows more money from the bank to live off.

Can you spot the flaw in this strategy? Well, it's really not too hard, is it? The problem is that if the properties owned do not appreciate in value – or worse, they decline in value – the investor cannot borrow more money and has nothing to live on. Besides, any strategy that is purely reliant upon an investor borrowing even more money is not one that I could ever recommend.

The above having been said, the idea of borrowing a buffer when refinancing property to cover a small cash-flow shortfall from investment properties and even some moderate living costs is not a strategy I have an issue with. As I become older, my attitude to risk is a far more conservative one, so using debt only moderately and always maintaining a reasonable buffer is what I advocate.

Demand outstripping supply

It is important for investors in property to learn that while markets will always cycle through peaks and troughs, each significant market peak over time tends to be higher than preceding peaks, thus emphasising the importance of a long-term outlook. Due to the leverage involved in residential property investment, it is capital growth rather than cash flow that creates wealth.

Therefore it is vital to invest in areas and property types where the demand will increase through population growth and real household income growth, and through a steady influx of foreign investment. You need to find areas where demand will grow to the extent that it comfortably outstrips supply. Over the long term, this is how wealth is achieved through real estate, which means looking at capital cities where the population is guaranteed to grow over the very long term and where the labour market is founded upon a solid base and a diversified range of industries.

The yield trap exists in property too

There is much talk of the benefits of investing in properties which generate a high percentage yield. We do need to note, however, that high yields tend to exist in residential property where capital growth has been restricted due to uninspiring levels of demand. Very similar principles apply to property as they do to shares.

When property market prices are high, percentage rental yields tend to be lower (and vice versa), but over a long time horizon we might expect rental yields to revert to something close to a mean or average, and therefore what we actually want is properties which experience great capital growth. The rental income will generally take care of itself over time if you buy well, so look for the property types in the highest demand not poor quality or junk properties located in regional areas.

Something to remember is that counter-cyclical property investors get great yields anyway! If you elect to invest counter-cyclically in property when sentiment is low, you can attain attractive yields even on prime location property – just as share investors who invest after a crash get great dividend yields on blue chip shares. Smart investors are able to find strong yields through investing counter-cyclically. By electing to invest in property which has recently experienced sharply rising rents but not capital growth, just like share investors, counter-cyclical property investors expect to receive both future capital growth and a solid yield too.

Counter-cyclical investors can achieve strong enough yields.

Smart investors tend to find rental yields above the quoted average and manufacture higher yields too by adding value to properties through cosmetic renovation. Thus if average properties in prestige suburbs can attain up to 5 percent yields we should question how much value there may be in seeking out yields of 6 percent if this involves investing in an area which over the long term will not experience as great a level of demand?   Quality, well-located boutique blocks of apartments in the inner suburbs of Sydney, for example, will over the coming decades experience a sizeable increase in demand due to population growth, while construction will continue to remain inadequate and tremendously costly.

OK, so I may have bored you with the theory. What does it mean in practice? What can growth do for us as investors? Being an Anglo-Aussie myself I frequently refer back to what is happening in England for clues, as some of the property markets there are more developed. While many property investors in the UK regions who bought in the period after 2005 are the unfortunate owners of property with negative equity, prices in London continue to surge to the highest they have ever been.[2]

Blue chip inner suburbs of capital cities outperform... over the long term.

Ask people who bought a house back in the 1980s and 1990s in Britain how they've fared and they say: 'I have done well'. Why? Because the property is worth more in dollar terms than they paid for it. Buy have they really done well? Most likely they have no idea because mostly they have few other investments and no worthwhile benchmark against which to measure performance.

Typically, house prices moved upwards through the inflationary 1980s, and appreciated further again as credit growth expanded in the 1990s, but have tailed off in most areas outside London over recent years. Expect to see similar trends unfolding in Australia, with properties in prestige suburbs of the major capital cities over time being significant outperformers both in terms of rental income and capital growth. Lower yields, maybe, but far, far higher income. Understand this fundamental difference and you can be a winner too.

Further property market analysis

The thing to appreciate is that while capital growth in property appears to be haphazard or at times completely random, it is certainly not so. In this chapter I have only begun to explain a few of the demographic shifts and imbalances which will cause certain suburbs to boom in the future and other suburbs and property types to stagnate and fall into decline.

Our company *AllenWargent* produces a huge amount of analysis concerning the macro-economic picture on a state level, the cost of debt, population and demographic shifts, supply versus demand at the suburb level and much more. What we have found over the years is that predicting where and when property prices will grow is much more scientific than people seem to believe, and we will explore this further in chapter 12.

Most people adopt a do-it-yourself approach to investment preferring to go with a gut feel, or worse they follow some of the dart-boarding recommendations offered by property pundits in the media. It is no real surprise that people get it badly wrong as there are so many poor recommendations in the real estate media about investing in mining towns or regional towns which do not have a prayer of outperforming the key capital city suburbs over the long run.

Some property books have even instructed investors to ignore the role of capital growth altogether as it is not possible to predict where it will happen. Therefore, so the theory goes, just buy any old property so long as it has a high rental yield at face value. This leads people to buy dumps in far-flung towns because cheap properties can have high yields (if, that is, the tenants actually pay the rent).

Whatever happens, do not follow this poor advice! In the next chapter I will explain to you how to identify the cities and property types and locations which you can invest in to create wealth. This will take a good deal of research but when all is said and done this is a small price to pay for achieving your own financial freedom.

Chapter 11 summary

» Property can be a great long-term investment

» Only invest in markets with very strong long-term fundamentals

» The housing markets will continue to cycle

» Aim to be fully invested through two market cycles in order to be wealthy

» Use leverage with great care and always maintain a healthy buffer for unforeseen cash flow problems or market downturns

12
Be Your Own
Property Buyer's Agent

12

Be your own buyer's agent

OK, so I said that I believe that would-be property investors should use an expert. However, I will include a chapter here on being your own buyer's agent. Why? Because I know that whatever I may say in these pages, there will always be a significant number of people who decide that going it alone will save them money and therefore it is worth the risk. So be it.

If you are going to go it alone in property investment, you will at the very least need to get a basic understanding of the macro and micro level economy and how it will interact with the real estate markets. In this chapter I will present to you just a flavour of how you can go about this and then how you can use this information to find the right property types and locations to invest in.

The economic backdrop

Through the 1970s and 1980s much of the developed world was living through a period of relatively high inflation. In terms of what this meant for property, nominal prices almost everywhere seemed to rise quite consistently, largely because the price of everything rose. That is not to say that it was an easy era for property owners, however. At times interest rates ran very high, while recessions and unemployment made life very difficult for some homeowners.

The compensating good news for those who were able to hang onto their properties throughout this period was that the high rates of inflation saw much of the value of household debt inflated away. However, not all property types outperformed inflation significantly - many poorly located properties did not.

> We have undergone a structural shift into an era of
> low interest rates and low inflation.

The 1990s were a different matter entirely where we moved through a structural shift towards lower rates of inflation and lower interest rates as central banks began to target inflation rates or bands. The result of this was an unprecedented rise in the levels of household debt as banking systems were deregulated thus allowing lenders to create debt more freely at competitive rates.

The net result was that for different reasons dwelling prices continued to rise fairly relentlessly through each of those three decades with some corrections, and until around 2007 this trend looked set to continue through another decade unchecked. Times had been so good for so long that folk began to believe in dwelling prices as a one way bet, while in the US in particular lenders found ways to write loans to people who previously had not a prayer of seeing a mortgage. Some real estate pundits were duped into believing that even properties in regions with weak economies could keep rising in price, seemingly defying gravity. Unfortunately in many cases lenders issued loans to people with little chance of ever repaying the loans, known as 'subprime' lending.

The property investment landscape has changed radically since 2007.

The global financial crisis which played out from that time saw another dramatic change in the landscape and we have moved into a new era once again. Before the financial crisis a number of property market commentators had been head faked into believing that because property prices had risen so consistently over such a long period of time, the location and the property type that they chose to invest in was unimportant.

In many cases advisers have recommended buying the worst types of property being those which were in very low demand and in secondary locations. These properties can be superficially appealing because they are cheap to buy and their historical lack of strong capital growth can mean that the rental yield might on the face of it be higher. Since 2007, a great many of these regional and secondary markets have performed poorly as we expected, and many mining towns are set to perform in an even worse manner.

The property markets have once again moved into a new era.

Today there is no longer high inflation to inflate away the value of mortgage debt, and the structural shift towards lower interest rates and the associated boom in household debt is behind us. Other trends such as the massive growth in dual income households have also now taken their full effect and will not be repeated.[1] In short, the easy gains in property which we as investors have benefited from over recent decades are no more, and you need to genuinely understand how times have changed if you wish to continue multiplying your earnings in the future.

The best case outcome for most regionally located properties or those in secondary suburban locations is that they increase in price in lockstep with the growth in household incomes, perhaps at a few percent per annum on average at best. In many cases, even this may be wishful thinking. The problem with smaller regional towns and cities is that weaker population growth can easily be absorbed by land release, jobs and income growth tend to be weak and consequently there will tend to be very little sustained upwards pressure on property prices. To outperform in the future you need to implement a different strategy.

Post financial crisis property investing

Large and growing capital cities have a built-in significant advantage over smaller towns and cities and this advantage is becoming greater with each passing year. If you understand a little about economics and demographics you will quickly understand why this is the case and can use this information to your advantage. Large cities such as Sydney, London and others around the world have long had an inherent advantage of attracting migrants and new inhabitants, which is indeed why I have invested so heavily in these markets myself over the years. In many cases these are the only cities which migrants are familiar with within their respective countries, and the larger cities offer greater potential for employment which also encourages internal migration.

Over time, the populations of the cities we tend to recommend investing in grow at a fast pace, tracking at around 80,000 persons per annum in Sydney's case, which will see close to another 1 million people living in the harbour city in another decade's time.[2] London is also expected to see its population swell to some 9 million persons by 2021 which equates to a truly massive new demand for housing.[3] By the way, I practice exactly what I preach and own a large portfolio of properties mostly comprised of investments in Sydney and around London.

These are huge population growth numbers which create great strain on infrastructure and consistent upwards pressure on the existing stock of dwellings. The problem for regional towns and cities is that rather than larger employers and inhabitants seeking out cheaper alternatives in regional locations, they are continuing to focus increasingly upon being located close to the centre of the capital.

While this may seem ill-advised, studies have found that there are some sound economic reasons behind the decision-making process, largely related to the fact that productivity tends to be far higher in densely concentrated capital cities. This is partly to do with the ability of employers to fill roles more easily from a diversified labour force and much to do with the way in which businesses at close proximity interact with each other. The larger capital cities are becoming self-sustaining jobs magnets, while regional areas are struggling to attract interest and growth.

> When investing in property look towards capital cities with sustained and assured huge future population growth.

Just as we have seen elsewhere, compound interest is an extremely powerful force, and the virtuous cycle is becoming self-fulfilling in favour of the largest cities. For every 100,000 new persons that choose to call a city their home, we need to build approximately 40,000 more homes, more hospitals, more parks, shopping centres, more junior schools, senior schools and further education units, more roads, more infrastructure, more service stations and more restaurants, more entertainment outlets and more supermarkets.

Dwelling construction itself tends be very effective at creating employment, not only for construction workers, but also for retailing and shopping centre staff, healthcare staff including doctors and nurses, schooling and teachers and other sectors. As previously noted therefore, construction can itself have a strong multiplier effect across the local economy. For every $1 million spent on construction, this tends to create around $3 million of additional output in the local economy, representing an economic multiplier of three.[4]

In decades gone by many Australian state economies were largely reliant upon natural resources to generate income and therefore prosperity. However, developed countries have gradually shifted towards more knowledge and services based economies over time, with mining in Australia now accounting for only 2 percent of jobs. Large cities have another great advantage in this regard too, as they serve as the financial and service sector hubs for their respective countries.

> Developed economies are transitioning towards knowledge and services based industries.

London, for example, has been Britain's greatest success story, becoming a major financial centre for the European region, partly thanks to its location in the world and its time zone, being unique in its ability to service transactions between America and Asia. Over the decades Britain has generated some wealth from its coal and North Sea Oil, but increasingly financial services have been the driver of Britain's economic growth and prosperity.

In Australia's case, if you look back only three decades, around three quarters of the stock market by value was accounted for by resources companies, yet today mining and resources companies account for only a quarter of the value of the index. It is true that commodities are still of great importance to Australia's economic standing and do account for a significant proportion of the national income. However, overall the largest sector of the economy is now services, and with the construction of the new suburb at Barangaroo, Sydney is setting itself to become a major new financial hub for Asia.

> Sustainable property price growth must be founded upon real wages growth.

Ultimately, sustainable growth can only be sourced from productive enterprise and value being created. Three decades ago in Australia this simply meant ripping an ever-greater volume of minerals out of our weeping planet. However, today much of our wealth is created through technological ingenuity and intellectual expertise, particularly in financial services. Sustainable property price growth needs real wages growth and growing demand. Speculating in remote areas, outlying cities or tourism-dependent regions where real wages growth is negligible carries a material risk premium.

I have spent a great deal of time over the last decade studying demographic and economic trends in great detail and I have only just begun to scratch the surface here. The key takeaway for the point of this book is that capital cities are self-sustaining jobs magnets which generate far more wealth than regional centres or smaller cities will ever be able to. Not only that, this trend is becoming steadily more and more entrenched, perhaps irreversibly so.

Trends within the capitals

As noted in the preceding section, we have spent a huge amount of time studying economic and demographic trends, and what we have found is that even with the large capital cities, specific and measurable new trends are increasingly evident. There was a theory doing the rounds a couple of decades ago that the internet would make the world less reliant upon being in a certain location. In theory, this is true, and we could all live far from the capital cities, opting to work remotely. However, it has simply not happened in any meaningful way.

When you analyse the statistical evidence of what is actually happening, we find that precisely the reverse has been true. While there are a few 'sea-changers' most people actually do not want to live remotely and younger generations more than ever before are seeking out ways to live closer to the action, near to the centre of the largest cities. These locations are often sought out even where there is a significant premium attached to living in these favoured areas.

Figure 12.1 – Employment density and population growth trends

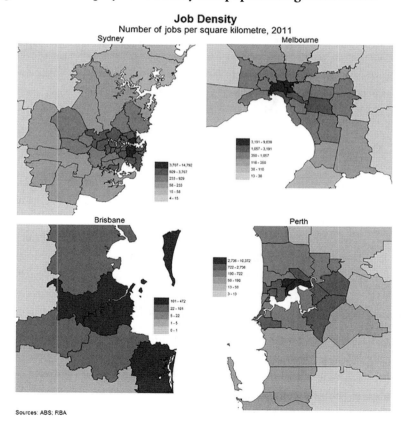

Sources: ABS; RBA

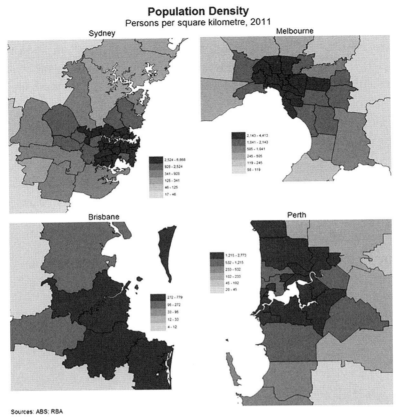

Population Density
Persons per square kilometre, 2011

Sources: ABS; RBA

Demographic study after study has found similar themes to be playing out.[5] Jobs growth is increasingly to be found in or close to the centre of capital cities, and this is particularly so in Australian capital cities, while public transport from outer suburbs is unable to service long-distance commuters effectively. Further, population growth is increasingly heavily focused on inner- and middle ring suburbs.[6] The combination of these two factors is putting huge pressure on inner ring dwelling prices, to the extent that prices are continuing to rise faster in inner city locations as compared to outer suburb locations, an obvious conclusion reached by the Reserve Bank itself.[7]

What is more, this trend is going to continue. Demographic studies have concluded that since outer suburb locations in capital cities have poor access to jobs, even where an hour is allowed for public transport or driving time, urban sprawl should be curtailed and more land should be made available for development where possible in inner- and middle-ring suburbs.[8]

There has been a generational shift towards placing a premium living in inner suburbs with access to the city.

In any case, this is what younger people are choosing anyway. One generational change has been that younger employees do not want to commute too far for work and are prepared to pay a premium to rent property located close to the centre of capital cities. In many cases they could afford to buy a starter home in a distant outer location and then look to trade up later on, but often they simply do not want to.

Often they would rather forego the starter home for a more exciting life closer to the city, and in many cases their first step on to the property ladder is via buying an apartment closer to the city either to live in or as an investment property. There is nothing inherently wrong with living close to the city of course, provided that young people do remember to set some money aside for the future by investing it wisely, although I fear that often this last point is forgotten (looking at the inexorable rise in retail spend on cafes, restaurants and takeaways, the evidence appears to be quite damning).

Rightly or wrongly, this is the way the world is heading. The population as a whole is prepared to pay an ever-greater premium for the privilege of living close to the centre of our capital cities. I suggest that if you want to escape from the rat race, rather than mortgaging yourself to the hilt to do the same you should aim to own a portfolio of investments and rent them to this growing demographic which wants it all and will pay a high premium to live close to the city.

This is only a starting point for consideration, of course. You still need to time the market and there remain a wide range of factors which you need to consider in order to make sure that you buy the right property, and look for locations and property types where the supply is effectively capped but demand is growing rapidly. But focusing on properties from which the inhabitants can commute to the employment hubs within 15 minutes by train is likely to be a very good starting point.

Falling household sizes

We have just begun to consider above of the types of locations which you might consider for buying investment property. Let us now drill in a little further. There has been a trend over the last century of falling household sizes, from well above four person per dwelling to under 2.5 persons.[9] This trend of falling household sizes may have run its course, but what has gone before will have a number of key impacts.

Figure 12.2 - Falling household sizes

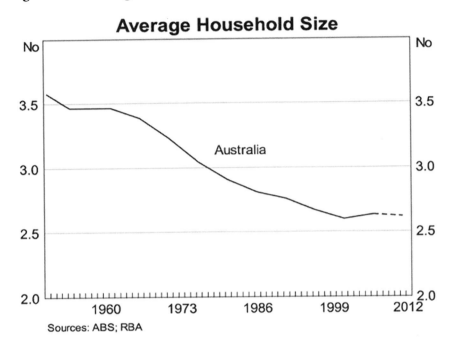

Source: Reserve Bank of Australia

Firstly, and most obviously, with smaller average household sizes which have been caused by a number of factors, we need far more dwellings to house the same number of people. This is creating tremendous pressure on the existing stock of dwellings. Secondly, there is a greater demand for medium density dwelling types such as townhouses, flats, units and apartments than there has ever been before.

This has partly been due to affordability as the population places an ever greater premium on being located in the right suburbs close to the city centres, and it is partly to do with a generational shift towards this style of living. Living in a flat was once seen as a secondary choice only for those who could not afford a house. Cleverly rebranded as *apartments* in a stroke of marketing genius, these attached dwelling types are often now seen as a favourable choice whereby they can allow tenants to live close to the city with a great deal of low-maintenance and secure convenience.

Houses and apartments can both be great investments
depending upon your goals.

This is not to say that houses are by any means an inferior investment. Due to their inherent scarcity value and high land value content a house will likely generate the highest level of capital growth over the course of a cycle, and remember that it is capital growth which creates wealth, not cash flow. However, if owning houses is to be your strategy then you need to find houses which will be in increased demand which means relatively close to the city and likely this will mean a high entry price and a low yield. Houses on quarter acre plot in distant outer suburbia are unlikely to be the popular property choice of the future.

One of the key reasons that you might look towards medium density dwellings is affordability. A house might be the best investment you can ever make as I know from my own experience, but if you cannot easily afford to service the mortgage then you will be limited in how many of these investments you can hold. Rental yields for well-located houses can be significantly lower, and finding tenants for prime location houses who are prepared to sign up for high-cost leases can be more difficult too. Periods of vacancy for these higher-end property types can be very painful.

Types of apartments to buy

There is an old saying in property investment:

'Land appreciates, and buildings depreciate.'

I am often fascinated by traditional sayings and adages and wonder where they first came from. In most cases, you find that they exist for a good reason. What this adage is hinting at is that there is only ever a finite supply of land in locations where people want and need to live close to employment centres. While some cities, including Sydney, have used reclaimed land to reasonable effect this is sometimes offset by rising sea levels reclaiming land in other parts of cities. In cities with growing populations the supply of desirable land is effectively all but fixed yet the demand for that land grows, and in an inflationary economy this inevitably pushes land prices higher over time. So far, so straightforward.

As for the buildings depreciating part of the adage, there is more than a grain of truth in this too. If you leave a building alone for long enough without paying good money for it to be maintained and repaired, eventually it will fall into complete disrepair and fall down. Property ownership can be a liability to the extent that there are ongoing costs of this nature associated with it. For this reason, to get compound growth working in your favour you simply must buy property which is in increased demand resulting in capital growth. For this property type rents tend to increase and compound over time too, leading to a happy outcome for the landlord.

Looked at another way, however, the building does not necessarily *fall* in value. The replacement cost of a dwelling increases with inflation as labour costs and materials costs rise, and therefore a house which was built 50 years ago for a few thousand dollars has not really depreciated in terms of its dollar value. So, how to use this information to your advantage? The answer is often to buy apartments which are located in prime locations in capital cities, but those with a high land value content which means buying a property with a level of scarcity value in a relatively small or boutique block.

Capital growth is sourced from high demand and scarcity value.

Take the inferior investment proposition of a high rise tower block which has 500 apartments in it. The block of land is generally relatively small and the land value content of each individual unit is likely to be very low, perhaps representing only a few percent of the market value of the property. This is not the type of property to buy. Almost by definition, there is very little scarcity value in this type of property, because there are hundreds of other properties exactly like yours! When you come to sell, there may be half a dozen or more units on the market exactly like yours.

Some people insist that a house is always a better investment than an apartment because a house sits on more land. While this may be correct in theory, in practice if the land is located in a secondary outer suburban or regional area where demand is lower, prices will still only increase in line with household incomes in the best case scenario.

If you do not believe me or are unsure about this, take a drive out some remote areas and see how cheap a plot of land is compared to the capital city. Do you see what I mean? Real capital growth after inflation is non-existent where there is a relatively low demand for the land. The property value in secondary locations is all in the building. I would take a prime location apartment over a distantly located house every time provided that it fits my other criteria for purchase. The capital growth over time will be much stronger because there is a much higher *and growing* demand for living close to the city and employment hubs.

Regional properties

Here is another old adage of real estate:

Cheap today is cheap tomorrow.

The problem with buying cheap property is that it is usually cheap for a reason. Just like gold investors who buy gold and still only have a bar of gold at the end of the process, folk who invest in cheap regional properties because of a seemingly tempting initial rental yield still only have a cheap property at the end of the process. While inflation can see the value of associated mortgage debt decline steadily over time, rarely will regional properties significantly outperform the inflation rate over the long haul and therefore it is very hard to build wealth in such a manner. And that is before you even consider that holding properties for a long period of time tends to incur repairs and maintenance costs.

On the other hand if you can buy property in a prime location for which demand is growing, then the rental income can continue to grow in perpetuity and dwelling prices can continue to grow ahead of inflation too. If you cannot afford to buy property in a capital city then you might choose to look at regionally located property and this may be preferable to taking no action at all, but history shows that capital growth over time will be longer in capital cities with strong population growth.

Especially given the trend towards falling household sizes and an increase in the number of divorces and this middle-aged singles I always favour buying even a one bedroom apartment (in a boutique block) in a quality capital city location in a city such as Sydney or London over a house in a poor regional location, and the capital growth results will be better over time. A spacious one bedroom apartment can be suitable for a young couple or a downsizing couple too.

Successful property investment is about understanding demographic shifts, and all research shows that as thriving capital cities develop they become self-sustaining jobs magnets which attract further population growth. Companies become compelled to locate their headquarters and offices close to each other in the centre of cities. As we have seen this becomes a virtuous circle. Remember that as the population of a large capital city expands and more jobs are created, we also need to build more schools, dwellings, hospitals, parks, shopping centres, transport links, and train stations, which in turn creates further jobs in the construction industry.

The impact of the new construction has a beneficial multiplier effect across the city economy, creating demand for building materials and transportation. For every dollar spent on construction, three additional dollars of demand are created across the economy.[10] Regional locations historically have not benefited from such strong jobs growth, wages growth or population growth and as such property price growth has always lagged way behind.

Capped supply

On the supply side, prime location land in the inner suburbs of capital cities tends to be fully built out. New development can only take place through demolishing existing dwellings or rezoning industrial sites. While this can be achieved land remediation tends to be an extremely costly exercise in the modern era with such high compliance, health and safety, labour and materials costs, and this underpins the value of established dwellings at a relatively high level.[11] With no new vacant land to be released close to the centre of capital cities demand outstrips supply placing further upwards pressure on property prices in those locations.

> Look for properties which are restricted in supply
> but where demand is growing.

Regional locations suffer here too as there almost invariably exists significantly more land to be released for development. While statistically median prices can appear at times to rise as new homes are built, the actual capital growth rate in established regional properties is generally poor as compared to those in the inner cities.

On the other hand, in outer suburbs and regional locations construction of generic project style homes may actually become cheaper over time as new construction techniques are used such as 3D printing, increased use of mass production for certain building materials or, for example, concrete being poured on site in the style of old per-fabricated buildings first seen after the war. While in theory this could happen in inner suburban locations too, rising land prices and land remediation costs ensure that the price of new dwellings remains elevated. Over time, the difference between the haves and the have-nots of the property world is becoming more pronounced, and the trend is for this gulf to keep becoming wider and wider.

Inner versus outer suburbs

We have briefly considered above whether you should invest in inner suburbs or outer suburbs of capital cities. There are multiple considerations here, but basic geometry tells you that inner suburb property should outperform. One of the key characteristics of real estate is its fixed location, hence the popular quotation:

'Location, location, location'.

While property rights can be and are exchanged over time, the location of a property remains constant and the ongoing demand for the land constitutes a prime determinant of prevailing market price. There is a geographical economic theory in real estate circles known as the *bid-rent theory*, which dates back some decades, it being derived from a Ricardian theory on the most productive agricultural land.[12]

In the simplest terms, the original theory and bid-rent curves implied that the price and demand for property was highest within the concentric rings located closest to the central business district (CBD) and decreased the further away from that central point you travelled. Location theories hold that centrally located land is commonly worth more as retailers aim to maximise profitability and therefore will bid more for the land close to the city. Land on the outer is often deemed to be more viable for industrial use and demand is lower. Meanwhile, as different land uses compete, residents are also prepared to pay the highest rent for land close to the city where work and entertainment is traditionally located.

Land values appreciate faster over time in inner suburbs.

All else being equal, prices could be highest in the inner city and gradually recede the further from that point you move out to the inner/middle rings suburbs and the outer locations. High prices in central locations also encourage a higher density of building as compared to the lower density and more sparsely populated locations further from the city's centre. Over time, however, it should be expected that improved transport links can increase demand from higher income earners further from the centre of the city, in particular increasing demand in the well-located middle ring suburbs too.

Despite some obvious limitations there is some reasonably sound logic behind the bid-rent theory. For one thing, simple geometry shows that when looking at concentric rings or something approximating thereto, there must be far less land in the inner zone of a city. Correspondingly, there is a significantly greater supply of land available to be developed in the outer, which you can clearly see with your own eyes as you drive through any capital city.

Look for a scarcity of available land.

The original grid system in Australia created an artificial land scarcity and the standardised city blocks encouraged rapid resale and speculative activity.[13] As you can see on any map of the country the artificial land scarcity in Australia was also exacerbated by all of the earliest cities being located beside water. If you travel away from the city in the wrong direction, you'll quickly end up in the blue stuff.

Over time it has become clear that in countries like the US and Australia, that all else is not equal when it comes to residential property. Even from in the 1880s you can find clear references in original sources to residents in Australia having a strong preference for suburban living slightly away from the centre of the city.[14] Social housing has often been located in the inner city zones, for example, while wealthier households have often sought space in the middle-ring suburbs. Further, the traditional bid-rent curve is distorted by other factors such as households preferring to be located near favoured schools or other recreation. One of the true experts in housing market economics Michael Oxley observed that:[15]

'A major objective of rational land-use planning is to take account of the external cost and benefits. If land-use planning achieves its objectives the actual pattern of land use will differ from that predicted by simple market-orientated location theories'.

Another artificial barrier is in place with our city land supply, which is related to zoning and land release. And herein lies Australia's greatest challenge. Take a look, for example, at the population growth in some of Sydney's leafy inner- and middle-ring suburbs and you will find that the population levels are remarkably static for a capital city with such a burgeoning population growth.

While new construction and renovation does occur to some extent and significantly so around certain transport hubs and urban activation precincts, the total supply in certain popular suburbs is often all but fixed due to effective height restrictions on new builds. Even on land which is zoned as 'high density', it is often difficult to build upwards due to blocking the views of other existing residential buildings. Sydney investors in particular are piling into this type of stock because they understand that the supply will be fixed with the demand increasing by the year.

The challenge for countries like Australia and the United Kingdom is to convince people that living close to the Central Business Districts is not essential, which means providing quality transport links to places of employment (our cities are not totally monocentric as is often argued, so this includes to transport links to and from secondary CBDs and other employment hubs), improved infrastructure and other entertainment.

Our cities are centralising rather than decentralising.

There have been a great many suggestions as to how this might be achieved and affordable housing can be provided for our growing populations. Ultimately, in aggregate, demand is growing, and the route we are presently embracing is simply people paying ever-higher prices for a constrained supply of housing stock close to the city. Our research in London, Sydney and other cities has continued to show that prime location property does indeed continue to outperform consistently and not by a small margin.

Figure 12.3 – Prime locations outperform over time

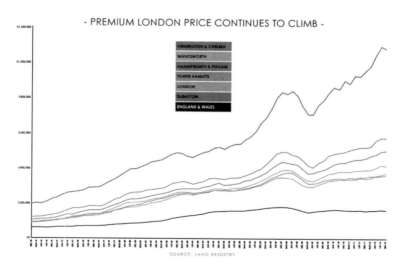

Chapter 12 summary

» The long term price of property is driven by supply and demand

» Look for strong population and employment growth and a scarcity of available land

» Studying demographics shows us that our cities are become increasingly centralised

» Household sizes have declined over the past century

» For a range of reasons more people are opting for medium-density living

13

How To Build A
Multi-Million
Dollar Property
Portfolio…Safely

13

Thinking big

Interesting choice for a chapter title, isn't it? I chose it quite deliberately. Well, why not think big? When you start out investing the concept of building a multi-million dollar property portfolio may seem like an impossibly distant goal. However, consider what you now know about compounding. If you are able to choose assets which increase in value year after year, your gains gradually become larger and larger. That is to say, the journey gets easier every year. One of the magic things about real estate as an investment is that if you choose the assets which you invest in very specifically and very carefully, you can secure enough capital growth to withdraw some equity to use for further investments.

> 'You only have to do a very few things right in your life so long as you don't do too many things wrong.' - Warren Buffett

A word of warning here, however. Note that I used in the chapter title the word *safely*. I have read plenty of books which talk about the so-termed 'fear of debt' holding back investors and that they should in fact use as much debt as they possibly can in order to invest in more and more properties. Perhaps it is right not to fear debt, but debt is a powerful double-edged sword and should always be respected and only used with great care. Just like our belief systems, debt has the power to create wealth, but it also has the power to destroy it.

The 5 key elements to building a multi-million dollar portfolio...safely

1 - Discipline

The first key element in being able to build a very sizeable property portfolio is discipline. Without the discipline required to save your first deposit or two, you will not be able to get started in investing in the first place.

2 - Always buying well – not having a single dud in your portfolio

The next step is actually buying the right property. I noted in a previous chapter that I believe investors should use an experienced buyer's agent in order to secure the best possible investment for capital growth. While a beginner may save some money by not using a buyer's agent, the likelihood of making a key mistake is multiplied tenfold (and possibly more).

Property can be a fairly forgiving asset class at times, in that most properties will show some capital growth over the long term. However, I know from years of my own experience the pitfalls that can be experienced by investors. When I look back at my early investments, I cringe at some of the many mistakes I made.

Provided you buy in strong capital growth areas, over time, most mistakes will be forgiven by a rising market, but in spite of this, if you want to achieve financial freedom quickly you should make as few mistakes as possible, and this is particularly so in the modern era where capital growth rates will on average be lower than those seen in the past. Remember the way in which it is possible to build a sizeable property portfolio quickly is to find areas which deliver capital growth quickly so that you can draw out a moderate amount of equity to divert towards new investments.

> Make a few big financial decisions and make
> sure you get them right.

There was an unusual theory doing the rounds some years ago that it did not really matter too much where you bought property because capital growth cannot be predicted. The theory was that you should buy for a strong cash flow and spread your investments all over the place so that some of them should get good growth.

This is completely wrong and totally back-to-front. The greatest advantage you have as a property investor rather than a homebuyer is that you are not compelled to invest anywhere unless you believe that you found a superior location where capital growth is assured. You can choose your suburb from thousands of possible choices and you can elect to invest counter-cyclically in cities which have not recently experienced a boom. To say that you should invest anywhere and just hope for capital growth is absolutely incorrect and misleading.

3 - Time

As implied in the chapter title we are only interested here in how to build a multi-million dollar property portfolio *safely*. In theory, you could 'build' a multi-million dollar portfolio immediately, simply by borrowing the full purchase price - if, of course, you could ever find an institution who would lend you such an amount! However, you could not do so safely and the transaction costs would put you immediately 'behind the 8-ball'. Property investment is a long-term game and the only way in which is possible to build a large portfolio safely is through the use of time as time is your friend rather than your enemy and to maintain a reasonable buffer.

> Time is the friend of the outstanding investments
> and the enemy of the mediocre.

In all my years of investing in property, I have never sold a single one. I have just continued to hold them for as long as I possibly can in order to continue to benefit from the compounding effect of capital growth, for year after year. Unsophisticated? Whatever, very efficient and devastatingly effective! When I look back at the purchase price at some of the earliest investments my wife and I own, I can scarcely believe how cheap the prices were! Yet, I can also absolutely assure you that the prices always felt very expensive at the time.

In fact, that is forever the case when buying property and prices never feel cheap at the time of purchase. Yet through allowing time to compound your wealth, you can undoubtedly succeed. There is no risk at all in the earliest investments I bought today, because the mortgages held against them are so small in relation to the value of the asset, even when I have refinanced them to buy new investments.

4 - Patience

To build a very large portfolio of assets, you need to demonstrate patience. This means that you need to be able to hold on to assets and wait for them to deliver you capital growth rather than buying and selling frequently. Buying and selling property attracts significant transaction costs in the form of stamp duty, legal fees, estate agent fees, capital gains taxes and other costs.

You should avoid the temptation to try to do too much too soon. If you leverage yourself up too strongly, you may speed up the results from your investing and reach your goals sooner, but you also introduce more risk. Property markets can and do fall in value. In fact, they do so regularly through each property cycle, and therefore it is important to keep a reasonable buffer at all times.

5 - Review your strategy and portfolio's performance regularly

I know that I have said that in general you should never sell an appreciating asset, but what if you have a genuine dud in your portfolio? This can happen if you bought poorly, especially if it is outside a capital city in a remote region. For example, sometimes industries suffer which impacts a certain region adversely. In this instance it may make sense to sell your asset and redeploy your capital into a more productive property investment.

Getting it right every time – the key data to analyse

Building a huge property portfolio is fundamentally very simple in nature. Firstly, save hard and buy a quality investment property in a suburb which you expect to boom in value. Secondly, when that property has increased in value, contact the bank in order to refinance the property and draw out some equity. And thirdly, use the equity created as a new deposit to invest in further properties which you expect to experience capital growth.

In essence, building great wealth through property is straightforward, yet it is clearly not easy. If it was easy, why do the overwhelmingly majority of investors only own one or two investment properties and fail to achieve financial freedom? The short answer is that they do not carry out the right research, they buy the wrong properties and thus they never achieve the accelerated capital growth they need in order to create the equity they need to buy further investments. It is that simple.

The science of sourcing capital growth

Property pundits in the media appear to use a dart-boarding approach to recommend which cities and regions will experience capital growth, going with some kind of gut feel or sometimes acting in their own vested interest. It is small wonder that their predictions are so bad – they are not based on any hard data at all. What we have found over the years is that property price growth is far more predictable than people believe but you do have to understand macro level economic data as well as micro trends down to household formation rates, and study the balance of dwelling supply against the demand for housing at a regional level.

Each week and each month at our company *AllenWargent* we update our chart packs, thus providing us with a huge range of data which we use to analyse what is happening and what is going to happen in the markets at both a macro and at a micro level. You may not be inclined or have the skill-set to analyse every set of data listed here, but to give you a few pointers, below are a few of the data sets which we analyse in our weekly chart packs. Our chart packs come under seven broader headings.

1 – Macro level economic data

We always begin with the macro picture and then drill down to the micro level data. Firstly, we want to know what is happening in the broader national economy and at the state level, since you cannot disaggregate real estate markets and household balance sheets from the economy which supports them. For example, among a range of other data sets, we chart the following each month:[1]

- Gross Domestic Product (GDP) growth

- Gross State Product

- State final demand

- Exports data

- Retail trade by state

- Private new capital expenditure and intentions

- Engineering construction activity

- Count of businesses

2 – Interest rates and inflation

Interest rates are always of vital consequence in investment. As explained in chapter 9, interest rates act a little like gravity on all financial markets and this is particularly so in real estate, since movements in interest rates directly impact mortgage affordability. In order to understand where interest rates are heading next you need to understand the drivers of both tradables and non-tradables inflation and how interest rate movements will be used to keep the rate of inflation close to the target range. In our chart packs we analyse:

- Quarterly Consumer Price Index (CPI)

- Monthly inflation gauge

- Cash rate futures yield curve

- Commodity price index

- Stock market indices
- Other financial markets

3 – Population and demographics

If you want to be a successful property investor, study demographics as enthusiastically as you can, for if you can anticipate demographic trends you will always remain a step ahead of the game. Each month we chart the following data sets by state, region and city:

- National population growth
- State population growth and interstate migration
- Regional population growth
- Overseas short term arrivals and departures
- Overseas permanent and long-term arrivals and departures
- Sale of motor vehicles by state
- Household formation rates and household sizes

4 – Employment markets

In order to buy property people generally need jobs, and therefore property investors should aim to analyse and then follow projected employment growth. We analyse the labour force data by city, by state and by region, including producing the following data sets:

- Employment growth by industry
- Full time and part-time jobs growth and participation rate
- Unemployment rates
- Wage price index and household income growth
- Private sector and public sector wages growth

5 – Housing finance demand

In relation to property market *demand*, we analyse the following monthly data sets in particular:

- Housing finance data
- Investor loan finance by state

- Mortgage indices by provider
- Credit growth by sector and financial aggregates

6 – Housing market supply

In relation to property market *supply*, we analyse each of the following by city, state, region and suburb, as well as keeping track of all news in relation to rezoning.

- Building approvals
- Dwelling commencements
- Building activity by state
- Dwelling completions
- Rezoning proposals and developments
- Vacancy rates by state, region and suburb

7 – Dwelling price indices

And, finally, of course, we also track what is happening to property prices by state, city, region and suburb:

- Residential property price indices by data provider
- Property price forecasts by city

A lot of research? Well, yes it is and it takes many hours of time for us to prepare and analyse each month. I have only scratched the surface above and we prepare a stack of other data sets besides these. It may take an investment of time but to be blunt it is this time investment which puts us at such a huge advantage over all other property buyer's agents who, as a general rule, have very little understanding of the economy and how interest rates and labour markets interact with property prices.

It is small wonder our clients have continued to experience outstanding results and we will continue on this path personally too. I have always believed that in order to create more value for yourself, you should first aim to create more value for others. Therefore, if you want to get more idea of how we analyse the markets I post many of the interesting findings from our chart packs on a daily basis to my blog page at http://petewargent.blogspot.com for free.

Ultimately if you want to build wealth through property, much of it comes down to having great discipline to save and patience to await the results. However, you still *must* buy the right property to get the capital growth you need to achieve success. And if you want to experience success, always remember these three vital key points: research, research and much more research!

Where to go for more

This book is predominantly focused on the motivation and psychology of building a portfolio of assets so that you can begin to explore designing a life for yourself that is not totally dependent upon a pay cheque or job. If you want to learn more about the mechanics of investing in property successfully, I recommend reading my investment book *Get a Financial Grip*, while my book *Four Green Houses and a Red Hotel* also takes an in-depth look at exactly where you should be looking to invest in property. As property moves in cycles, the best place to invest next will depend upon when you are reading this book. You can contact me via my blog page to find out more.

Chapter 13 summary

» Building wealth through property investment is fundamentally very simple - but it is not easy!

» To build a large property portfolio you need patience, discipline and time

» Capital growth can be forecast through a comprehensive understanding of the right data

» Buying the right property every time comes down to three key points: research, research and more research

---

Part Three
When It Doesn't Go Well...Re-Boot!

14
Getting Started:
The End Of Mass Consumption

14

'The constant effort towards population, which is found even in the most vicious societies, increases the number of people before the means of subsistence are increased.' – Thomas Malthus.

The Malthusian trap

In 1789, at around the time that Australia was being first populated with Europeans, Thomas Malthus devised one of the most famous and popular of all economic theories, the Malthusian Trap.[1] What Malthus concluded was that the human population was expanding faster than its ability to provide food for itself and therefore population growth would stall. His theory was centred upon the idea that the human population has the potential to grow at a geometrical ratio (such as 2, 4, 8, 16, 32, 64, 128…) – and by this stage in the book you should be very familiar with the limitless power of compound growth!

The problem, noted Malthus, was that the supply of food we as a race were able to provide for ourselves was growing at an arithmetic ratio (as in 2, 4, 6, 8, 10…). The logical conclusion was that eventually there would be more humans than food available to feed them, and thus famine (or war and disease) must eventually cap the population growth.

Malthus was proven to be wrong for a couple of reasons, the main one being that technological improvements allowed us to produce more food. As so often is the case, one of the most popular economic theories of all was wrong (which is why the saying 'don't follow the crowd' has so much truth in it) although sadly some parts of the world are still stuck in the Malthusian trap. In some sub-Saharan African countries the population may grow very rapidly before being checked by war, famine or disease. However, the population of the globe at the time of Malthus was less than one billion – and today, the world's population is closer to 6.5 billion. So the Malthusian Trap theory was clearly wrong on a global level.

The global population is set to continue expanding at pace and this creates opportunities for businesses and for investors.

Over the next few decades the population of the globe is expected to reach 9 billion by 2050. What Malthus had not reckoned upon was the ability of humans to find technological solutions to problems. The world has seen a number of huge improvements to agricultural processes over the last two centuries, which has meant that it is more than possible to feed the 6.5 billion people on the planet, where the political landscape does not preclude this from happening.

Malthus also felt that it was impossible that humans could voluntarily elect to have fewer children and yet this is exactly what has happened in a number of developed countries. The trend seems to be that countries have very little concept of birth control while they are developing. However, once a country reaches a certain level of prosperity or affluence, living costs in popular regions can increase and families voluntarily elect to have fewer children.

Malthus revisited

All key historical and economic theories tend to be revised and revisited subsequently, and the idea of the Malthusian Trap is certainly no exception. Revisionist historians, known in this case as neo-Malthusians, claim that while the specifics of Malthusian theory may have been inaccurate, his general idea was correct. Instead, they claim, the limiting factor (or 'principal means of sustenance') on human population growth may not be food, but in fact the natural resources of the earth such as energy and oil.

Changing demographics

Like many developed countries, Australia has reached the level of affluence whereby we are tending to have fewer children. The 2011 Census showed that the average Australian family has just 1.9 children.[2] Broadly speaking, whilst you might have expected an average family to have three children in 1980, today you would expect them to have just two. Recent data from the *Australian Bureau of Statistics* has also shown that the average household size has continued to decrease, heading down from over 4.5 persons a century ago to an expected average household size of 2.3 persons by 2026.[3]

Australia faces a population problem of a different kind. Our so-called Baby Boomer generation is now moving into retirement, with longer life expectancies than ever before. Unfortunately, the average pension or superannuation balances are far too low to cover the number of years it is expected most Australians will live in retirement.

This places a great stress on government budgets as they need to cover even more pension and medical care costs for the growing millions in their retirement years. There is only one viable solution to this, of which the government is well aware: we need massive population growth to find new taxpayers to fund the retirement of those who are no longer working, and to pay the other mass of government commitments. So while we are having fewer children on average, the absolute population levels are going to continue to grow drastically. In 2011, for example, the population of Australia grew by approximately 400,000 people![4]

Increased life expectancies, spiralling medical care costs and inadequate pension balances are not just an Australian problem, they are a problem across the developed world.

Incidentally, growing social security costs are by no means a problem only in Australia. The longer life expectancies across the developed world, combined with poor pension savings, place great stress on government spending, which to date has only been reflected in vast government debt. Take the most glaring example of the US where the government debt clock today reads more than $17,000,000,000,000. You are not misreading that - the figure is $17 trillion. Since the US came off the gold standard in 1971, the country has taken on even more debt to pay for wars, education, infrastructure and social security. There is increasing debate as to whether this is sustainable, which is a subject to be dissected another time. Until such time as any drastic measures are taken, governments will effectively print more and more cash to inflate away the debt and stimulate economic growth.

Central banks will attempt to combat deflation.

One thing which we can expect to see over the next decade is a bias towards continuing inflation in a number of debt-ridden developed countries. So, the tricky situation for Australia is that we have a double whammy. Firstly, we have an inevitably booming population. And secondly the existing population needs more dwellings to house the same number of people. The obvious conclusion is that we need to start constructing millions more dwellings.

With higher levels of household debt around today too what we can expect is a prolonged period of interest rates at well below the long-term historical averages as the Reserve Bank attempts to stimulate activity in the housing construction sector. Greater construction of housing will be required to replace the hole which will be left as Australia's mining construction boom moves past its peak. The above trends suggest to me two things for investors. Firstly, it may be an excellent idea to own medium-density dwellings close to the employment hubs of the large cities like Sydney. And secondly, the healthcare sector of the stock market is likely to perform well as the population ages.

Finite resources

Some years ago now I went on a world cruise on *Cunard*'s Queen Elizabeth and while on the voyage I attended a series of six hour-long lectures on the subject of climate change. Note that I was the youngest passenger on the ship by approximately three decades, and a couple of thousand Baby Boomers travelling around the world purely for pleasure is hardly likely to be the most receptive audience to the idea of reducing emissions!

The lecturer was fairly dispassionate in his analysis of the data, being neither for nor against the argument that man is contributing to global warming or climate change, but allowing the statistics to do the talking. After the sixth and final lecture we were largely left to draw our own conclusions. On careful consideration, I drew the conclusion, as perhaps many others have, that if everyone in the world simply resolved to do a bit more, our steady destruction of the planet could be halted or even reversed. It certainly got me thinking.

In the years leading up to the financial crisis, there was a small but growing chorus of voices warning that we were heading for a global economic and ecological crisis. Most people did not want to listen, arguing that free markets are generally self-correcting and would be able to tackle the key challenges that faced the world. After the financial world imploded in 2007, perhaps more than a few minds were shifted from that stance.

Global economic growth is likely to be lower in the decade ahead.

Richard Heinberg wrote an important book called *The End of Growth* in which he argued that not only was the world weighed down by resource constraints, the world was also being hampered by too much debt.[5] Global levels of household debt had exploded in the two decades running up to 2007, and many countries were teetering on the brink of default as a result of excessive levels of government debt too. People began to question household lending more after a decade of predominantly good-time reporting.

For perhaps the first time journalists across the world began to report natural disasters such as floods and hurricanes and began to link extreme weather to climate change. Across Europe countries such as Portugal, Ireland, Italy, Greece, Cyprus and Spain faced possible debt default, while the US continued to push hard against its $17 trillion government debt ceiling.

It has become increasingly clear to many commentators that the world as we once knew it was unsustainable – too much debt, too much population growth, excessively wasteful use of natural resources and unacceptably high levels of carbon emissions. Some still live in denial but gradually the debate is shifting from denial towards possible solutions. The world has finite natural resources and this shortage will drive up certain commodity prices. Until 2007, the world was stuck in a debt versus growth trap. To date the only way out seems to have involved governments taking on more debt, and yet how will that debt be paid off without economic growth?

There will be challenges, but there are always opportunities.

I do not mean to be fatalist about all this in terms of global economics, but it does seem that in the decades ahead the world will need to become acquainted with the idea of slower economic growth than we have been used to. For much of the time since the global financial crisis it has been the case that policy has leaned towards pushing deckchairs around rather than allowing the debt-induced pain to find its ultimate home.

But let us look on the positive side, because there are many positives to be found. We will have a boom in the global solar market and in other forms of natural energy. When I travel across to the United Kingdom, I see that Britain is finally beginning to embrace wind turbines. Finally we seem to be moving towards a new model which aims for economic growth without using up all of the world's resources, while central banks are actually taking an interest in responsible lending and acknowledging their role in leaning into asset price bubbles. As individuals we need less 'stuff' and should spend more time on the things in life that really matter. We should get comfortable with the idea of owning less rather than always desiring more.

What does this mean for us as investors and individuals?

Firstly, although the price of some commodity prices will spike due to there being a finite level of resources, I do not believe that owning shares in mining and resources companies is the way to get ahead in the period following the global financial crisis. Certain commodity prices including iron ore and coal had exploded into a huge bubble that was always likely to deflate as soon as the supply response from mining companies really hit its straps. Instead, share market investors should look towards self-perpetuating industrial companies and those in the expanding knowledge and services sectors.

Mining and resources companies have a finite level of reserves and once they are depleted, they must spend more capital to explore and develop new projects, and for this reason dividends over the course of a cycle from resources companies are likely to be weaker. And if we are genuinely moving into an era of lower growth, dividends must take on a greater importance than they have had in recent decades.

Secondly, we should acknowledge that economic growth in the future may not be accelerated along by booming household debt in the future as it was in the past. Too many households are tapped out, and in aggregate debt levels cannot increase at the same pace as was once the case. As already analysed in chapter 12, if you want to be a successful investor in real estate you can no longer simply invest in remote regional locations and wait for household debt to increase thus pushing dwelling prices higher. That era is over.

In real estate, dwelling price growth in the future will need to be driven by existing equity and real, sustainable wages and household income growth from technological and industrial expertise. In short, capital growth will be found close to the centre of thriving capital cities, not in remote regional locations.

Thirdly, we should personally spend less money on junk we do not need. In truth, folk should be doing this anyway, but until relatively recently there has been little incentive to do so since success for many people appears to be measured on what they *own* rather than who they *are*.

In terms of the ecological challenges facing the planet, while I can hardly claim to be a role model in this area (I do own cars in Britain, and fly long haul for work fairly regularly), it does seem to me that the world can only benefit from all of us resolving to do our bit. In Sydney, I no longer own a car and have only been using car-pooling companies and public transport. It is something a bit different, but I see it as something of a challenge to be enjoyed rather than a chore! I have not eaten meat or fish for more than half a decade, while I do my bit by trying to spread the word on the benefits of a vegetarian lifestyle. More than that, I just try to make as many small positive changes as I can with regards to my carbon footprint. We all should.

Times change and trends change.

In years gone by, of course, I actually worked in the mining industry myself, where any mention of the words *climate change* or *carbon emissions* were pure anathema and would have been met with outright mockery. But the world changes. First, ideas are met with ridicule, then they are violently opposed and gradually they come to be accepted.

Keep doing your bit and spreading the word, and eventually the world will slowly but surely begin to adapt. In 2012, my old man stood as a Green Party candidate and is also now a vegetarian. If you had told me that in 1992, I would most likely have laughed in your face! It is always interesting how the world moves on and evolves towards new ideas. Remember that whether we like it or not the world changes, so it is often better to move with the times and embrace change rather than to fight it.

Resources and technology

Equities expert Peter Thornhill often gets on his hobby horse and does a piece on the theme of 'if I was Prime Minister'. One of the many things which he ridicules is how the world has known about its finite natural resources for decades, yet even today we still build cars with four or five litre engines. This could so simply be solved by amendments to the tax regime, but even now there appears to be little incentive to change.

Of course, as always this all comes back to the principles of pleasure and pain. In the early 1970s it was calculated that all the oil in the world would have run out by 2015 at the rate of consumption then occurring. Yet instead the world found new technologies to extract more oil from the earth and other new technologies which could make use of the oil resources we did have more efficient. Fuel efficiency today is far better than it was in the 1970s and therefore the oil we do have will last longer. Today, it is technology and ingenuity which determines the true value of a resource.

In decades past it was instead often believed that if you could corner the supply of a resource then you could control wealth. For example, in the silver market, the Hunt Brothers attempted to corner the silver market in the 1970s causing the silver price to spike from $6 per ounce to more than $48 per ounce.[6] However, the Hunt brothers had over-leveraged themselves and a change in regulations related to leverage saw silver prices crashing back down again by 50 percent in a matter of days.[7]

The world has moved on since the 1970s. Today it is largely technological and intellectual expertise which determines the level and value of a physical resource or company. Based upon forecasts made in the 1970s the world should have essentially run out of oil by now. Yet improvements to technology not only meant that we learned to extract more oil, technological improvements also allowed us to make the utilisation of oil resources more efficient.

To create value for yourself, you must first create value for others.

The world has changed. If you attempt to use the old methods of achieving wealth such as cornering the silver market, you will fail. Today, you need to be able to add value to others in order to create wealth. This is known as economic alchemy, turning something of little value into something with much more value. In days gone by, people thought they could turn lead into gold. Today you need to find ways to add value to the lives of more people.

A property investor can provide quality accommodation to renters which is one way to add value. If you want to build a business, you need to find a ways to add as much value as you can to as any people as possible and as efficiently as possible.[8] When you stop to think about it, a business creates value by improving the quality of the lives of others or through making their lives easier in some way. In the forthcoming chapters 18 to 20 I am going examine how you can use your own ingenuity to become self-employed or start your own business in your own area of expertise should that be what you choose to do.

Spending less

One of the key rules of personal finance and investment is to spend less than you earn. If you fail to adhere to this simple key rule then you will fail to get ahead and achieve your goals. It matters not whether you a teenager starting out or a wealthy individual, if you do not spend less than you earn then you will be by definition going backwards and you will be unable to snowball your wealth effectively!

This ties in neatly with the concept of the end of mass consumption. Buying junk or luxuries that you do not need as a form of comfort for a lack of job satisfaction may provide temporary pleasure or relief, but the long-term result for your personal finances and for the planet is more likely to be one of pain.

Nutrition

It has been found that smokers and drinkers frequently have poor or even shambolic personal finances.[9] Part of the reason this is may be deceptively simple, that being that apparently small daily expenses add up to a surprisingly large figure over times resulting in a detrimental outcome for personal finances.[10] Limit the poisons and toxins which you put into your body.

Apart from your food and drink nutrition, you should also aim to feed yourself a healthy daily diet of quality information. If you spend your time reading doom and gloom media and websites this is likely to impact your global beliefs adversely, regardless of the merits or otherwise of the content and associated online comments. The same is true if you spend your time mixing with negative people. Their negativity and limiting beliefs gradually begin to rub off on you.

If it bleeds, it leads.

The fact of the matter is that there is a demand for negative news. Some people will always want to believe that the sky is falling and will seek out confirmation of their preconceived bias. And if you look hard enough there is always negative news to be found. There will always be some weaker economic data to eke out regardless of the true strength of the macro economy.

Over the last half decade, certain websites and media outlets have projected daily content of nothing but doom and gloom, yet over that exact same time period investors like me have expanded our wealth continually through using compounding interest to our advantage and making smart snowballing investments. I have expanded my business too while the same websites keep on churning out the same old daily doom and gloom.

Mix with positive minded people as much as you can. One thing which I have seen work for young people is to form networking groups of like-minded and positive people such as entrepreneur groups or investor clubs. The positivity and support of like-minded people can have a greater positive effect than you might imagine.

Invest in your human capital

In investing we talk a lot about expanding financial capital which is a simple idea, really. You save some of your income each year and invest it for your retirement. Although one must make an allowance for a future increase in the cost of living, if you invest wisely thanks to the compounding growth effect, your retirement should be a comfortable and well-funded one. In the ideal but sadly non-existent financial world where nobody becomes ill, dies, gets divorced, goes on a spending spree, loses money on bad investments...then building a retirement portfolio is very simple.

Let us now think instead about human capital. Coined by economist Theodore Schultz in the 1960s, in purely economic terms human capital is said to be 'the sum value of our human capacities'.[11] This is a very useful concept. Just like other forms of capital, you can invest in your own human capital, through education, practising skills and professional training.

Figure 14.1 – Human capital

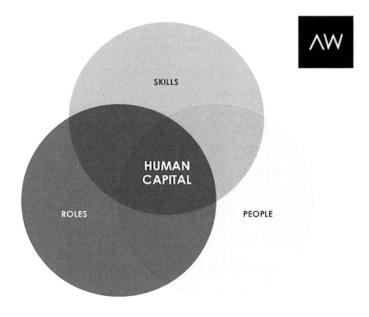

A purely academic economist would tell you that human capital is a way of measuring an employee's skill set, for the more skills and experience you can get under your belt, the greater your earnings potential. If, therefore, the value of your human capital is said to be the present value of your future earnings capability, you might expect that at the age of 18-21, while your financial capital might be low or even negative, your human capital might be at its highest point since you have decades of earning power ahead.

In practice, what often happens is that as we move through education and in some cases higher education and professional training, our skills and therefore the salary we can expect to command in the future increases. When you are younger and you have time on your side, when allied with professional skills, this can make the level of your human capital high. For the want of a better example, this is what happened to my salary between the age of 18 and 32.

When I left school I was mostly interested in playing cricket and drinking Guinness, and had a factory machinist job in cold England which paid £4 per hour or £8300 per annum. Onwards to my University years and I undertook an array of worse part-time jobs in factories producing anything from timber products to perfume and then in my backpacking year, I earned $15 per hour as a van driver and mail-sorter in Sydney.

But then as I started my professional training contract in London I saw a nice jump in my salary, which then almost doubled after three years of tough exams and painstaking auditing when I qualified as a Chartered Accountant. Moving up through the ranks at Deloitte and then transferring into the mining industry saw my salary increase - not exactly in a straight line, but quite significantly as my skills and experience increased.

Human capital increases and then can decrease again later in life.

The basic point is that while human capital tends to be high when you are younger, it then tends to decrease as you approach retirement, since you have fewer earning years remaining. Consequently from an investment point of view you should aim to be an accumulator with your long-term investment capital (including your pension) in your younger years while tending to take a more conservative approach as you move into the income phase as you approach retirement.

The old rule of thumb used to say 'subtract your age from 100 and put this percentage of your portfolio in shares, and put the balance in bonds'.[12] But unless you've had 100 subtracted from your IQ you will know that in the real world individual circumstances differ and no such hard and fast rule can really be applied.

Just like financial capital, human capital has different rates of risk and therefore potential returns. Some occupations, such as Chartered Accountancy, are expected to be relatively low risk and steady in terms of income flows, which makes formulating a regular investment plan straightforward. Meanwhile other occupations (such as acting, for example) may be perceived as riskier but potentially with greater rewards, both financially and personally. Other occupations are commission based and can see more earnings volatility.

Risk assets

Typically therefore, a younger person might be more inclined to invest heavily in the so-termed risk assets since they have the benefit of a longer investment time horizon. Apparently 'safe' term deposits may produce a reliable though small income, but over the long term actually tend to be much riskier since they provide no growth potential. Upon approaching retirement your financial capital should have increased as your human capital gradually decreases, and the focus often tends to shift towards income investments.

Time horizon

This is an important point, particularly in the light of day-to-day commentary which focuses almost unstintingly on recession risk, economic headwinds, investment market corrections, and so on. Remember that what is risky for one investor is not necessarily risky for another. Risk is often largely related to financial goals and time horizon.

Stock markets will periodically boom and crash, but for those who invest wisely in dividend-paying investments the long-term risk is greatly diminished. By way of another example I read that vegan property investor Les Moore, aged 100 this year, retired nearly 55 years ago having invested heavily in properties around North Sydney and Manly.[13] Since the median house price in Sydney in 1960 was around $4000, these were clearly not risky investments for Les Moore, although they may of course have appeared to be so at that time!

Diversify your risk.

Diversification is one of the key rules of investment and since human capital is a form of investment, then you should avoid having all of your eggs in one basket here too. To go back to the example of my own career, I recall that when I worked in mining (a copper mining company), many of us were offered shares and options as a long-term remuneration incentive package from the company. When the copper price tanked some years ago, the company was forced to make some executives redundant, while the value of their shares also dropped at the same time, and their options flipped out of the money too.

This represented for those executives a highly leveraged bet of both human and financial capital on one outcome - that is, one company successfully mining, selling and shipping copper off to China at high commodity prices. While this focused approach can certainly pay off handsomely for some, for most of us it is often better not to have too much correlation between your human capital and financial capital. If you are specialised in one career, it may be wiser to invest your financial capital in non-correlated investments.

Take out appropriate forms of insurance.

When investing in the share market you might opt to you have a form of insurance (e.g. put options) and so it is with relation to your human capital. Life throws up unforeseen events such as illness or disability which can severely impact earnings potential and therefore there are forms of insurance that can be taken out to protect against such an adverse event.

Investing in your human capital has many similar principles to investing financial capital. Invest in your skills and compound your education and the value of your human capital and your future earnings potential goes up. Aim to have some level of diversification, limit your downside risk, and invest in yourself for the long term.

Chapter 14 summary

» We have moved into a new economic era, potentially one of lower growth

» Position yourself wisely by embracing the end of mass consumption and spending less than your earn

» Invest heavily in your own skills and human capital

» Wealth creation in business is increasingly shifting towards intellectual, knowledge based and service sector expertise

» Invest for the long term in quality assets

15
When It Doesn't Go Well
(Not 'If'!)

15

Niall's story

Niall had always had a range of interests, and was well known among his friends for his willingness to try anything once. Several years ago he had become interested in investment when interest rates were at the bottom of their cycle and bought an off-the-plan city rental apartment when the market seemed to be in an upswing. This was unusual for Niall because he had previously been quite negative about the prospects for the property market and the economy in general, but he'd been convinced to take the plunge after a number of his friends had made some apparently strong returns.

In the following two years the market jumped by more than 30 percent, which excited Niall and he subscribed to a few property and share investment magazines. With the property market continuing on its great run, Niall decided to pull out some of the equity in his property.

He spent a portion of this redrawn equity on a new car and a little more on a holiday, while he set aside $50,000 to invest in a portfolio of shares. Having read about the importance of diversification he knew that he would not be so stupid as to invest the full $50,000 in only a couple of companies. Instead he split the money across a portfolio of ten companies and continued to monitor the market daily.

Markets move in cycles, and they always will.

By this time, the property market was starting to get a little overheated and property developers were gaining approvals to build apartments all over town, resulting in a temporary oversupply of dwellings. Niall became a little uncomfortable when his property manager phoned him to say that no tenant could be found, and that the rental dollar amount per week would need to be dropped by 10 percent in order to fill the vacancy.

At the same time, the central bank was becoming uncomfortable with the level of speculative activity in financial markets and rising inflation and gradually began to hike interest rates. Combined with a few adverse stories about the health of the global economy this triggered something of a global sell-off. Niall was bemused to see the value of his share portfolio drop quickly to $45,000 and then over the next year it slipped further to $40,000.

To add insult to injury the market value of his property slipped back by around 8 percent, reversing some of Niall's previous paper profits. Niall liquidated his share portfolio for a $10,000 loss and sold his investment property for a small gain. There had been a number of stories about a forthcoming recession and he felt that he should move his money into gold to hedge against a possible collapse of the financial system. Unfortunately after all fees and expenses the gains from his property investment were small. He bought a small amount of bullion and the rest of the funds gradually ebbed away from his bank account.

Getting back on the horse

It is perfectly normal to become interested in something for a period of time and then lose interest in it. When I was in junior school I became strangely compelled by the idea of playing chess for a couple of years, but then when I reached an intermediate standard, I lost interest again and went back to football. As an early teenager I was utterly obsessed with golf and got my handicap down to quite a low level, but then gave the game away when the sheer intensity of my University studies took on an increased importance (or something like that, anyway).

There is nothing particularly unusual in that. As humans we are designed to have a range of different interests and learn new things, and that is healthy. However, investment does not lend itself well to people who take a passing interest in a certain asset class before moving on to other investments, because it will often be the newcomers to the market who get wiped out when the market inevitably reverses. To some extent I believe that investors can be successful in almost any asset classes provided that they resolve to master it.

> Aim to learn from people who have achieved the goals you want to achieve.

More than that, taking care of your financial future is something which you must remain committed to because its effect can be pervasive on the quality of all parts of your life. If you see an author write a book on finance or a new investment fad and then move on to write about other unrelated subjects this is probably a warning signal, if not a red flag. I understand why it can happen – I would like to write books on other subjects myself in the future – but be very wary of passing fads or crazes in investment.

Be even more wary of apparent experts who have never built an investment portfolio of their own. They rarely have a clue what is best for the average investor because they have not been through the process themselves! What I can tell you for certain is whatever your investment strategy is there will be days when you experience downturns, adverse results, mistakes and failures, because that is simply a part of what the process is.

Success does not occur in a straight line and even the greatest investors of all time look back at some of the decisions that they have made (or often decisions they have not made – errors of omission rather than commission) and cringe. There is nothing unusual about this. It is normal. But it is important to re-emphasise that what determines success or failure is having a solid long-term plan for success and resolving to get back on the horse and never, ever giving up.

Learn from your mistakes

We all inevitably make mistakes when it comes to our lives, our personal finances and investments. The great challenge is to learn to treat these mistakes as education rather than make them a reason to fear taking action in the future.

Never say 'oh dear'. Instead say 'ah, interesting!'

Some days the world seems to be against you and everything can seem overwhelming. If that is the case, and on some days it will be, resolve to get some small successes under your belt. Taking a first step inevitably leads to bigger things, bringing you both satisfaction and increasing your confidence.

Success in life and investment is achieved by setting yourself big and inspiring targets but breaking those target down into smaller and more achievable tranches. More achievable means more believable. One practical tip is at the start of each day to draw up a to-do list just for that day. It is amazing the difference that this simple action can make to the way in which you view your progress and the satisfaction which can be drawn from the knowledge that you are simply getting things done.

Dealing with adversity

Perhaps the biggest determinant of how successful you will be in life is how you deal with failures and how you treat adversity may be the single biggest influence on the results you can achieve. If you respond to failures or adverse results with a sense of resignation and begin to believe that it is not even worth trying then you will have almost lost before you have even begun.

> Success rarely occurs in a straight line and
> failures are not personal to us.

The past does not necessarily equal the future, yet too many folk become resigned to failure after comparatively few attempts, and worse, they take their failures personally. They begin to use phrases like 'this always happens to me' or 'I never seem to make the progress I want'. The problem is that such learned helplessness becomes self-fulfilling, because they stop trying and therefore stop achieving, thus confirming their previously acknowledged belief that they cannot succeed. It becomes a vicious and insidious circle.

> Everyone experiences failure so it is how we respond
> to adversity which really counts.

If you experience a failure or adversity, consider instead what you can learn from the situation. Actively picture yourself doing better next time. If you can change your beliefs to believe that success is reachable you can certainly achieve things that others believe are impossible - but even then you will inevitably experience hurdles and setbacks on the way, and it is how you respond to these setbacks which determines your eventual outcomes. Achievers in life do not see problems as permanent, they do not see failure as personal, and they do not believe that their problems are pervasive.

Positive thinking exercise

It is interesting how some people in life appear to take great comfort in being miserable and downbeat, whining almost ceaselessly about how unfair the world is. I find it incredibly self-centred when people in some of the world's wealthiest countries like Australia can complain about how unfair life is when not an hour from our coastline, countries have populations which live in genuine poverty yet consider themselves in many ways more fortunate and happier.

Ultimately in life, there are two types of people, there are lifters and there are leaners. Which do you want to be? I believe it is a fair assumption that if you are reading this book, you are inspired enough to want to be a lifter.

Nevertheless it is true that humans are programmed to experience negative thoughts. We seemed to be designed that way unfortunately, and some days everything seems too hard or too much! However, just like our responses to failure and adversity are within our own control, so it is with our response to negative thoughts.

Over the years I have read scores of motivational books. Naturally, some have been great and others have been utter dross - not all of the information you read will be relevant or useful to you, but some might be life-changing. Very occasionally I get good pieces of advice from people and I write them on a slip of paper to put in my wallet. Below I describe an exercise that I found which has genuinely worked wonders for me.

> We all have negative thoughts, but it is how
> we deal with them that is important.

For seven full days, try to have no negative thoughts. Obviously this is not 100 percent possible, because we all have negative thoughts some of the time. For that reason you are permitted to 30 seconds of negative thoughts at one time. If you catch yourself going over 30 seconds, however, then you must go right back to the start and begin the exercise again. Even if you have completed six days and then you have 40 seconds of negative thoughts, the clock is reset!

Such a simple idea, and yet if you are like me and prone to irrational bouts of glum moroseness, this can be a supremely effective exercise if you can genuinely commit to it. Some people are lucky and do not suffer from too many negative thoughts and they will find this exercise easier than the rest of us. Ultimately, we have two choices in life - we can choose to be happy and positive or we can elect to be sad and negative. Choose the former!

Ways to change your state

When I was living in East Timor, I initially spent some months sharing a house with a group of African guys and gals who were great fun and a rather lively bunch to say the very least! I did discover something about myself though, and that is that while I am generally an upbeat character, I am forced to admit that I can also be quite a moody cove. I guess I have always known this about myself, but when you share a house with a group of others you tend to learn a lot about people very quickly, including yourself. I can at times become quite withdrawn, I realised.

The truth is that we all at times feel frustrated, sad, angry, morose, upset, lonely, anxious, depressed or miserable. Just as surely, however, we can all develop triggers for changing our state or the way we feel. The trouble is that people often respond with unproductive triggers by reaching for a cigarette, eating too much chocolate or junk food, engaging in retail therapy, gulping down alcohol or taking illicit substances. In others words, people often use addictive and destructive behaviours in order to change their state. This has a short term nullifying effect on the way you feel, but does not lead to long-term empowering results.

What we need as humans is to find ways to change our state into a positive frame of mind, but to use healthy and productive triggers in order to do so. Music is a great example of a powerful medium for changing the way in which we feel, which is why some sports teams like to have music playing while they train. Dancing or singing is another (although if you sing as badly as I do, then this may actually lead to greater pain).

Write down a huge list of other ways to change your state, that do not involve food, drink or drugs, perhaps 30 or 40 other triggers. Here are just a few of the ways that I thought of that can work for me:

- listening to AC/DC on my i-Pod
- calling my Mum on Skype
- buying presents for my nieces
- going for a relaxing hot tub or spa
- driving somewhere and listening to music
- heading to the beach for some body-boarding
- doing 30 minutes exercise on a cross-trainer and some weights
- watching sport
- going down to the pool for a swim
- telephoning my mates for a chat
- going for walk around the Botanical Gardens
- look through some old photo albums or newspaper clippings to enjoy some great memories

Of course, listening to *Highway to Hell* might be great for me yet it might be an actual living hell for a fan of classical music. Clearly you have to think of ideas that will work for you! I have only come up with a dozen ideas here, so why not write down some of your own? In fact, I suggest making a huge list of ways to change a negative state of mind and resolve to use them to change your mood for the positive. We all have up days and down days, but it is the way you react to the negative thoughts that matters most.

What are negative emotions telling you?

I would be willing to take a bet that you regularly experience negative emotions. The reason for that that is simply because we all do! Over the years I have come to understand that what determines results in life is not so much how we respond to successes, rather it is how we react to the inevitable failures. As an investment mentor I have needed to learn to listen very closely to what my clients say. When people are not achieving the results they desire it is likely that they are experiencing negative emotions. This may be no bad thing, for negative emotions exist in order to send you an important message.

The key to emotional mastery is to listen to what your emotions are telling you.[1] Negative emotions are sending you a message, so it is important to acknowledge negative feelings or emotions and appreciate them for alerting you to their message (or even thanking them if you are feeling especially spiritual). Then you must seek to understand what the negative emotions are trying to tell you and, finally, take the appropriate action in order to turn matters around to your advantage.[2]

A client of mine named James came to me with a problem, that being that he felt overwhelmed about his financial situation. He had received so much conflicting advice over the years, some of which had not been very good, and James increasingly was beginning to feel helpless about his financial future.

Listen to what message negative emotions are trying to tell you.

I explained to James that feeling overloaded is a common negative emotion and it was important for him to try to understand what message the emotion was delivering to him. Feeling overwhelmed can occur when you have experienced negative outcomes which have taken place outside of your own control, since you can begin to believe that there is little you can do to change outcomes. The key message of feeling overwhelmed is that you need to get back to basics and prioritise what is important to you and to focus on putting together a list of action points which you can take towards achieving those priorities.

James advised me that his priority was his three children and in particular that he had the funds in place to pay for their further education. In this instance, it was therefore important for James to put his previous bad experiences behind him and to re-prioritise putting a plan in place to be prepared for his children's future.

Another client of mine, Shaun, called me and said 'Pete, I believe I am great at my job but I feel so inadequate when it comes to my personal finances.' Yet when I asked him a few questions it became clear that Shaun was extremely knowledgeable about finance and investment and was by no means in a bad place financially.

Acknowledge the message of negative emotions.

Feelings of unworthiness or inadequacy are common experiences and are often caused by individuals having set themselves unfair rules for determining whether or not they are adequate. The key message which the emotion was delivering in Shaun's case was that he did not yet have the full skill set to achieve what he wanted to in the field of share investment. Shaun had an ambition to be a full time share market investor and trader but he was not yet in a position to fulfil his goals.

The important thing to remember about feelings of inadequacy is that the emotion is simply delivering you a message that you need to find tools or ways to do things better than you have been able to achieve to date. It does not mean that you should wallow and allow the feeling to become pervasive of self-fulfilling. I suggested to Shaun that if being a great trader was his primary goal then his best course of action would be to seek out a trader with a proven track record and use them as a role model or coach.

Still another client of mine, Jackie, told me that she felt continually scared about her financial future. We spent some time discussing her situation and it came to light that Jackie was due to come into an inheritance and she was completely flummoxed about what to do with it or how to cope with the responsibility. The emotion of <u>fear</u> is a very useful one to us as humans. It tells us that something is about to happen and that we should prepare for it.

Fear sends us a message that we need to be prepared.

Unfortunately the way that most people deal with fear is to deny that they are fearful, become paralysed or allow the fear to become destructive, which is the wrong way to react. Fear is a very useful emotion because it is telling you that you need to take action and become mentally prepared for a future event. People are generally fearful when they are unsure how to deal with a situation, so the answer is to get as prepared for the future as it is possible to be.

There are yet more negative emotions!

I have briefly touched on three common negative emotions above. There are more, of course. If, for example, you are feeling mildly agitated that you are not achieving as much as you think you should be, or you feel somewhat uncomfortable with life, this is likely to be a signal for you that you need to clarify what it is you really want to achieve and then to take some concerted action towards achieving your goals. Similarly, if you are feeling frustration, then this is actually a good thing – it is a key signal that you can be doing better than you are and you should take heart from this!

Other, more intense negative emotions also exist, including guilt, disappointment, hurt or even anger. In each case, it is vitally important to remember to listen to what message the negative emotion is telling you and to turn this into a call to action rather than to wallow in the negativity. What might these emotions be telling you? What can you do to remedy the situation?

Take action in order to remedy negative emotions.

If you are experiencing or feeling hurt it is likely that your expectations may not have been met, or perhaps you have been let down. If you are feeling hurt then you need to consider what it is that you have really lost (if anything?). Do you need to communicate with the person who has hurt you and explain your sense of loss? Or perhaps you will instead realise that the loss is not real.

If what you are feeling is disappointment this is likely to be an indication that you feel that you have been let down or that you could miss out on something forever. This often happens to investors when they have missed out on a market boom and they feel that there is nothing they can do to rewind the clock and participate in the boom.

While one cannot turn the clock back, what can be done is to learn from the situation and resolve to do better next time. Remember that we all make mistakes, that markets move in cycles and the proverbial apparent investment of a lifetime actually comes around approximately every month. The solution to feelings of disappointment is to learn from the emotion and set new inspiring targets and goals for the future.

As humans we do not like to experience guilt, as it is an emotion which tells you that you may have violated one of your own most important standards. If you do experience guilt, it is important not to hide from it – instead acknowledge the emotion and take some immediate action to ensure that whatever has taken place to cause the emotion will not recur in the future. Too often people wallow in feelings of guilt which leads to learned helplessness. Guilt is a direct message that your past behaviours were not right for you and should not be repeated in future, and the emotion should be treated as such.

The severe negative emotion of anger signifies that one of your standards has been violated, either by you or by someone else. Being angry can be one of the most destructive emotions and it is therefore important to *change your state* as quickly as possible - see earlier in the chapter to remind yourself of how you are going to do this. It is vital to understand that while you may be angry because someone has violated one of your standards, it does not automatically mean that they have violated one of theirs – your rules are not necessarily the right rules!

Are your rules necessarily right?

If you are regularly angry then you either need to change your perceptions (do other people even know that they are breaking your rules?) or change your actions (let them know what your rules actually are!). Uncontrolled anger is such a strong negative emotion and is rarely conducive to success or happiness. Therefore it is important to understand what message the emotion is actually trying to deliver to you and take corrective action as quickly as possible.

One final negative emotion which perhaps surprisingly seems to be becoming increasingly common in today's hectic and electronically connected world is that of loneliness. Feeling lonely is an emotional signal to you that you need to reach out and connect with people, but to do so in a constructive manner. Perhaps you could join a club which is commensurate with achieving your goals? If you want to get fit, join a running club. If you want to become a great investor, join an investment club.

In all cases, the important point of this section is that the emotions you experience happen for a reason. You will continue to experience negative emotions and so will I. That's partly because we are human and it is also because negative emotions are delivering a message that something is not quite right and needs corrective action to be taken.

The problem for so many people is that they wallow in the negative emotion and make matters worse instead of better! Always remember that the level of your success will largely be determined by how you deal with negative outcomes and emotions. Therefore, you must acknowledge and listen to what message negative emotions are attempting to deliver to you, understand the message, and then take corrective action accordingly. What else can you do if you appears to be stalling or lacking in progress. Go back to your goals! What keeps driving us forward as humans is inspiring targets and tangible goals which excite us and provide us with the energy to keep going no matter what.

Chapter 15 summary

» The singular ability to 'get back on the horse' will separate the successful from the rest

» Do not dwell unnecessarily on inevitable negative thoughts

» Find a long list of ways to change a negative state of mind

» When you experience negative emotions, these emotions are delivering you an important message

» Listen to the message your emotions are delivering you and refine your actions accordingly

---

16

Recognising
Market Cycles

16

Ray's story

Ray had never invested much in share markets before, but his pension fund had always performed reasonably well over the long term, and it had always seemed to move nicely higher over time. Ray heard from a friend about an investment opportunity in a mining company he was employed by, and his good buddy had told him the stock was about to boom in price.

The mining company was only a small exploration venture and it had never made any profits to date, but Ray's friend advised him that there was some favourable market sensitive news due to be released in the coming week regarding a legal decision related to one of the mining company's tenements. Ray acted on the news by investing $20,000 in shares in the company, picking up 40,000 shares for 50 cents each.

Sure enough the following week news was released on the stock exchange which went in the company's favour, but the market seemed to act as though it was already aware of the news and actually moved down a tick to 49.5 cents. Ray was confused but decided to hold on to his shares anyway because he had confidence in his friend's recommendation, despite not knowing anything about the future plans of the company or indeed anything about its financial health.

Financial markets move in cycles.

Over the next year, the market went on a strong bull run and a number of speculative mining shares jumped in value, and Ray was delighted to see the value of his investment increase to nearly $30,000. His friend was even more enthusiastic about the company's prospects now! Ray was quite excited by his 50 percent return on investment which had all come from capital growth and none of it from dividends (the company did not generate any revenue so it had no profits to pay dividends from) and decided to buy another $15,000 worth of shares, this time at 75 cents.

In time, a broker report was released to the market by a stock broker which had acted for the company when it had raised some capital for mining exploration two years previously. The broker report suggested a 'Buy' recommendation with a target price of $1.25, which caught Ray's eye. He was getting the hang of this now, and as the share price moved towards $1.00 he felt he should top us his investment further for fear of missing out.

Ray now had invested a total of $50,000 in the company having acquired 75,000 shares. Ray had never invested anything like this amount in a company before, but he wasn't too worried as at a share price of $1.00 his investment was worth $75,000 and he was now well in the black to the tune of 50 percent. Unfortunately over the next few months the wider share market reversed and went into a bearish trend, which was unfamiliar territory for Ray.

Ray watched in bemusement as the share price declined with short shrift to 80 cents and then back to 50 cents. Throughout this time Ray had very little idea what the company was actually doing or how much funding the company needed to maintain its exploration activities. Instead, he was only interested in watching the share price. Over the next week, the share price fell to well below 50 cents and Ray had now lost money, and as the price continued in its downtrend he felt paralysed and unable to act. The price had been up to $1.00 he rationalised and it could surely get back there again, so he would hold for the long term in the manner of a wise and patient investor.

Unfortunately the bad news did not end there, as the company released news to the market that it would need to raise funds from the market in order to continue. Its recent quarterly releases to the market had shown that the company was rapidly depleting its cash which the market had interpreted as problematic. Indeed, this was what had accounted for the crash in the share price, but Ray had not been reading operational update releases, and in truth he was only watching the share price chart.

The company announced that it would issue several million shares in order to replenish the cash it needed to pay for its directors' salaries and bonuses as well as provide further exploration capital. The company hadn't really progressed too much in terms of its drilling exploits and the market seemed to be losing interest. The new shares issues were to dilute the value of existing shares and the share price dived to 30 cents. If Ray had read the stock exchange release he would have noticed that the broker who acted as the underwriter for the capital raising was the very same broker that had issued the bullish company valuation report together with its buy recommendation.

> Loss-making companies will lose share
> price market value over time.

Over the coming years Ray held on to the shares as the company returned to the market again and again to raise further funds to pay for its exploration activities and its staff salaries and bonuses. The friend that had recommended the stock pick to Ray had been made redundant by the company and was seething that the Directors had remained at the company and were even continuing to draw annual performance bonuses.

Although the share price fell to 20 cents and then 15 cents Ray could not bring himself to sell. He was now simply praying for a miracle and praying that the market would 'come back' to save him. He even tried averaging down and in desperation threw another $15,000 at the company at a price of 10 cents. Eventually the share price was diluted down to 2 cents and the company announced that its once promising exploration of its tenements had failed to discover a resource worthy of pursuit.

Not a single share traded in the company for longer than an entire year, and eventually Ray heard that the company would be de-listed from the stock exchange entirely. Ray was less than amused to hear that the directors had long since taken redundancy packages and had started up new mining exploration ventures elsewhere.

Ray's annual pension statement arrived through the mail and he was interested to note that his pension scheme had experienced another good year. In fact, over the past six years since Ray began his misadventure into investing in the mining company his pension fund had returned a healthy 12 percent per annum.

Through the course of that six year share market cycle Ray could have doubled his initial investment capital and built a solid investment portfolio through simply buying an index fund. Instead Ray had acquired 225,000 shares in a company which no longer exists. He had lost $65,000 of his own cash and fallen out with a former friend. Although his pension continues to perform reasonably well, Ray is convinced that the share market is risky and a mug's game, and he no longer invests in equities outside of his pension.

Oliver's story

Oliver was a lawyer who earned a high income in the city. He was not a fan of the idea of property investment and had shied away from owning a home through his twenties, preferring to wait until he was a little older before taking on a cumbersome mortgage debt commitment.

Gradually, however, it did begin to grate with Oliver that at dinner parties and at the pub how his friends often yapped incessantly about how much their properties had gone up in value over the past few years. He tried to steer the conversation onto more interesting topics or point out that they had made no 'realised' gains but his friends continued to be annoying and discuss how clever they were for essentially just taking on a lot of debt to buy property.

As time rolled on the property markets continued to climb and although there was the odd article in the press about the dangers of increasing household debt they were quickly crowded out by excited pundits and property journalists (themselves probably property investors, bemoaned Oliver) which reported monthly property market price movements as though they were the weekend football results. When the market began to climb more sharply for the fifth year in a row, the press began to make quiet noises about a property bubble forming.

Don't listen to the crowd when it comes to property – do what is right for you.

Oliver's friend Mick, a tradesman, had pulled out equity over the year to invest in a number of properties and often brought up in conversation how much money he had made from property investment. It seemed obscene to Oliver, for the equity that Mick had built from his portfolio of seven properties was now running into the millions while Oliver, despite earning a very high salary income as a lawyer, had made very little financial progress at all. After tax was deducted and Oliver had paid the rent on his city house and living costs, there seemed to be relatively little left over each month and it was easily spent on his lavish up-market lifestyle.

Over the next two years, the property market began to boom with values rising by a further 25 percent. By now Oliver was passed the midpoint of his thirties, and was thinking that he really ought to buy a house. The trouble was that the market had continued to rise and Oliver could not afford to buy the type of house that he had become accustomed to as a renter. He told his friends that the property market was in a bubble and he would wait until it became cheaper again before he bought, but the next year property prices increased yet again by another 10 percent.

By now the press was all over the property bubble story and Oliver was convinced that there would be a crash. Everyone he knew seemed to be in the property investment game. New apartments were springing up all over the city but they were selling out in a matter of hours, almost exclusively to investors rather than homebuyers. When the press reported that prices were continuing to rise and had now averaged 10 percent growth for seven years in a row, Oliver felt that he had no other choice but to at least get a toehold on the ladder.

Buying a house in the area in which Oliver lived was by now totally out of the question, but he could not bear the idea of listening to more crowing from his peers about how much money they were making from property. Appalled at the price of city property, Oliver thought he would buy an investment property in a tourist region, with the idea that he could use it as a holiday home once in a while. It seemed like the next best thing as compared to being a homeowner.

Some property types are far riskier than others.

Tempted by glossy brochures and a slick sales presentation Oliver paid $900,000 for a new two bedroom apartment, which seemed awfully expensive but did have nice views. The salesman had produced some charts predicting future infrastructure and jobs growth for the area which sounded promising.

Within the next few years, however, the economy moved into a downturn, jobs growth stalled, unemployment was rising fairly sharply, and although interest rates were cut several times, property market sentiment dived. Oliver was alarmed to read in the newspaper stories of two-tier marketing schemes and interstate investors being duped into paying too much for new properties, but figured that he was only planning to hold for the long term, so there was no point in paying too much attention.

There could be seven to ten recessions in the next fifty years – don't act surprised when they come.

Unfortunately over the next two years the economy went into a technical recession, property prices declined steadily across the nation, while many of those in certain tourist regions were hit with calamitous losses as holiday homes were sold. Oliver began to become increasingly concerned and when he next visited his apartment he checked out what prices apartments in the area were selling for. He was devastated to discover that prices were no higher than $490,000, and became convinced that he had been conned. How had the bank ever given him a mortgage for a property which they had once happily valued at $900,000?

Although the tourist region markets picked up marginally over the next two years, Oliver remained in a negative equity position and eventually sold the property for a $220,000 loss. Meanwhile, property prices in the city where Oliver lived had rebounded and were now making fresh all-time highs by the month. Not only was Oliver priced out of the region where he lived he had been left with a large personal debt and was forever convinced that the property markets were a Ponzi scheme rigged by con artists.

Making sense of the cycles

Both Ray and Oliver are convinced that investing is a bad idea – they may both be right, and yet neither are right. What did they do wrong? They listened to the wrong people, bought the wrong assets at the wrong time, and had no long-term plan. Both were speculating on asset prices moving in their favour in the short term yet had no coherent plan for what they would do if the reverse proved to be true.

In this book, I have promoted the idea that timing is not everything in investment, rather if you buy the right type of investments then time in the market can solve many if not most of your problems. Nevertheless, it does pay to understand market cycles because you can look to buy more when markets are cheap, with the same applying to both the share markets and property markets. I will explore in a little further detail below how market cycles work.

Dow Theory

In this book, I have put forward the idea that the best and most efficient investments can often be those which you can hold onto indefinitely. If you want to understand in more detail how share market cycles develop and play out, and how you recognise what stage of the market cycle we are in, I recommend reading my book *Get a Financial Grip*. Summarily, there are three phases of a typical share market cycle:[1]

- accumulation phase
- public participation phase
- distribution phase

The accumulation phase is when investors in the know are actively buying stocks against the general sentiment of the market. During this phase, stock valuations do not change much as these investors are in the minority, absorbing stocks that the market at large is supplying. Eventually, the market catches on to the moves of these astute investors and a rapid price change occurs, which indicates the second phase. This happens when the crowd begins to participate in the market, and this phase continues until eventually rampant speculation occurs. At this point, astute investors begin to distribute their shareholdings to the market and prices begin to fall.

Sophisticated investors aim to be fully invested through the bull market before lightening their holdings before the market reverses. In practice this is far more difficult to do than it sounds, because within each secular market cycle there are smaller movements and cycles within cycles which consistently head fake market traders and investors.

A great example was the share market crash caused by the financial crisis, which threw up a couple of epic bull trap scenarios. A bull trap occurs when a market which has been falling levels out and then begins to rise again, tricking investors into believing that a new market cycle has begun.

Figure 16.1 – Bull traps

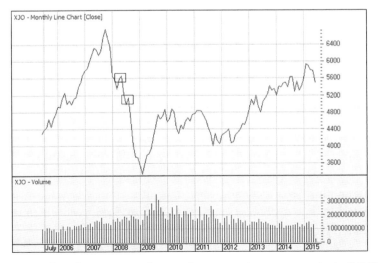

The grim truth is that even professional investors have a great deal of difficulty in analysing market cycles, so unless you have a written plan and a great deal of discipline, an averaging approach suits most average investors best. That said, there is absolutely no reason why even an investor adopting an averaging approach shouldn't look to add more to their share investments when the market is demonstrably cheap on a historical basis. How do you know when a share market is cheap? There are a number of measures, but two of the simplest are to look at market-wide price/earnings or PE ratios and to consider dividend yields.

If PE ratios are historically very cheap, then it is likely to be a good time to load up on quality equity investments. At the time of writing share market appear to be only offering moderate value so you need to have a plan which allows you to survive a potential downturn. In other words, it is not likely to be a great time to pour all of your money into the market quickly! In a similar vein, if dividend yields are historically high, then it is also likely to be an attractive time to load up on quality investments.

You will never be able to time the market perfectly since that is not possible to do, even for the greatest of experts. However, what is possible is to adopt a sensible long-term approach to investing in quality assets and buying more when the market is clearly on sale. To learn more about the different approaches to investing in the share market, I recommend reading my book *Get a Financial Grip*.

Why property markets cycle

There are a number of common explanations of why property markets move in cycles:

- It has been seen that monetary policy, particularly the tightening of interest rates, has been effective in the past at stifling undesirably strong levels of property price growth

- Governing bodies have been blamed at times for becoming addicted to the 'feel-good factor' or wealth effect associated with rising dwelling prices

- Construction activity can increase rapidly during a house price boom as developers chase profits, leading to a temporary oversupply thus exaggerating market downturns

- Construction activity can decline rapidly and be quelled during periods of falling prices leading to a tightening market and eventually an undersupply - and the next upturn begins

One of the most compelling factors, however, is simply the human psychology element. Not only does each new generation see an influx of new market participants who have never experienced a housing bust, humans are emotional creatures: we tend to extrapolate the present into the future in an irrational manner. When times are good, we think they will be good forever which sends the market up to an irrational and overvalued peak, which then inevitably has to correct. Each boom sets us up for the next bust, just as each bust sets up for the next boom. The long-term trend of quality well located property investments, however, remains an upward one.

Investment markets are impacted by fear and greed.

All investment and financial markets are to some extent impacted by fear and greed. When markets are falling fear abounds and those presently invested frequently look to sell in a panic, concerned that prices will be cheaper again next month or next year. When prices are rising greed begins to take over and market participants push prices higher and higher. The market often moves into the rampant speculation phase as a fear of missing out (FOMO) kicks in, which is exactly what Oliver experienced in the short story above.

Eventually the irrational exuberance comes to an end and the market begins to fall again. It is these very human characteristics which cause markets to overshoot both on the upside and on the downside and why markets will always continue to cycle despite the best efforts of central banks and governing bodies to keep markets stable or in equilibrium.

The property market cycle in more detail

In this section of the book, I am going to delve a little deeper into the concept of property market cycles and housing market economics to help you understand why the market behaves as it does and how you can use this information to your benefit. Although there is often a disapproving tone from market pundits about dwelling prices rising and falling in cycles, there are good reasons why market cycles occur, and indeed to some extent cycles are beneficial to the functioning of a healthy market.

A market which is perfectly in equilibrium should see prices remaining steady in real terms, yet what happens in practice is nearly always somewhat different. Take the example of Sydney. The population of Greater Sydney could rise by anything up to around 90,000 or more persons in any given calendar year.[2]

The growth in the population naturally puts pressure on the established housing stock and an increasing shortage of existing dwellings puts pressure on market rents, forcing monthly rentals and market yields higher.

Dwelling prices tend to rise following increases in rental yields.

As rental yields rise, being a homeowner or a landlord becomes comparatively more attractive than being a renter, altering the investment decision in favour of purchasing a dwelling as a homebuyer or an investor. As more participants enter the market by buying a dwelling, prices begin to rise. Due to the human emotions involved in all markets, prices can begin to rise relatively quickly eventually becoming detached from the underlying fundamentals.

Property developers study market cycles very closely and land-bank holdings in anticipation of the market cycle moving upwards. Developers aim to release new housing developments to the market when prices are at attractive levels allowing them to generate an acceptable return on their invested capital and reasonable profit margins. This is why the construction sector of the economy cycles too.

If, for example, a central bank wants to stimulate dwelling construction to offset weaknesses in other sectors of the economy, it will need to cut interest rates in order to push dwelling prices higher, financing costs lower and bring developers back into the market. Markets do tend to overshoot on the upside and on the downside, and if development continues too far then an over-supply of dwellings eventuates.

Markets overshoot irrationally on the upside and on the downside.

All of this sits against the backdrop of the wider economy which has implications for movement in interest rates, the strength of the labour force and myriad other factors which impact household confidence. The way in which the economy interacts with the housing market at both a macro and micro level can appear to be quite complex, and it is these very factors which I attempt to elucidate for readers in my free blog page each day.[3]

There are a few key points of note here. Firstly, housing markets in large capital cities are a very different beast to those in smaller cities or regional towns. Housing market economist Michael Oxley explains how in a large capital city a boost in dwelling construction will rarely have the same impact on supply that could eventuate in a small or regional city since the ratio of new stock to established stock in a large city tends to be relatively insignificant.[4]

> 'With only 6 percent of all houses in London being newly built, the idea that there being an increase in the building of new houses, even a massive increase, will have an effect on prices, is highly implausible'.

For example, if Sydney is in the midst of a construction boom it might still only be adding 50,000 new dwellings in a year, which is very small proportion as compared to an existing city population which is rapidly approaching 5 million. Further the new supply can easily be absorbed by the growing population over time. On the other hand, observe what happened across parts of Ireland through the financial crisis property bubble. With near full levels of employment, house prices had tripled in a short period of time and unprecedented levels of over-building took place.

When the inevitable Ireland crash finally did take place, some housing estates had to be demolished. I have met Irish property investors in Sydney who have told me that they have owned property in Ireland for half a decade that has never once been let to a tenant. This is an extreme example and accentuates why I believe that real estate can be too risky a proposition not to engage an expert. You need to be able to identify inner capital city locations - not city centres where there is no height restriction of tower blocks - where dwelling supply is effectively fixed, but demand is growing due to a rapidly expanding city-wide population growth.

> Strong population growth can underpin capital city property markets.

If there is one situation you never want to be in as a property investor it is owning property in a town or city where the population is declining. If you want to see examples of what can happen to dwelling prices in cities where the population is declining, check out how dramatically prices have fallen in parts of Detroit, which is to say effectively down to zero in many cases. I have seen similar outcomes in parts of regional towns in the United Kingdom while London prices simply kept on rising through the financial crisis, which should have been a salutary lesson to promoters of regional property.

If you want to succeed in real estate investment over the long haul, I suggest that you ultimately need to be playing in a large pond. It can be a reasonable strategy to start out investing in a small city if that is all you can afford, but capital growth over the long term will always be more robust in landlocked inner suburbs of large and thriving capital cities.

Shorter cycles?

Typically a property market cycle might take around seven years or so to play out in full, with prices flat or in a downturn for a period of two or three years, before rising again. Historically it was reasonable to expect that each trough in prices would be comfortably higher than its preceding equivalent, but in this era of lower inflation this may not always be so in the future. Indeed, average dwelling price growth we should expect to be lower in the future too as we are in an era of higher household debt and lower inflation.

In today's faster moving world with more instant feedback, combined with the fact that high inflation will no longer carry housing markets forward in long and sweeping cycles, it seems reasonable to expect that housing market cycles might be shorter and more staccato in nature than was the case in times past. Boom cycles will still occur periodically but may be of a lesser magnitude than was the case historically. In order to create financial freedom through real estate investment, you will not only need to own a portfolio of properties, you will need to own those well-located capital city property types which will comfortably outperform the averages.

Chapter 16 summary

» Financial and investment markets will continue to cycle in the future as they always have in the past

» There are signs and indicators which you can use to recognise where markets are in their cycle

» Property market cycles historically took around seven years to play out

» Future market cycles may be shorter in nature and booms of a lesser magnitude

» Correct asset selection will be vital to future success

17

Don't Give It All To The Taxman!

17

'I pay what I'm required to pay, not a penny more or less. Now of course I'm minimising my tax. If anyone in this country is not minimising their tax they want their heads read, because I can tell you, as a government you're not spending it so well we should be donating extra'
– Kerry Packer to Australian Senate, 1991.

Paying tax

One of the things which holds people back from building wealth is that they pay too much in tax at source. There is certainly nothing wrong with paying a fair level of tax. After all, we are all citizens of our country and should pay some tax in order to pay for essential infrastructure, such as schools, roads and hospitals. One of the reasons that it is so hard to build wealth from your salary is that the government deducts its share of the tax at source. The government gets paid first, and then you are paid the balance.

Tax benefits of owning a business

In Part Four of this book, we are going to look at how you can begin to turn your passion into your business. In contrast to being a salaried employer, if you own a business, legitimate expenses are deducted from sales revenues and then the company pays tax on the balance after expenses. This can be a major advantage to the business owner and is one key reason that business owners are often able to build greater wealth than a salaried employee. However, if you are an employee, you still have the opportunity to build significant wealth if you can invest a fair proportion of your net pay into wealth-producing assets.

Capital gains tax

The buy and hold strategy is designed to lower risk by buying quality shares and holding them for the long term.

One tremendous advantage of a buy and hold strategy is the reduced impact of capital gains tax. Warren Buffett refers to unrealised profits - paper profits on shares that have not yet been sold - as an interest free loan from the Treasury.[1] Consider the following table, where a share trader has doubled $10,000 five times in five share trades, each time realising a gain within a year and incurring capital gains tax at an assumed rate of 30 percent:

Figure 17.1 – Gains taxed at 30 percent

Starting capital	Capital doubled to:	Tax at 30pc	Finishing capital
$10,000	$20,000	$(3,000)	$17,000
$17,000	$34,000	$(5,100)	$28,900
$28,900	$57,800	$(8,670)	$49,130
$49,130	$98,260	$(14,739)	$83,521
$83,521	$167,042	$(25,056)	**$141,986**

In the table above, after doubling his capital five times and paying his due capital gains tax at an assumed 30 percent the investor has been left with a total capital of $141,986. Next consider the below table, where a share trader has again doubled his capital of $10,000 five times. This time, he has held each trade for more than a year and has thus only incurred capital gains tax at an assumed lower rate of 15 percent (due to a capital gains tax discount for assets held for more than 12 months).

Figure 17.2 – Gains taxed at 15 percent

Starting capital	Capital doubled to:	Tax at 15pc	Finishing capital
$10,000	$20,000	$(1,500)	$18,500
$18,500	$37,000	$(2,775)	$34,225
$34,225	$68,450	$(5,134)	$63,316
$63,316	$126,633	$(9,497)	$117,135
$117,135	$234,270	$(17,570)	**$216,700**

While he has incurred tax that has still eaten into his gains, his final capital of $216,700 is more than the investor in the first example. Finally, consider the table below of an investor who has doubled his capital of $10,000 five times through one trade that he has held over a period of years. He will pay capital gains tax of 15 percent on the whole amount of the gain in the final year:

Figure 17.3 – The power of compounding unrealised gains

Starting capital	Capital doubled to:	Tax at 15pc	Finishing capital
$10,000	$20,000	$-	$20,000
$20,000	$40,000	$-	$40,000
$40,000	$80,000	$-	$80,000
$80,000	$160,000	$-	$160,000
$160,000	$320,000	$(43,500)	**$276,500**

While the tax payment in the final year is undoubtedly painful, the final capital of $276,500 is an excellent result, and far outstrips the capital of the other two investors who have traded more regularly. This is the essence of successful value investing and in many ways it echoes the approach of the property investor who never sells in order not to trigger a capital gains tax liability. The tax bill in year five may be significant, but the final capital balance is a handsome compensation.

Buy and hold for efficient gains

The numbers in the above table aren't all that important, but the principle certainly is. If you can adopt an investment strategy which involves buying quality assets and holding for as long as possible, then the income and capital growth can continue to grow and compound for you in perpetuity. The more you trade, the more transaction costs and capital gains taxes will eat away at your ability to achieve the financial freedom you desire. Timing the market always seems easy in retrospect because you are reading the chart from right to left. In real time and when you are reading the chart from left to right, timing the market is much harder to do well.

Other tax benefits of investing

There are other tax benefits to investing, which I recommend you learn about. These include tax deductions on loans for investment purposes in some jurisdictions, and franking credits on dividend income. I covered these areas in more detail in my book *Get a Financial Grip*, so I will not delve too deeply into this subject here.

In truth, everyone has a different situation when it comes to their personal taxes and therefore it is difficult to give specific pointers in a book, but as a general rule there can be great tax advantages for those who operate in the business and investment spheres, particularly those who adopt a long-term approach to investment which is not based around trading assets. Employees on the other hand are somewhat constrained in what they can do to minimise their tax.

Use a good accountant

While I am in favour of saving money where possible there are certain things that are worth paying a good professional for and paying for a good accountant is one of these things. I use Deloitte as my accountant. You may not need a Big Four accounting firm for your personal tax, but I recommend finding someone with expertise that can save you tax. If, for example, you are invested in property, find an accountant with experience in property investment tax treatment. It is not worth skimping on accounting fees and using a back-street accountant just because they offer the cheapest fees. It will cost you more in taxes and penalties if you receive a below par service.

Chapter 17 summary

» There are tax advantages to being in the business and investments sectors

» The most efficient way to build wealth is usually to buy quality, income-producing assets and hold them forever

» Find a good accountant and stick with them

Part Four
Getting Down To Business

18

Making Your Vacation
Your Vocation

18

'The secret to success in life is to make your vacation your vocation.' – Mark Twain.

Making your vacation your vocation

These were very wise words from Mark Twain. If you can make your vacation your vocation, then you will never really feel as though you have done a gruelling day of work in your life! If you think back to your school days and the so-termed extra-curricular activities that you undertook such as playing sport or a musical instrument, you may recall that people tend to be far more successful when they are passionate about what they do.

It tends to be little use a parent instructing a child to undertake violin practice at home five nights every week if what they really want to be doing is playing football outside with their mates. Why? Because the child will see the violin practice as a chore rather than something to be enjoyed and approached with fervour, and as soon as they are old enough to do so, they are likely to give up the violin playing altogether.

Of course, the reverse also applies - if what a child desperately wants to do is to play music rather than sport, then it may often be better to allow them to do so, because they are likely to be passionate about their practice and, as a result, more likely to derive success and enjoyment from that field. Success in business, just as in the investment markets, is achieved by using the 3 golden rules of success, in particular, if you find pleasure in your field of business, you are more likely to be successful. To re-cap, the three golden rules as they apply to business are:

- Golden Rule #1 – The **80/20 Principle** – focusing on the key business decisions, industries, products and customers, recognising what works and doubling down on it

- Golden Rule #2 – **Snowballing** or compounding your successes

- Golden Rule #3 – **The Pleasure-Pain Principle** – by following your passion

Be guided by your passion.

How often do people fall into careers which they never felt any passion for even before they started out? All the time! I know more than a little about this myself. I trained as a Chartered Accountant, which at times was great fun, but I am still doubtful as to whether many people grow up with a burning desire to be an accountant. Over the years in my career I enjoyed various parts of my job, but I found lacked the opportunity to be creative, the hours were very long and inflexible, and the further up the corporate ladder I climbed, the more of my week I spent dealing with appraisal meetings, profitability conferences, efficiency drives and other corporate mumbo-jumbo.

The pay was good, but all research into the subject shows that pay tends to only motivate people so far in a career. Job satisfaction surveys repeatedly show that levels of remuneration only have a relatively small input into happiness in the workplace. In short, you need to be passionate about what you do! While it does not necessarily float everyone's boat, what I was passionate about was economics and finance, writing, share investment and real estate. I practised all of these things in my spare time regardless of whether I was paid for them because I am genuinely passionate about them, and so I resolved to make a plan to make my vacation my vocation.

The Zulu Principle

A couple of decades ago an English accountant (there are a few of us around!) by the name of Jim Slater published a book entitled *The Zulu Principle: Making Extraordinary Profits from Ordinary Shares.*[1] Slater's premise was that becoming an expert in one specific field could help share market investors to secure outstanding returns, echoing Buffett's concept of focus investing.

Slater dreamed up the concept of the *Zulu Principle* after his wife read a book on the subject of Zulus and having done so was able to demonstrate a superior knowledge to him on that very subject.[2] He rationalised that if his wife read every book she could find on the subject of Zulus she could relatively quickly become an expert in that field and perhaps even a leading authority within a relatively short period of time.[3]

Slater's point is that through 'identifying a narrow and clearly defined area of knowledge' then applying that knowledge learned in your area of expertise can help you to profit from your expertise.[4] This is very much true, although as I considered in Chapter 10 the fact of the matter is that most average investors do not have the skill-set (or inclination to learn the skill-set) to analyse a company and its financials in detail, which is pre-requisite for achieving outstanding returns in this way. After all, even a focused investor will be pitching their analysis against that of dozens or perhaps hundreds of professional market analysts.

The Zulu Principle holds that you can become a true expert in one field.

Nevertheless, I do believe that Slater's concept does have a great deal of merit. You are far more likely to be successful in a field of investment or asset class which you feel you understand because this will help to reassure you when the market is in a downwards cycle. Further than that, the Zulu Principle holds that if you can identify a narrow and clearly defined area of knowledge then you can profit from your expertise.

In my line of business, for example, I may be an expert on how to profit from investing in Sydney apartments in a particular price bracket, in a certain range of very carefully identified inner-ring suburbs. On the other hand, I do not really know very much about strata-titling blocks of apartments in the Whitsundays, but then nor do I particularly want to. If you can become a true expert in one field then you can add value to others in this particular area of expertise.

In London, my business partner achieved the same for investors aiming to achieve outstanding returns from investing in London property. For example, in early 2014 we bought a range of properties for investors in London suburbs such as Ealing, Hayes and Woolwich which would stand to benefit from the construction of the new Crossrail link.[5]

Later in the year, the mainstream media began to get wind of the capital gains and publicised the story, but by then the big gains had been made. Our company's expertise added value to investors and improved their returns. We do not pretend to have expertise in investing in remote regional areas and nor do we want to. Following Slater's premise of the Zulu Principle, it is possible for you to become an expert in your field of passion. If you are able to do so, then you can resolve to turn your passion into your business.

'But I can't go into business...'

I have talked in some depth in this book about the power of belief systems both to create and destroy achievements. I have done so because it is clear to me that whether or not an individual is able to transition from full time employment into business successfully is ultimately decided by their beliefs. So many of us have been trained through our upbringing and formal education to believe that a job is the only valid path to success (and perhaps that entrepreneurship is somehow a slightly less acceptable path) that we do not question the underlying assumptions.

A key theme of this book is that while setting up a business may be challenging for those who have been conditioned by years in the workforce, by first building a portfolio of assets which can go out to work for you in perpetuity, you can gradually begin to focus upon expanding your skill-set so that you can generate substantial income in your own business or area of passion too.

The advantages of being in business

One of the inescapable problems with being an employee is that your salary remains linear. Each day you must wake up and return to work anew in order to earn your pay cheque. You only get paid once for each day of work and if you stop turning up for work, generally speaking it will not be very long before you stop getting paid. Regardless of whether you are an employee or a business owner, if you want a pay rise or more revenue then you must find ways to make yourself more valuable to more people, and do so more efficiently. If you want to become very wealthy, you must learn to make yourself *invaluable,* by honing your skills to dramatically improve the lives of others.[6]

Going into business is another way in which it is possible to use leverage to your benefit. If you can develop a product or service that adds huge value to the quality of the lives of others, you can then create more value for yourself. A business has the potential to generate recurring income as well as potentially leveraging other people's time to increase profitability. If you can find ways to reach more people, more quickly and more effectively then money can begin to flow to you.

To create more value for yourself, find ways
to create more value for others.

Another problem with salary income is that it tends to be more heavily taxed as you move up the pay scales, with around half of an employee's gross earnings in the top slice of income ultimately forming part of the government's sizeable tax take.[7] There can be legitimate ways for employees to reduce their taxable income as I explored in more detail in my book *Get a Financial Grip*. However, as a general rule, tax levied on salary income is deducted at source and there are relatively few defences for the employee.

Broadly speaking an employee goes to work in order to be paid, yet the government takes its share of your income leaving you to spend the balance. A business owner may instead deduct legitimate expenses from their revenue and only pays tax on the net profits after deductible expenses. One of the key messages of this book is to find ways to minimise your expenditure in order to free up capital for investment. If you are a business owner, you should do the same, and try to ensure that most of your expenditure is directly attributable to your business so that it becomes a legitimate deduction for your business.

The well-trodden career path

You may know some people who are natural-born entrepreneurs. At school they often stood out as kids who were always interested in making a bob or two from some profitable scheme or other - at my high school, selling chocolate bars for a small profit was all the rage. Natural entrepreneur types can perform reasonably well in high school exams, but tend to lack enthusiasm for traditional higher education, instead wanting to get 'out there' into the real world of business.

In some senses, young entrepreneurs are the lucky ones, for they know that they do not want to be stuck in a job for their whole lives and can afford to take chances when they are young with nascent business ideas and ventures. One of my housemates in my University days set up a business even before he finished his University course – he had no need for a degree, he wanted to get out there and set the world alight!

This was a fair few years ago now, of course, and his first company designed web pages back in the days when this was a much sought-after skill. He continued with various business ideas and plans until eventually he hit the jackpot by owning a series of website businesses which generate him millions of dollars in free cash flow per annum. With a great deal of capital at his disposal he's free to explore new ideas and businesses. It is interesting to note that small business owners who start when they are young can afford to have less profitable business ventures or companies which fail because they have not yet built up the dreaded addiction to or dependence upon the monthly pay cheque.

'Fortune sides with him who dares.' – Virgil.

If you think about my friend's financial profile, he was able to take risks early in life because at the age of 20 he did not have a wife, children, a large mortgage or car loans to worry about. Rather, he just needed to be able to feed himself, which means that taking on business ventures can be a far more thrilling prospect than seeking out a traditional 9-5 job. This is also why most people today are never able to take the step to owning their own business: they feel unable to take the risk of moving away from the security of the monthly pay cheque.

As people move further up the pay scale, the more entrenched this belief inevitably becomes, for the pay cheques generally become larger and is harder to walk away from, and the financial commitments also increase. Once you have a mortgage and children to think about, even the idea of giving up full time work becomes a distant dream for many. This need not be so, but it is probably true that you would want to have a solid portfolio of investment assets behind you before you consider taking a leap into business.

Moving away from full time work?

Can the dream of moving away from full time employment to part-time employment or business owner still be achieved in these circumstances? The answer is yes, absolutely, but in reality for many, it cannot be achieved overnight. If this is to be your goal, then the first step is to build a portfolio of income-producing and appreciating assets such as a substantial portfolio of investment properties and shares. Once you have built a solid and substantial financial base then this can gradually allow you to shift your focus away from the need to work full time to generate an income and towards securing other revenue streams such as from a business.

What is your passion?

As I previously noted, I had a reasonable idea of what my passion was and what my ideal day would be. But I also had a full time job and a decent monthly pay cheque as the Financial Controller of a mining company which was difficult to walk away from. One of the reasons why it seems impossible to people that they might ever be able to go into business is because they think that they must quit their job and then immediately replace their income with business income practically overnight. It seems far too risky a notion so they never take the chance and they never find out whether they could have been a business owner.

I suggest trying to think a little differently. Instead of worrying about whether a venture into the world of business might fail, instead consider how over time you can begin to replace you salary income with a business income gradually. I will refer to my own short story by way of an example. My wife and I were both lucky in one sense as we were both quite successful in our early careers and by the time we were in our mid-twenties we were both higher-rate taxpayers (you could consider this to be lucky or unlucky depending upon your perspective!). The problem was that neither of us felt great passion for our careers, so we decided to plan how we could do things a little differently.

Your salary will not make you wealthy, but investing can.

My wife had bought herself a house when she was only 21, and it had skyrocketed during the UK housing boom of the 1990s, tripling in value very quickly. Real estate was something which she believed she had some experience of and had had some success with. Over the years we continued to add property after property to our portfolio in prime locations close to London and the centre of Sydney. While we were doing so we also committed everything to becoming the most educated and experienced share market investors that we could.

But even with a substantial portfolio of assets to our name and a large pool of equity, it was still difficult to walk away from the security of our twin pay cheques. I knew that my passion and area of expertise was in the areas of finance and investment, but I was not yet sure how I could turn this into my day job. This is where the concept of *modelling* can help. I found a number of people who were already successful in the field I was interested in and I modelled what had worked for them.

Find mentors who have achieved the goals you want to achieve.

One way in which it becomes possible to move away from full time work is to begin creating small sundry revenue streams for yourself. There are many ways in which you can do this. Investing in income-paying shares is one great strategy. Another one of the things I did was to start writing books which generate recurring revenue – that is, you write the book once, but the royalty income continues to flow in for as long as the books are sold. I also began to write a free daily blog and paid articles for media websites. At first, I generated a helpful income stream from advertising on my blog page, but I later removed the advertising because I felt that they detracted from what I was writing.

While writing books, media articles and blogs can generate recurring revenue, generally speaking they are not actually terribly efficient ways to make money. The author of a book typically only receives a small portion of the cover price, and in my case I donate 10 percent of my royalties to charity too, so selling books may not be a particularly lucrative exercise when you consider the huge number of hours that writing a book takes. And while blog adverts generate some revenue they are generally quite annoying and can be quite detrimental to tone of your blog page.

A third revenue stream I created was through mentoring clients on how they could build a portfolio of assets in the same manner in which I had. I restricted the numbers to half a dozen mentees at any one time who paid me a monthly fee for my services. In return I provided email and phone support and constructed bespoke investment strategy documents for them.

All businesses take time to grow their revenues and so it was with these revenue streams. Instead of quitting my full time job completely and resolving to go straight into business, I went travelling for 15 months, first driving around Australia for a year and then travelling around some 25 other countries. Once I had quenched my thirst for travel, I also did some contract work overseas which generated more useful income.

In short, in order to help myself move away from full time work, I wrote books and media articles, generated income from mentoring and providing investment strategy advice to clients, earned a small amount of advertising revenue from my blog page and undertook some shorter part-time contracts overseas. The combination of these revenue streams in addition to my investment income and growth from my share and property portfolios meant that slowly but surely, I eventually began to feel ready to go into business. It certainly did not happen overnight, and I progressed only with baby steps at first.

Together with a business partner, I set up an international property buying business with offices in London and Sydney, the two real estate markets which

I knew inside out and also the two markets which I personally felt offered the best long-term prospects for investors (which is why I have been so heavily invested in those locations myself over all these years). We felt that the best way in order to earn income from the business of real estate was to use our expertise as property buyers and investors in order to help others to achieve their goals through real estate. This was not only an area of my expertise, but also something which I felt and still feel passionate about.

> Do something you are interesting in – you will do it better.

Today's world is full of professionals who are too busy working to have time to mind their *own* business, and real estate buyers agencies operate in a growing industry. Our business was set up to help time-poor professionals and investment funds fulfil their financial goals through investing in quality, well-located real estate. Property and housing market economics are fields that I am passionate about and it gives me a real buzz to wake up every morning and receive emails from people who are achieving their financial goals and living their dreams through smart investment. It beats the living daylights out of waking up each morning with a large and resigned sigh in contemplation of another 60 hour week in the office!

One step at a time

The goal of moving away from full time work can seem such a huge one that it may feel insurmountable. But, just as climbing Everest must start with establishing a base camp, the goal is one which can be achieved simply by taking one simple step at a time. Firstly, as previously detailed, it is important to begin building your financial base, a portfolio of assets which can continue to appreciate and pay you income whether you are working or not. This helps to take the pressure off your reliance on business success.

Then you can begin to consider in more detail what it is that you are truly passionate about and how you would live your ideal day if money were no object. You do not have to simply quit your day job and dive into business headlong, although of course plenty of people do. This could be a stressful approach and induce stress of a financial nature too.

Instead, aim to think of how you can steadily build a profile which will allow you to generate income from your expertise. For most employees, trying to think of a steady transition from one state to another may be more achievable and realistic than taking a running jump from a well-paid role and starting a new business venture from scratch.

Where to start out?

If you are currently employed but want to move in setting up your own business or being self-employed the task can seem daunting. I know, because I remember this clearly from my own experience. The thing to remember is that, just like anything else in life worth achieving, setting up a successful business is not something which happens overnight. Instead, it takes many hours of application and effort.

Always endeavour to remember golden rule #2: the power of compounding growth. Start small, make small improvements and gradually increase your leverage over time. The problem facing too many people is that they believe that the only way in which they can ever be self-employed is to immediately replace their salary income with an equivalent level of business income, and the real world just does not work like that.

Start small and grow steadily.

In the early years of business revenues and distributable profits can be quite scarce which is precisely why I recommend building a portfolio of assets first which can continue to grow and compound for you before you go into business. As an accountant, I have often read business plans which begin with absurd projections for the first few years, making huge allowances for owner-manager salaries, support staff, company cars, and a raft of luxurious IT equipment, well-appointed offices and more. If that is the type of business plan you want to take a crack at, then best of luck, but the odds are well and truly stacked against you!

In truth, it is possible to start businesses at the mid-tier level, but you would need a large fund of seed capital in order to achieve it, either through your own means or by raising funds from investors. I will make the assumption here that if you have the ability to facilitate capital raisings from investors or fund the start-up of a larger enterprise from your own hip pocket, you are unlikely to be reading this book in the first place!

When people come to me asking how they can get out of the rat race and working for themselves I often ask them to consider writing a book about their passion or area of true expertise. First, I ask people to consider these questions:

- What is that you are passionate about?

- What do you know more about than anyone else?

- In what field can you add the greatest value to others?

- What would you be doing on a Monday morning with your time, if you could be doing anything you choose?

The considered answers to these questions should act as your guide.

Write a book?

Back in the 1960s Stanley Millgram undertook a series of experiments which aimed to test human response and obedience to authority.[8] He instructed the test participants to deliver electric shocks to human 'guinea pigs' who answered what were effectively trivia questions incorrectly.[9] Unbeknownst to the participants the electric shocks were not actually real, but the results were very real…and scary. The conclusion of the Millgram experiments was essentially that the majority of people would deliver a lethal electric shock to another human being simply because a bloke in a white jacket has told them to.[10]

The implications of these experiments are terrifying when considered in their wider historical context. We are far too trusting of authority. However, the main point of relevance for us here is that the general public tends to ascribe more credibility to published authors or journalists on their chosen subject of expertise, whether they deserve it or not.

A published author dons the proverbial equivalent of Millgram's white jacket and is immediately afforded credibility and authority in their field. I will not cite examples here, but finance and investment is a classic case in point – pundits with no genuine financial or investment expertise or qualifications publish books on the subject and can temporarily achieve quasi-guru status without any substance or experience at all behind their content.

> If you want to build credibility, write a book.

Now obviously I am certainly not saying that you should pretend to be an expert in any area in which you are unqualified! There is certainly no pleasure or satisfaction to be gained from living your life feeling like a fraud. Indeed, if you fail to deliver your message convincingly then you will only ever achieve suboptimal results, while unconsciously you will fail to promote yourself as a genuine expert. What I am saying, however, is that published authors receive more mainstream media attention and credibility than they might otherwise be ascribed and therefore it might make sense to take advantage of this fact.

A great place for would-be business owners to start out therefore can be to write a book about their passion or area of expertise. This is my third book – I wrote my first book when I was 33, and in many ways I wish I had written my first book a few years sooner than I did. I knew I had the expertise and real world experience, and I knew I could write the best personal finance book on the market, but what I lacked was the confidence.

I knew in advance of course that people would take pot-shots at me (they did), would query whether I was a true expert in my field (they did that too) and tried to pull me back (and that!). The fact of the matter is there will always be people on hand to pull you back. But what is to stop you from rising above mediocrity?

Writing a book does not tend to earn most authors a great deal of money. Typically the author might receive a small percentage of the sale price as a royalty, and as writing a book takes up much, much more time than you might think, you would need to sell a lot of books to make it worth your while from a purely financial perspective. It may also be difficult to find a suitable publisher for your book. If this is the case, self-publishing may also be a good alternative. The point of writing a book is to establish a level of authority in your chosen field.

Becoming a published author helps credibility.

If you do not want to take the step of writing a book, or find it difficult to find a suitable publisher, the good news is there are other alternatives.

As a positive example of what writing a book can do for you and the doors it can open, I read about Dale Beaumont, a young Australian with a passion for education and self-development for young people. Beaumont was frustrated at how the media would not take him seriously because he was only nineteen years of age and he lacked credibility in the eyes of the press. Dale's point was that it was precisely *because* he was nineteen years of age that he could relate to young people and had something worthwhile to say.

Undaunted, Beaumont co-authored and published his first book *The World at Your Feet* with his friend Brent Williams at the age of only nineteen.[11] What a transformation! Within a short period of time, having previously been dismissed or ignored by the media, Beaumont and Williams were featured on the television and in newspapers and could begin to reach other young people with their message. Dale also has a tremendous work ethic which anyone who has a goal of being their own boss should aim to learn from. He went on to produce no fewer than 15 books in his *Secrets Exposed* series, incredibly eleven of those books being published in the calendar year 2007 alone.

The format Beaumont used was to interview key experts in each field covered and dedicate a chapter to each, and it worked, with him going on to sell more than 250,000 books. Interestingly, when people asked what the 'secret' was to pumping out eleven books in a year, Beaumont's answer was illuminating - he looked blank and said simply: 'Secret? There is no secret. It just takes a lot of hard work!' - *touché!*

> The real 'secret' to getting ahead is hard work, and lots of it.

I note that not everyone is a great writer and not everyone actually enjoys writing. If that is the case, why not consider writing a short book or an e-book which you can sell online or give away for free to your followers, connections or database of contacts? Offering a free e-book is a good way to build a list of email contacts which later can form a part of your client database. Be careful of course not to violate rules regarding electronic spam – you must allow anyone on your database to unsubscribe from your content if they so elect.

Getting a book published

If you are to achieve the goal of publishing a book you will need a great deal of perseverance (you have read this far, so I believe that you most probably have what it takes) and you will also need to be well organised. The best advice I can give about writing a book is to break down your target into smaller achievable goals. If I told you to go and write a book which totals 80,000 words the target may seem distant or remote and therefore impossible. The way to reach big targets successfully is to set yourself a number of smaller and achievable targets.

> Break down large goals into smaller and thus more believable and achievable and targets.

For example, if your target is to write an 80,000 word book in your specialist field then break the target down into 20 chapters of 4000 words each. OK, so it is still a big target but you should be able to conceptualise writing a 4000 word chapter much more easily than you can visualise producing an entire book. If you can commit to writing just 2500 a words day, you can write or draft a whole book in only one month. Sure, the editing and research will take longer, but that is the fun part!

Of course, it is not quite that simple. Writing a book is one thing. Writing an outstanding book is quite another. It takes a great deal of thought, research, commitment, writing, editing, and time. However, think back to what we have already covered in this book - nothing that is genuinely worth having in life comes easily, and what I can tell you is that the satisfaction and results you can achieve from being a published author will forever outweigh the hundreds of hours you pour into the writing, editing and promotion processes.

I acknowledge here that not everyone can be a good author, and for some people writing is nothing more than an almighty chore. I have never had a problem with the motivation to write books because I am passionate about writing, enjoy the challenge and love words. But I appreciate that it is not so for everyone. I know, for example, that my business partner Paddy Allen has never been all that keen on writing – he finds it challenging and not particularly enjoyable. The flip side to that is that he is a very sociable and personable person who enjoys networking events, much more so than I do, and so in that way we complement each other well.

Play to your strengths.

So what can you do if writing, grammar and English comprehension are not your strongest suit? Outsource! Clearly I do not mean get somebody else to write your book for you in its entirety, as that would not work in your favour at all. What I actually mean is, why not engage a writer who has published books before and get them to assist you through the writing and editing process? You can either agree to give them a dual writing credit as your co-author if they contribute significantly to the content, or you can simply engage a writer to make coherent sense of your ramblings and pay them on a fee-for-service basis.

Blogging

If writing does not come naturally to you, a great way to start out is simply by writing a blog. You can easily find a blog host for free. Again, I do not suggest writing a blog as a source of income alone, although I know of people who do. Trying to manage paying blog subscribers is a headache you probably do not want or need, while adverts pay reasonable revenue to websites with high volumes of traffic, but equally can be rather annoying. You may be tempted to put adverts on your blog but personally I recommend resisting this urge. These apparently random adverts cheapen the tone of your blog, distract from your own content and can promote products which are contrary to your own ethics or the true content of your page.

I believe that an internet blog can be a quick and effective way to bring quality content and your own profile to a wider audience. If the content is interesting and useful enough then people will keep coming back if you provide quality content regularly. You can choose to promote your content to followers using other social media sites such as Facebook, Twitter, LinkedIn or other avenues, while encouraging your readers to become email subscribers can expand your reach.

When you start out in the blogosphere it will no doubt feel as though you are talking to yourself, or perhaps if you are lucky to yourself and a couple of family members. This is by no means necessarily a bad thing! It can help to learn the ropes, make a few mistakes and have a few laughs while relatively few people are watching.

Start small and compound your growth.

Always come back to the key concepts of this book – get the key things right most of the time through embracing the 80/20 Principle, and remember the power of compounding or snowballing. Your humble blog page might start out with a few hits here and there from a few random locations in Singapore or Sweden, but if you resolve to concentrate on quality rather than quantity, the sheer power of persistence can see your webpage become a go-to source for other people who are interested in your field of passion.

Tips for successful blogging

First and foremost, you need to be passionate about what you are blogging about, because if you are not then readers are unlikely to be excited by your blog either! How do you get readers to keep coming back to your blog rather than being a once only visitor? The most effective way is to become a useful source of information and opinion on your chosen subject or field of expertise. You need to write a blog which people will not want to stay away from because they believe that they will be missing out on essential information or content.

For this reason, you need to consider what problems your reader has with your area of passion and how you can help them to solve those problems. On my blog page, for example, I aim to help readers to improve their investing skills by providing useful, free daily content which explains the economy and financial markets in a way which can help them to understand and profit.

Provide useful content.

While you want your blog to be a source of useful information, you also need to build some rapport with your readers and engage with them via an over-arching viewpoint or outlook. One effective way to engage with readers is to allow comments on the blog, although with the amount of spam comments around these days you may find that the time involved in approving or deleting comments quickly becomes tiresome. Your posts should have eye-catching subject titles to encourage readers to click on them. It's a simple fact of the blogosphere that a blog post with an eye-catching or arresting header will attract more hits that one with a moribund or generic title. Quality is also more important than quantity when it comes to blogging.

Choose quality over quantity.

Few people take the time to read long articles in today's era of short attention spans and info-mania. A useful guideline is to keep blog posts to no more than around 700 to 1000 words. Use plenty of white space rather than long paragraphs, and a few pictures or charts to break up the sea of text can be a very useful idea.

You will find your own ways to build readership over time. Linking to other blog posts or articles that you have written can help to keep readers engaged with your blog, while social media is a great way to promote your content. Once you have built your readership to a good level, if the quality of your content is high enough then you may find that websites with large numbers of subscribers, companies which want to promote their products or even mainstream media sites invite you to contribute to their output. If you can achieve this then the leverage which you can achieve from providing quality content can expand and compound dramatically.

Ultimately, your blog is an opportunity for you to showcase or display your superior knowledge in your own area of expertise or field of passion on a daily or weekly basis. If you are passionate enough about what it is that you do then this should translate into your writing. Remember, to paraphrase the philosopher Alan Watts, if you are passionate about something then it is likely that others will be too. You need to find a way to engage with those people because they could ultimately be your future customers.

Blog advertising

I am not sure about you, but I hate visiting websites where you are overwhelmingly bombarded by annoying adverts, usually for stuff that you do not want or need. I want you to consider building a blog which ultimately leads customers to use your products, not to click on adverts for other junk. Adverts can detract from the quality of your blog and annoy readers.

While adverts might bring you a little advertising revenue this is scant compensation for your blog spamming readership with infuriating invitations to drive traffic away from your own site elsewhere. Why would you want to do that anyway? You ultimately want readers to buy your products or services, not somebody else's! My recommendation would be to ditch advertising on your blog altogether except for your own services and products, which we will consider in more detail shortly.

Although you may start out using a free web host the ultimate goal should be to lead people to your business website where they can opt to use your services or buy your products. You can either link through to your business website from your blog page or simply migrate your blog page to a tab on your own business website. What you can do is build a blog following and then use your blog page to direct traffic to your business website once your business is established. This offers far more leverage that pay per click adverts for junk that people do not really even want or need.

Media profile

Ultimately to become a specialist in your field you want to gain media or other exposure. Just as with any other area of your life, media profile can grow and compound because the more you are in the media the more you gain credibility. And the more credibility you can amass, the more you can be in the media – it becomes a virtuous circle.

Chapter 18 summary

» You can become a true expert in one area that you are passionate about

» Do not spread yourself too thinly

» Look for ways to build credibility in your chosen field

» Writing a book – even a short book – is an outstanding way in which to build credibility

» The real secret to getting ahead is hard work, and lots of it!

19
How To Get Started In
Business

19

'I think we're having fun. Our customers like our products and we're always trying to do better.' – Steve Jobs.

Starting out with a little

One of the reasons that in the modern era the majority of people will always be employed rather than owning their own business is a misunderstanding of the funding requirements for a small business. If you begin to make a list of all the things you could need to start a business, the amount of seed capital you might require could be almost limitless – an office, staff, plant and equipment, a company car, a monthly marketing budget, and so on.

The flexibility afforded by starting small can be advantageous.

Starting out small in business has some tremendous advantages. A business which starts with capital funding is immediately under pressure to generate returns to repay loan interest and meet overhead. A business which starts out small can be allowed to evolve and be more flexible, and it can be acceptable to make some mistakes and to learn from what works and what does not along the way.

Starting out small with baby steps and over-servicing a few customers can be a great recipe for success, instead of trying to run before you can walk or leaping in at the deep end. If you can begin by providing an outstanding service to a few customers, they may then become repeat clients or refer you on to their friends and colleagues.

Physical products or services?

One of the first major decisions you need to make is whether you are going to run a services business or one which provides a physical product. Over recent decades, developed countries have generally moved increasingly towards service industries to the extent that services now form the greatest part of economies such as Australia or the United Kingdom, far larger than, for example, manufacturing or mining and resources.

Will you sell a physical product or a service?

My recommendation when starting out in business would be to find an established industry rather than trying to re-invent the wheel, and particularly, to find an industry which is growing. Then you can aim to win a market share of that growing industry. As it has been the services sector of the economy which has been growing over recent times, then this may be the ideal place to start.

Of course, this is largely down to personal preference and some people feel more inclined towards selling physical products. The thing about selling physical products is that you need stock. Stock ties up capital, you need a certain level of funds to get started and you will need to have somewhere to store your inventory. It is possible to overcome these challenges and if you are passionate about your product you will certainly find a way. Some start-up businesses use a just-in-time approach to orders or simply aim to acquire their stock after the point of sale. I am not saying that you should not go down this path, but you do need to be reasonably confident that you can make a success of a product line before spending thousands of dollars on buying inventory which you may not be able to shift.

Look for ways to solve other people's problems.

Think for a moment of how much industry today happens electronically. Once we had bookstores and record shops. Today people buy e-books and download their music from the internet. The internet has made the power of leverage available to those who have the ability and imagination to use in to their advantage. It is often said today that wealth is simply an idea, and I agree with this to a point. Creating a successful business is largely about how you can solve problems for people and add value to their lives, and the more you can improve people's lives, the more they will be prepared to pay you for your skills.

Take my path as an example, if for no other reason that it is the one in which I am most familiar with. By profession I am a Chartered Accountant, a trade which lends itself ideally to a services style business. There are many ways in which I could have set up a business based around accounting. In the modern age, for example, there are start-up businesses which need accounting or book-keeping services but do not want to pay for a full time staff member to carry out the work.

An accountant could therefore set up a business which executes accounting services for an hourly rate, and as the businesses expands it could bring in additional sub-contractors to process journals and reconciliations or perform more detailed accounting work. This is a good example of a services industry which helps time-poor people and start-up businesses today, and it can be a lucrative line of business for an entrepreneur.

For me, though, there would be just one small problem with setting up a book-keeping business: it would bore me to the back teeth! Remember, perhaps the most salient point of this book is to design a life that you are passionate about. In truth, I actually quite enjoyed book-keeping when I was a junior accounting clerk, but if I were to set up a services business providing a book-keeping service I would quickly become bored to tears.

To excel at something, you need to be passionate about it.

I am passionate, however, about investing, finance and the markets, studying demographics and analysing the economy. This is not everyone's cup of tea, for sure, but I would be doing all of these things whether I was paid for them or not. I knew that I had enough expertise to write high quality books and a blog on the subject of finance and investment, and I believed that I could improve the lives of others by helping them to invest successfully.

The business we decided to set up was a property investment services business which helps investors to buy property as an investment successfully enough to outperform the market with their returns. This is a sizeable and growing industry in cities like Sydney and Brisbane in Australia as time-poor professionals increasingly look to find experts to guide them through their property investment journey.

We intuitively knew that we could offer much better service than the competition by providing vastly superior market analysis and helping investors to translate this into building wealth. And we still do. Our detailed market analysis is simply miles ahead of the rest and we use this to our advantage, sharing some of our many findings for free in media articles. Interestingly, although buyer's agencies are a growth industry in London too, it is a relatively fledgling sector by comparison. Traditionally in Britain, when people look to buy or invest in property they do so themselves, whereas Australians are more aligned with the American model of engaging the assistance of a professional.

Looked for established industries which are growing.

Educating the market about a new product may be a worthy goal but you will probably find it to be an uphill battle and will likely fail to translate your efforts into revenues which are fully reflective of your hard work. As noted above, you are likely to be more successful by slotting into an existing and growing industry, and through aiming to win a share of that industry. Find out what the best existing businesses in your field are doing and do it better.

We aimed to solve our London problem in two ways. Firstly, we looked at sourcing foreign buyers or overseas based buyers as clients. While Australia has foreign buyer restrictions on its property market whereby non-residents can typically only buy new housing stock, huge chunks of the London market tends to be sold off to foreign investors (part of the inner city boroughs feel like one giant hotel at times). Foreign investors need buyer's agents because they frequently do not have the ability to visit the city in order to buy property, and nor do they have the expertise to know where exactly to buy.

Still today a fair portion of our business is for foreign buyers, which is a win-win situation – we can add value to foreign buyers and improve their lives since they do not have to pay for airfares and hotels to visit a city which they also tend to have little or no expertise in. The other way in which we aimed to solve the fledgling industry problem in Britain was to target residential investment funds, of which there are many in European markets. Funds have access to large pools of cash for investment purposes and need experts to deploy their capital into prime property markets efficiently and effectively.

The 80/20 Principle holds that you will likely source 80 percent of your revenue from only 20 percent of your clients, suggesting that the secret is to focus on finding those few good customers.[1] And when you do find them, double down on them by trying to find more of the same types of customers, rather than spreading yourself too thin by trying to be all things to all people.[2]

To summarise these key points:

- Fee-for-service businesses are generally easier to set up than those selling physical products

- You have a greater chance of success in an industry which you are genuinely passionate about

- Adapt your passion towards a business model which operates in an existing industry and is in a growth sector

- Aim to secure a share of this market

- Find out what the best businesses in your field are doing and aim to do it much better than them – this concept is known as *modelling*

- Consider carefully who your ideal customer or client is, and then aim to find these customers

- To be successful in business you need to use your expertise to radically improve the quality of the lives of others

Franchises

If you are starting out in business one option is to purchase a franchise. Buying a franchise is a short-cut to establishing your own business model as a respected franchise should come with its own product, business systems and procedures, as well as solving your marketing and promotion challenges.

There are advantages and disadvantages to the franchise idea. For example, if you buy a sandwich store franchise from a large multi-national chain, you might benefit greatly from their national advertising campaigns, but you also need to avoid the potential pitfalls. Firstly, buying a franchise of a well-known brand is likely to be relatively expensive and you need to be sure that you do not overpay.

Secondly, as Warren Buffett would tell you, the key to a business being successful over the long term is to have a business model with a strong economic moat which keeps marauders at bay or away.[3] There is little value in building a wildly successful sandwich store if the franchise owner implements no restrictions on the opening of new franchised stores. If there are no such restrictions then the moment your business begins to flourish and rake in significant profits you will find another store springs up next door, or at least, somewhere too close by for comfort.

> A sustainable business needs a strong economic moat.

You will have understood by now that a key theme of this book is that whatever line of business you go into you need to be passionate about your product. For example, I could choose to source a *McDonald's* franchise and open a burger chain branch in Brisbane. *McDonald's* franchises are by no means cheap, but I like Brisbane and its attractive climate, and I certainly know that there a strong and growing demand for fast food in Queensland. *McDonald's* maintains its economic moat through spending tens of millions of dollars on advertising, so I should be reasonably confident of generating ongoing revenues.

However, there is one minor problem, and that is that I am not really passionate about the product, at least, not in a way which would lead me to promote my new burger and fast food franchise in a positive light! A key thing to understand about business or self-employment is that whatever might appear to be the case when you are in paid employment, when you are working for yourself you replace your annoying boss with a boss of a different kind.

If you are self-employed it may be that your new boss is simply 'the job'. If on the other hand you are in a fee-for-service line of business, your customers become your new boss. Since you are aiming to have plenty of customers, you may be replacing your annoying boss with multiple bosses. Therefore if you are not passionate about your product then being in business is likely to be an unfulfilling experience and you would probably be better off in the workforce over the long run.

Funding options

There is a popular notion that in order to start out in business, you need a substantial business loan. Nothing could be further from the truth! In fact, taking out a business loan can be an extremely stressful course of action which adds pressure to a new venture which must provide the budding entrepreneur with an income upon which to live, but also has a new additional hurdle to overcome, that being the repayment of the interest and principal of the business loan.

The statistics show that a significant percentage of new business fail due a lack of cash flow, and a business loan merely adds to this risk. If you fail to repay the loan through the business, depending upon the terms of the loan and the structure of your business you may end up being personally liable to the bank or other source of funds. In truth, if you look at the actual statistics in terms of how new businesses are funded, the methods used are far more widely dispersed that you might imagine.[4] Traditionally it was said that business ventures are funded by 'friends, fools and family' as much as they are by banks, but in the modern era there are actually a wide range of funding methods used.[5]

Businesses can be started with relatively small levels of funding.

One of the outcomes of the financial crisis has been that in many instances debt has often been harder to source in than it was previously. It was once not at all uncommon for entrepreneurs to take out a credit card liability with a finite interest free period and then to transfer the debt across to a new product with a similar facility at the end of the interest free term.[6] Generally, that is harder to pull off today, which may of course be no bad thing![7]

An alternative to a business loan is to sacrifice some of the equity in your new venture. For example, you might relinquish a 25 percent share in your new business in exchange for some early funding, whether it be from venture capitalists, business angels or simply a friend or family member. While this can work, the payback down the track can of course be painful. 25 percent of a start-up business might not be worth too much in today's dollars, but a quarter of your business in a decade's time might be a hugely valuable investment and a painful sacrifice for you to make!

One of the more common complaints from vociferous economic commentators since the financial crisis has been that banks have been lending far too much money for residential real estate and providing far too little funding for productive enterprise such as new business ventures.[8] There is an element of truth in this – banks do have a preference for lending against housing because even if the mortgage-holder defaults and disappears into the ether, the house and land is fixed in its place and cannot go anywhere! After all most, though not all, properties are immobile. Lenders like this. You cannot easily disappear and take your house with you, and even if you could manage this, the land will still be there.

This tends to make lenders considerably more comfortable and as a result they can offer very long mortgage terms, at relatively low interest rates and often require only relatively small deposits. This is triumvirate of lending conditions that is unique to housing and as such it makes real estate unique as an investment. Every day Mum-and-Dad investors can use significantly more leverage – they can borrow more capital – to invest than is the case in other asset classes.

Banks are often understandably reticent to lend to new businesses at a competitive rate of interest without security.

The flip side to this is that a small business has yet to prove itself and has no proven track record of making consistent and predictable profits. As a result the business loan is likely to incur interest at a higher rate and be of a shorter term than a housing loan. Housing loans can be issued with a uniquely favourable conditions: 25 year terms or even longer, low borrowing rates and small deposits, but business loans offer none of these benefits.

One trend that has been playing out in recent years is that new business owners have become increasingly wise to these factors, and instead of using a business loan which incurs a necessarily high rate of interest, they borrow against a property they own to fund their start-up needs in that way. Recall that I stated earlier in the book that a new attitude to debt can be a powerful tool if it is used wisely. I recommended that while investment debt for real estate can be an effective method of leveraging results, debt for luxury assets or credit card consumer debt makes compounding work in reverse and lead your personal finances into a negative spiral.

While arguably taking out a business loan is so-termed *good debt* because you can use it to leverage results and returns from your business, it is also the case that the greater the debt hurdle is for a new business, the greater the likelihood that the new venture will fail. I would rather see investment debt used sensibly for well-located real estate investments which will continue to bring income and capital growth in perpetuity than for funding a business.

In life and in investment it is often true that the clearest thinkers can see the most outstanding results. This is one of the reasons that I believe using debt for share market investment can often be as much of a hindrance as it is a help. Instead of concentrating on the basics of acquiring high quality investments which can be held on to forever, the leveraged share market investor frequently obsesses over whether annual and even monthly returns are exceeding the interest charge hurdle.

Using a moderate amount of debt to leverage share market returns can be OK, particularly where the interest rate charged is low (which typically means a line of credit against a house rather than a margin loan), but generally those with the simplest plans are often the most successful over time. Investment debt in the share market can cloud thinking processes. What is right for me, may not be right for you, of course. However, I do want you to consider whether you can set up a new business venture with no new debt. With an absolute bare minimum of seed capital. This may sound challenging but I can assure it can be done, as discussed in further detail below.

Don't give up the day job!

As stated before, too often people think in black and white.

- 'How quickly can I retire?'
- 'When will I be financially free?'
- 'How long will it take me to launch a new business?'

It need not be so. In terms of financial freedom I encourage people to think more in terms of a see-saw or counter-balance. When you start out in adulthood you may be 100 percent dependent upon your salary income to survive and thrive. As you gradually begin to build a portfolio of assets you can slowly but surely become slightly less reliant upon your salary for building wealth, until eventually your investments begin to earn more than you can from your salary due to the snowballing effect. This takes patience, time and discipline, but eventually you surely will get there if you adhere to the task with gusto.

Why not try to think of your transition to self-employment in the same way? Some of the great business ventures have been started while the owners were still working in their day jobs. Clearly there is a delicate balance to be found here. It is not a smart idea to spend too much time focusing on a new business idea while you are being paid a salary if this detracts from your employment performance to the point where you are considered to be a drag. If you fail to add as much value to your current employer as you are being paid for, you may soon find yourself looking for a new job.

But this is not to say that you cannot sow the seeds of a small business idea while you are still in paid employment.[9] Think once again of a see-saw or counter-balance. As your business idea begins to grow you can become steadily less reliant upon your job, and this is particularly so if you have a portfolio of assets working for you too. The fact is that starting out a new business is hard and cash flows can be tight in the early days. One of the ideas which can helpful, which I used myself, is to switch to becoming a contract employee who works short term contracts instead of full time.

Clearly you need to have a reasonably strong commitment to the idea that you can eventually become self-employed in your own right in order to do this, but undertaking short term contracts can help to keep dollars rolling in while you are busy establishing yourself in business. Indeed, for anyone interested in starting out in small business, it is vital to understand the importance of cash flow, which I will consider in more detail in Chapter 20.

Premises – keep costs low

Years ago I worked in the mining industry in Australia and being a Group Financial Controller was based at a Sydney head office. One of the things I noticed before the financial crisis was how many small mining exploration companies which had yet to generate a single dollar in revenues let alone profits had head offices located in prime locations such as Australia Square Tower on George Street. Often when you visited these offices or walked past the reception area, there would not be a single soul at home, except for a very bored looking receptionist intermittently clicking 'Refresh' on their Facebook page.

Just think of the wasted overhead! Hundreds of thousands of dollars which had been sourced from investors via share placements and other capital raisings being squandered on prime location offices which were rarely used, and that is even before we get on to the subject of executive remuneration for loss-making ventures!

Keep operating costs down to a bare minimum in the early days.

Office costs for small business can be relatively punitive, which is why you might consider working from home when you first start a new business. In the modern era, working from home is quite feasible, provided that you have some space to use as an office and a strong internet connection. As you progress and your business gets up and running you may consider using serviced office space. Serviced offices can provide many of the benefits of renting a full office space including a telephone number, receptionist, a fax number and a street address which can be used to receive post as well as used as a registered office address, but at a fraction of the monthly expense.

Flexible staffing arrangements

Whilst working as a Financial Controller one of the most tedious tasks of each financial year for was the annual budgeting process. It still makes me shudder a little just even thinking about the countless hours of back and forth between cost centre bosses and head office. On the positive side of the ledger, I did learn a lot about how to maintain a very close control on costs in a business environment. One important matter which continually struck me was just how high staff and employment costs can be in the modern age.

When budgeting for staff costs if you just drop in a figure for a staff member's basic gross salary you will get a nasty surprise come the end of the year for the actual costs to the business are considerably higher. For example, there may be pension contributions to consider as well as bonuses, annual leave entitlements, long service leave entitlements, worker insurance costs, share option expense and more.

Part-time staff working contracts for discrete pieces of work are becoming increasingly common.

In small business you may not need to incentivise staff in the early days with share options or even bonuses, but there can nevertheless be significant ancillary costs of employing staff. When starting out in small business in the early days there may only be yourself and your spouse, or perhaps you and a business partner. When you require additional tasks completing it often makes sense to outsource or engage people on a freelance or contract basis. In some circumstances you may be able to agree with a contractor that they perform work for which you only pay them once your customer has paid you, which makes a tremendous difference to the cash flow profile of a small business.

Getting people to invoice you for actual work done can be an effective means of controlling costs and ensuring that you do not pay excessive employee costs for which you are not receiving a commensurate value for the business. When we started out in our business we employed contractors to undertake standalone tranches of work, and it generally worked well. While taking on an employee introduces a range of additional challenges, such as for example what to do when the employee takes annual leave for holiday, paying a contractor for discrete projects can work well for all parties involved.

Outsourcing and contract work is becoming increasingly common and offers flexibility.

Another idea is to look for graduates or students who are seeking work as an internship for a few weeks or a couple of months.[10] This is a good example of a win-win outcome as the intern can receive valuable training, experience and a reference for their CV, and you can benefit from their intelligence, enthusiasm and in many instances their superior and tech-savvy IT skills.

In the very early days of business you might be able to enlist some help from friends and family too, dependent upon your individual circumstances. If you go down this path, you still need to lay down a clear set of ground rules and may need to accept that others do not always share the same vision as you, particularly if you are not paying them a market rate for their time.

Websites – first impressions count!

Today it is entirely possible to set up a business website yourself for free. There are plenty of sites which allow you to do so, and they only begin to charge for premium or advanced functions such as increasing the bandwidth. If you are an IT whizz-kid, therefore, you might consider setting up your own website. One of the key premises of this chapter of the book is to get across the point that setting up your own businesses need not cost tens of thousands of dollars, and in many cases you do not need to shell out any cash up front at all until cash flow has begun to roll in. However, a word of caution here. I believe that a company website is one of the things that is definitely worth considering paying a fair price for.

Quality websites are worth paying for.

First impressions count. They always have and they always will. Judging people and situations quickly is a defence mechanism which is built into us as humans and helps us to simplify our responses to situations, and we cannot get away from this fact. For example, you probably know within one minute of meeting someone for the first time whether you find them attractive or not. Sometimes, of course, this first reaction may prove to be a costly error, but nevertheless, you probably do know!

It is very similar when you first encounter a business. If you think about a holiday or travel business, often the first interaction you have with that company is via its website. If you find the website to be slow, cumbersome, difficult to use, content-heavy or visually unappealing, your first experience of the business will not be a good one and the relationship is likely to degenerate from there.

Spending some money on a quality website is an investment which should see an ample return on your capital if done well and I encourage you to consult an expert for this process. Consider whether you have any business contacts who can help you design a great website for a reasonable price. My business partner has a friend in London who owns a website design business and he was able to design a quality website for us at a reasonable cost, while were able to help him out with our property services. That is another example of a win-win.

In our case we also engaged a business consultant to help with advising upon our business model, company name, our logo and branding. In the event the consultant recommended a business title which incorporated our surnames on the basis that we should be promoting our own expertise, while the logo that was designed for us has two letters which are designed to look like homes, in keeping with the real estate theme. Of equal importance the tagline of the business tells potential customers exactly what we do: 'Residential Property Buying Advisors in London, Sydney & Brisbane'. Straight to the point and no fluff.

Figure 19.1 – Example company logo

Ultimately how much you decide to spend on designing a website, a business plan and a logo for your business, including company letterheads and other associated products, will be dependent upon the level of funding you have available. If funds are short, then all of this can be done relatively cheaply, but do remember that a company website is often the first engagement which your customers have with your brand. If their experience is suboptimal then the quality of your business has immediately been compromised. Instead aim to blow clients away with your superior branding.

Business cards

When starting out my business partner Paddy and I joked that we wanted to avoid our business cards looking like they had been produced by the vending machine at Chelmsford train station. I am at risk of showing my age here, but a couple of decades ago there were indeed business card vending machines in public transport terminals! Times have moved on, but the point remains valid – your business card should be visually appealing and radiate quality. It should not look like something designed in a public transport depot.

Interestingly, business cards are generally considered to be less important than they once were, partly as a result of the increasing use of social media business sites such as LinkedIn. I must confess that when LinkedIn was first launched, although I did sign up for an account, I could not really see the point of it. At that time I was an employee with only a moderate interest in maximising my career potential which accounted for my apathy. When I wanted to transition from a mid-tier accounting firm to a Big 4 accounting firm my means of doing so was a specialist recruitment agent and not a social media connection site. I had little use, therefore, for the social media networking site.

What I can tell you is that this certainly all changes when you become a business owner or self-employed! I clearly lacked some foresight because the LinkedIn business is now said to be worth more than US$20 billion and all credible new business owners should have an account set up in order to connect with potential clients.[11] LinkedIn is useful because in the modern information age your key contacts will switch their positions, companies, telephone numbers, email addresses and fax numbers - if anyone actually still sends faxes - more frequently than they ever have before. Therefore a significant proportion of business cards in your Rolodex (do they even still exist?) are likely to be redundant or contain misinformation.

The value of a network can be almost priceless.

The great thing about LinkedIn is that once you have networked with someone for the first time, you can immediately be connected with them electronically forever - if you choose to be. If they change jobs or contact details, you will still be connected and you can continue to choose to share articles or information with them via the internet if you so desire.

All of the above said, people in small business should have a business card. Business cards are very useful for networking events, even if only to serve as a reminder to subsequently connect with someone on LinkedIn, and they add credibility. If you meet someone at a networking event and they provide you with a business card from a major corporation but you have nothing to exchange with them in return, rightly or wrongly you can come across as amateurish.

In terms of business card design, aim to make yours stand out from the crowd. I once went to a networking event where a lawyer got in contact with me solely because he wanted to know where we'd had our business cards designed, so impressed was he with their striking nature. I would of course like to claim credit for my superior refinement and style, but alas in truth our company branding was all down to my business partner. I don't have great taste in interior design either, come to think of it. When it comes to business cards, less can be more. While you want your business card to be striking, too much information can detract from its impact. As an example, our business card reveals only the following key information.

Figure 19.2 – Example business card - front

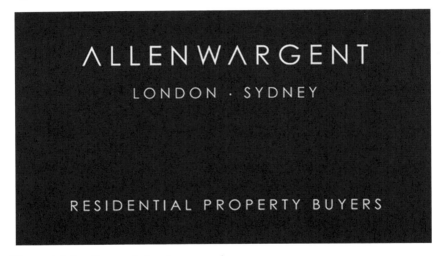

Figure 19.3 – Example business card - reverse

This is direct and straight to the point, and it tells you all you need to know about what the business in question actually does. As for the reverse of your business card, this simply needs to communicate all of the key contact details that potential customers and clients may need. Again, think direct and concise with all the key information clearly noted and nothing that is surplus to requirements.

Keep business cards and particularly the message of what your business actually does as clean, simple and as clear as possible. The only downside we found with our business cards has been that it is not possible to make notes on a business card with a black background. But perhaps this is also a plus? After all people should be taking note of your business cards rather than doodling on them! And in any case, all the pertinent information which they need should already be on there.

Email addresses

The name of our business is *Allen Wargent* residential property buyers and today we have offices in London, Sydney and Brisbane, although of course it was not always thus. How much credibility do you think we would have if you emailed me an enquiry about buying an investment property in Sydney and I replied from an email address denoted as allenwargent@hotmail.com? Or worse, if I pinged you back from petewargent@gmail.com? Hopefully the answer you came up with was: 'not very much!'

One of the first things to do when you have set up a new business is to register a website with the name of your business, potentially including the domain name in your country if you deem that necessary, and then to set up some email accounts for yourself and for enquiries. For example, in our business the first five email addresses by my business partner Patrick and I set up were:

- london@allenwargent.com
- sydney@allenwargent.com
- info@allenwargent.com
- paddy@allenwargent.com
- pete@allenwargent.com

Of course, we have more email accounts today, but that is how we started, out with these five basic accounts. The enquiry accounts can simply feed back to your main email account for the sake of efficiency.

Marketing and promotion

When marketing your business, you need to consider how you are going to stand out from the crowd. While it can be a good idea to model ideas that have worked for other successful businesses, ultimately your business needs to stand on its own two feet and offer a compelling reason for customers to choose *your* business ahead of the competition.

In our industry we had noticed that other buyer's agents often tried to be all things to all people. They offered property investment seminars, mortgage broking services, property management services, property strategy and investment advice, a home buyer service, rental searches, a search and acquisition for property investors and more. Any property-related service you might want, they would provide it. In essence, the larger firms were like the supermarkets of the industry, but we wanted our business to stand out from the crowd by offering a niche, bespoke or exclusive service to our targeted clients – property investors.

The best way to approach this is to begin by considering who your ideal customer is and work backwards from there. We decided that our ideal customer was a time-poor professional or overseas buyer who earned a good income or had strong equity but lacked the time and expertise to execute a property investment strategy. On the other hand, property management did not appeal to us so strongly, while the home buyer service we considered likely to be a lower margin product with a relatively poor return on time invested.

Your culture is also your brand.

Investors tend to buy property that makes good financial sense if the numbers stack up, but home buyers are on average a far more emotional breed – we could find a property which ticked 99 boxes out of 100 but that one missing item could always be a deal breaker and it would be back to square one.

I found a business mentor and paid for a course to spend some time on considering how to position ourselves in the market.[12] I considered this to be money very well spent. The problem I had was that I was getting dozens of enquiries from people who had seen me in the media or read my blog and investment books, but many were simply seeking free advice via sending endless questions. My mentor suggested that I mentally create four 'boxes' for my enquiries and categorised them accordingly:

- **Investment advice** questions – offer these clients a property investment strategy advice product or program

- **Property investment purchase** enquiry – offer the full buyer's agent service to these clients

- **Referrals** - such as home buyers or investors who want to invest in locations outside of our area of expertise – refer these on to an affiliate buyer's agent in the industry for a percentage share of their fee

- **None** of the above.

This simple piece of advice helped me no end and improved my efficiency in streaming the dozens of email enquiries I was receiving in the early days. Either enquiries would lead to a fee, in which case, great, or they would not, in which case I did not have to spend hours each week answering the same questions. In terms of market positioning, my business mentor suggested that we needed to position ourselves specifically in the market as a niche or boutique firm which aimed to offer a superior and bespoke niche service to our ideal clients. We amended our website for our Sydney office, for example, to state the following:

'We specialise in buying investment properties for clients in Sydney's eastern suburbs, the inner west and on Sydney's lower north shore in the $700,000 to $1.5 million price bracket'.

Clear, direct and succinct. I have seen it said in business books that people can love your business, hate your business or even sit on the fence, but they must always be crystal clear about what it is that you do. I believe that this is very true. By offering a specific description of what it is that your business does, your ideal clients know that you are the go-to guys in that sector or industry, while the customers which you do not want to attract will naturally be guided elsewhere.

Trade fairs

Trade fairs are generally a useful thing to attend. However, you should be very wary of spending thousands of dollars paying for a stand at a trade fair unless you are certain that you will recoup more than the cost in new sales. I have witnessed at first-hand businesses paying thousands of dollars for a stand at a trade fair for an entire weekend and make almost no sales at all. How about a better idea? Offer to speak at a trade fair for free. Design a compelling pitch a year in advance of an industry trade fair and offer to speak for no fee. This can be a great win-win as the trade fair gets some free quality content from you as a presenter and you can get to speak in front of dozens of potential clients.

If you are nervous about public speaking – and most people naturally are when they first do it – there are three proven ways to get better at it: practice, practice and more practice! Public speaking is simply a skill like any other and it can be learned. If you are chronically nervous join a public speaking group where you can learn to make mistakes and conquer you nerves in front of a small group first instead of in front of scores of potential clients!

Marketing budgets in the early days of business might be nil.

In the early days of business your marketing budget could be $nil, but this by no means must be a bad thing. Try approaching a bank for a small business loan and tell them that you need the funds for marketing. See what I mean? They are unlikely to extend it because banks understand that a successful business person will have the tenacity to start small and build a business without the need for too much loan credit. The good news is that in the modern era you do not need a substantial marketing budget in order to build a successful business, particularly if you can build a media profile and learn to leverage the power of the internet. However, this does take a good deal of time and commitment to achieve successfully.

Be brave, for if nothing is ventured, then nothing is gained!

If you sit at home and wait for publicity and results from marketing your business to come to you, you will be disappointed and on the first train back to the paid workforce. You have to get out there, be brave and try stuff. If people laugh at you or you get knock-backs, you have to be tougher again, because this will happen at some point! You need to bring it back to the Pleasure-Pain principle – if you want to success you need to associate pleasure to showing resilience and pain to feeling sorry for yourself when not everything goes according to plan (because it won't!).

Word of mouth marketing

The best source of business for a new venture is often from your existing clients. Therefore you should always aim to provide an exceptional service so that your existing clients come back to use you again and again. If you want to add value to your own life, first add value to others! Indeed, the key to building wealth and being successful is always to look to add more value than you charge every time.

When you have completed exceptional work for a client, aim to do two things. Firstly, ask them for a testimonial - hopefully if you have done great work for them, it will be a glowing one. And secondly, ask your clients to recommend your business to friends, work colleagues and family. While you should of course do this in a tactful manner and a way in which does not cause you to appear desperate, this is a legitimate marketing tool.

Our best clients are those who keep coming back to use our services every year. There is a great deal of satisfaction in that both for us and for them. We get repeat business, but better still we get to share in our clients' journeys from starting out as property investors right the way through to achieving and exceeding all of their financial goals and dreams.

Google advertising

A good friend of mine, Cate, was formerly a junior school teacher. However, her true passion was for health and fitness and she regularly ran marathons and ultra-marathons as well as competing in iron-woman competitions and other daring adventures which generally involved demonstrating unnatural levels of endurance. Eventually Cate decided that she wanted to set up a business as a personal trainer, which would combine her passion for education with that of health and fitness. Cate also wanted to become self-employed so that she could work on her own terms. Taking the plunge one summer, she decided to pay for a handful of Google ad-words and set up a personal website to which advertising traffic could be directed.

Advertisers can elect to bid for the Google keywords they want so that their sponsored adverts appear in the Google search engine results page. Google decides which adverts are displayed and in what positions based upon each user's maximum bid and quality store. Cate bid for the words 'personal trainer' and the name of the city in which she lives. Before too long she was receiving plenty of emailed enquiries and her business was up and running.

Over time, Cate was able to scale back her payments for Google ad-words as her personal training business established its reputation and began to grow by word of mouth. Today, Cate has more than 50 clients and has completely replaced her teacher's salary.

Social media

Social media today is an important tool for expanding your networking reach. Some of the key networking sites which all new businesses should look to use in addition to leveraging existing social networks include:

- Facebook

- Twitter

- LinkedIn

- YouTube

- Your blog page

- Your business website

- And more…

A new business does not need to go overboard in terms of social media. You should not, for example, spend so much time on social media that you actually forget to concentrate on the core elements of your business. However, all new ventures should make use of the sites listed above and others which specifically relate to your chosen line of business.

A key point on social media networking is that it should be done in a co-ordinated way. Don't use my social media content as a good example! My approach to social media over the years has been somewhat haphazard so I do not recommend using me or my business as a role model here. I have hardly used Facebook at all for productive enterprise, for example. I do use LinkedIn to connect with people but and promote articles, but perhaps not as frequently as I should.

In the social media world, you are what you share!

I enjoy using Twitter and use it regularly for keeping updated with news and views, and I often share interesting findings from our chart packs. But in truth I have also often tweeted inane nonsense about cricket, travel or pretty much anything else which springs to mind, which is not the recommended professional approach to business which you will find in any of the textbooks. That said, it probably has worked in my favour a little, because my esoteric tweets have kept people from becoming too bored with my Twitter feed. Some Twitter accounts are so relentless in their tweeting of business news or self-promotion that they can become more than a little wearisome.

The great thing about Twitter is that while it is has now become a global phenomenon, it is still possible to connect with key people in your industry and interact with them on a one-to-one basis. On the other hand, you should always think three times before tweeting a comment and be very wary of making bold political statements or being openly critical or rude. It is frequently amazing how far some people let themselves go when the blood rushes to their head. The problem with Twitter is that even if you delete a tweet, nimble-fingered folk can quickly take screen-grabs and retweet your *faux pas,* and thus those messages will exist in the social media Twittersphere forever!

All forms of leverage are a double-edged sword and must be used wisely.

Earlier in the book we noted that leverage is a double-edged sword. If you use debt to invest but buy poor or underperforming investments your losses will be magnified. And so it is with social media. Articles and social media comments can go viral, which is both an exciting and terrifying concept at the same time. If you write a great article for the media which goes viral, for example, your profile can be raised a thousand-fold. However, become involved in an online slanging matching or argument and the negative publicity can be felt just as keenly.

The reason for my lack of great efforts in the realm social media, to be blunt, was that through other media exposure we quickly generated more business and enquiries than we actually needed. This is a very happy position to be in, for sure, and is perhaps unusual for a start-up – most small businesses generally suffer from a lack of exposure and leads rather than having too many enquiries. My approach was therefore to focus on trying to win more of the clients we prefer, being private investors with ample funds to spend rather than homebuyers or clients for whom funds are tight. We developed a mechanism whereby we referred sundry work to an affiliate business rather than trying to be all things to all clients.

Are you a boutique business operator or a supermarket?

The analogy I like to use is that while others businesses may be the Wal-Mart or K-Mart firms, we want to be the niche business which people will seek out for specialist service. Of course, if building a huge business is your goal then you can look to address all of your enquiries and look to recruit staff in order to build your business empire! It all ultimately comes back to your goals.

If your goal is to build a huge business then you need to put systems, procedures and staff in place which can deal with a higher volume of clients and transactions. If, like me, your goal is to achieve a balance of work, play and travel then you may look to develop an outstanding niche or specialist business which clients will pay a premium to engage with.

For most business start-ups you should look to co-ordinate social media in a far more organised fashion than we ever have. Ideally you should link the Facebook, Twitter and LinkedIn pages of your business so that your content is published once across each of these sites in and coherent manner. There are different approaches to what you should post and how often which tends to vary depending upon what line of business you are in. You will find your own path on social media and discover what works and what does not.

> Social media marketing should be lively, clever, compelling and co-ordinated.

Quality of content is more important than quantity. I like to update my blog daily which keeps readers checking in each day (or subscribers receive a free daily email), but it is far better to provide a punchy daily insight than it is to bombard readers with thousands of words of content per day. Less is more, and if you provide too much, few people will read it.

Do remember to consider the 80/20 Principle when it comes to promotion. I have found that television, radio, selling books and writing for print media for me reaches thousands more people far more quickly than attending networking events, for example. If one million people tune into a television breakfast show, even if I am only on screen for six minutes I can connect with many more people much more quickly than I can by promoting an article on Facebook. Of course, when you start out, getting on television shows may not be possible. Want to know how to do it? Well, I recommend starting by…

Understanding the media

Social media is a great place to start out because it is free and anyone can do it. But if you want to maximise your leverage, aim to get coverage of your business into the mainstream media. For example, with a real estate business I look to promote my business in the following forums among others:

- Serious financial newspapers

- Mainstream newspapers

- Breakfast television shows

- Radio stations and shows

- Property, finance and investment magazines

- News media and property websites

I have contributed to or appeared across all of these outlets over the years. They all reach a slightly different audience and each requires a different skill-set, but all of them are valuable sources of publicity and profile in their own individual way. How can you aim to get in the media? First and foremost you need to raise your profile, build your online presence and establish your credibility.

Find out which journalists are writing about small business, entrepreneurs or articles on the industry which you are specialising in. Then you need to find a way to contact them, via a telephone call, email or social media to let them know what your business does and why they might want to write about you. Even if you receive no publicity immediately the aim of the game is to build a level of trust, respect and credibility with the journalists in your industry or sector of the market, so that in future when they need a quote or copy you are the person which they instantly know to turn to.

Start small and build slowly

We have covered a lot of ground here in a relatively short space. There is so much involved in the building of a successful business that the idea can seem overwhelming and this causes many to become defeated before they have even started. Just like anything else in life the solution to feeling overwhelmed is to break down the bigger goals into smaller and thus more achievable and believable targets. In the next chapter we will consider how you can use the 80/20 Principle to focus and double down on what is working and you can gradually snowball or compound your results over time.

Chapter 19 summary

» The idea of building a business can seem overwhelming, so start small and build your business step by step

» Keep business cards and your website direct and to the point, and don't overload them with esoteric information or too much content

» Cash flow is king and you must get paid promptly for any work that you do

» People can love your business or hate your business – but they must be absolutely clear about what it is that you do

20

Minding Your Own
Business

20

Be guided by your passion

The 80/20 Principle holds that you will get most of our results from a few of your actions. More than this, you are more likely to be successful at something you are passionate about. Imagine if your day revolved around doing stuff that you are genuinely excited about – this makes all the difference to the way you can live your life because you will automatically become more enthusiastic and energetic.

However, while this is true, you also need to get the details right, and to do so in business you may need to engage help or learn the appropriate business skills over time. Business is infinitely more enjoyable when everything is operating smoothly, making you money, and you are working with your ideal customers. It tends to be less so if you are working with awkward customers and you are getting bogged down in administrative procedures, complaints, cash flow challenges or compliance issues!

Structure and compliance

Broadly speaking business owners and self-employed persons have a choice of whether to operate as sole trader or partnership, or to set up a company within which to carry out their business. There are benefits and drawbacks to each structure. A company offers some level of flexibility in terms of distribution of profits (salary, director's fees or dividends) and potentially asset protection. A self-employed person who operates a sole trader may appear in essence to be similar to an employee, yet may still be able to claim legitimate deduction for expenses which are directly attributable to the business.

A company in its simplest terms is a set of legal and administrative documents which you trade and operate within, but there are significant implications for how this impacts the way in which you do business and pay taxes. As a separate legal entity a company can offer you some legal protection, although you may still require professional indemnity insurance to insure against you being sued personally.

> Get the structure of your business right at the outset
> – this can prevent headaches later on.

This is potentially a huge subject with myriad different angles which might be covered, and as such much of this topic remains outside the scope of this book. If you are unsure about the benefits of setting up a company and why you might choose to do so, speak to an accountant, particularly a professional who is familiar with company compliance as well as having a detailed understanding of corporation and personal taxes. While I of course encourage readers to always save money where possible, sometimes it is much more sensible to pay for expert advice, and this is one such case. If you are not familiar with company law and taxation implications, pay for an expert who is.

Your products or services

Think again of the 80/20 Principle and acknowledge the following key rule of business:[1]

> 80 percent of revenues and profits in your business are likely to come from 20 percent of the products your offer.

What this means is that you should focus on having few products but ensure they are outstanding. For example, our business is in real estate - plenty of other real estate companies diversify into property management, investment strategy advice, vendor advocacy and other revenue streams, but thinking the 80/20 way I quickly realised that what our business can do better than other for customers is to achieve great results for them as investors through buying the right investment property to suit their financial goals.

We stripped back the business so that we offered only one main service – sourcing and buying property for investors – which itself accounts for more than 80 percent of our revenue streams and bottom line profits. When it came to expanding the business, instead of offering more *products*, we opened *another office*. It is possible to spread yourself too thin in geographical terms too. From my own personal property investing experience I knew that the best markets were London and Sydney, and certain specific regions within those cities, so we started with offices in those locations.

We also wanted the offices to be in the best possible locations, so our London office, for example, is in Mayfair, and our Sydney office is in Martin Place. Location is everything in the world of real estate, and not only for investors, but for businesses too. Over time, we did add another product, a strategy consultancy deliverable where we advise on property investment strategy for clients. However, in the true spirit of the 80/20 Principle it is nevertheless the case that well over 80 percent of our revenue is derived from our main property research and acquisition product. This is one of the key takeaway points from the 80/20 Principle. Do not try to be all things to all people or try to diversify too broadly.

Double down on successes.

Instead, recognise what is working well for you and double down on it.[2] Where you have found there to be success in a certain product that you offer, instead of thinking of what other products you can provide, try to consider how you can maximise revenues from your existing successful product. How can you add value to more people with your successful product?

The importance of cash flow in small business

While I at times found working in the accountancy field something of a drag, I must say that the skill-set you learn as an accountant is absolutely irreplaceable. When young people today ask me about career choices, I tend to be wholeheartedly in favour of anyone who is considering getting a Chartered Accountancy qualification. Even if this not your true area of passion, the grounding that this qualification gives you can open so many doors for you to go on and achieve whatever you want to in business.

Accountants are often able to understand finance, how businesses run and company financial statements far better than others can – this is because they learn the basic principles of finance and book-keeping from the ground up. I recall that one of the most crucial things which we learned in the early days of accounting school was the importance of cash flow. I certainly have no inclination to write a handbook of accounting terms here, but it is vital for a would-be business owner to understand a few key terms, including:

- **Revenue** or **turnover** – the value of your sales

- **Net profit before tax** – the net figure of what is left of your revenue after all costs except for tax charges

- **Net profit after tax** – should be self-explanatory after you have read the preceding bullet point!

- **Cash flow** – the actual cash which transacts in and out of your business

Casting my mind all the way back to accounting school, one of the first things we learned was how even an expanding business which is generating huge profits and ever greater revenues can still go bust. How so? The reason is that businesses do not become insolvent because they make profits or losses, they go under because they run out of cash. A growing business which is guilty of overtrading can find itself unable to pay its liabilities as they fall due because their cash flow profile is not right.

For example, if a company sells 1000 widgets for $10 each expecting to make $2 profit per widget, the business may appear to be generating a nice profit of $2000. But if customers refuses to pay for the finished product widgets for several months then the business can run into problems because it has to pay for its new raw material inventory other manufacturing costs up front. In the early days the business may muddle through, but where the widget firm tries to expand quickly its up-front costs may fall due well before the receivables from customers roll in to balance the books. If no loan or bridging finance can be sought, the widget business goes bust...despite having no shortage of sales and profits recorded in the monthly accounts.

During the financial crisis I witnessed the heart-breaking situation of friends losing their businesses because they had clients owing large balances which they were unable to pay. Tempting though it is to focus on sales and profits, there is absolutely no point in making a sale to a customer who is unable to pay. In fact, doing so is likely to send *your* business into a funk as well as theirs.

> When business ventures fail it is due to a lack of cash flow, not a lack of profit. Cash is king.

In my line of business, because I help clients to invest, it is relatively straightforward for me to ask potential customers how much cash they have available. After all, if I do not know the answer to that question, then I can hardly help them to achieve their investment goals. Most businesses do not have that luxury, but you do need to be fairly certain that your customers are creditworthy because bad debtors are often what send business ventures to the wall.

Be very wary of customers who run up large debtor balances and do not be tempted to perform more work for them if there is even a small chance that they may never pay you. Equally, be wary of new customers who place very large orders. You need to be sure that they can and will pay you before you commit to making substantial sales.

Non-payment of outstanding customer balances are commonly a cause of a business venture failure.

It is not always possible, but the best way to improve the cash flows of a business is to get paid for your product or service in advance.[3] For example, my company now offers two products. One is a property investment strategy service, and for this we charge the full fee in advance for the simple reason that we do not want to tip hours of work into a preparing a strategy and investment plan for one of our clients only to find that they do not pay us later.

Can you get paid in advance?

However, it is not always possible to bill in advance. Our main service is a property search and acquisition service, and it would not be reasonable to expect clients to pay the full fee in advance for work that has not yet been carried out. In this circumstance what we do is charge an engagement fee which is a percentage of the total fee.

Can you charge an engagement fee or take a customer deposit?

An engagement fee serves two purposes. Firstly, it provides some small compensation for time spent in the event that a client decides to never purchase a property using our services. But more importantly, a client who is prepared to pay a small engagement fee, in our experience, is far more likely to be a serious buyer and not a tyre-kicker. Consider ways in which you can make these ideas work for your business too. It is not always achievable to have clients pay for your product or service dependent upon what line of work you are in, but one thing is certain is that if you do not ask you will not get.

To be successful in business it is absolutely vital to understand the importance of cash flow. This is why the primary financial statements of even the largest business include not only an *income statement* or profit and loss account (which details revenue, costs and profits or losses) and a statement of financial position or *balance sheet* (detailing assets and liabilities of the business), but also a *cash flow statement* which shows how funds have flowed in and out of the business over the reporting period.

Invoice promptly

When you set up a small business, it is a great idea to focus on what you are passionate about because this is what excites you and therefore you will excel at it. However, an entrepreneur has to do more than what they are passionate about. In a small business or start-up venture you may need to be the research and development officer, the sales team, the marketing team, the distributions manager, the book-keeper, the accountant and much more! Of course, you can choose to outsource areas of the business when you have the funds to do some particular tasks which you find tiresome or are administrative in nature. You may not have this luxury in the early days, however.

> Billing on a timely basis is vital. You must always get paid for what you do.

One task which people seem to put off more than others is *invoicing*. And they should not! It is vital to the survival of a small business to ensure that you are paid promptly for what you do. Some entrepreneurs do not enjoy the process of invoicing because they do not like to ask their customers for money. This is the fastest route to failure and your business becoming insolvent. If you do work, you simply must get paid for it, and get paid for it on a timely basis.

One thing which is worth remembering is that if you invoice clients on a timely basis they are more likely to pay it on a timely basis too. If you put off the task for a few weeks or months simply because you don't feel like doing it, you can be sure that your client or customer will be less than motivated to pay the balance quickly too (and who can blame them, really?).

Chase payments

If a customer owes you money then you need to chase it - simple as that. In small business it is common for clients to find all manner of ways to delay payment, but this simply serves to put more pressure on your own cash flows. In short, you either need to be mentally tough enough to chase up late payment of your invoices, or to engage someone else to do it for you.

Book-keeping, record keeping and accounts

Record keeping is potentially quite dull, but it is essential to do it right in order for a small business to be successful. Book-keeping is one of the tasks which can easily be outsourced by a start-up business, but I will make the suggestion here that you might want to learn how to do this yourself, at least in the early days. As your business develops you will probably find that your time is better spent elsewhere, but in the early growth phase of your business there can surely be no better discipline than understanding where your business is spending or leaking money and how frequently it is getting paid.

> Always maintain a separate bank account for your business.

All business owners should maintain a separate bank account from their personal finances in order to keep funds separate and to allow them to see how the business is truly performing. There is strong empirical evidence to suggest that entrepreneurs who keep a separate business account are more likely to consider funds within a business account part of the business, whereas those with co-mingled finances tend to view business funds as an extension of their own finances and treat those funds accordingly.

It also looks particularly amateurish to invoice customers using the details of a personal bank account. I recommend keeping a simple spreadsheet of your business bank account and categorising all forms of income and expenditure at the end of each month. This forms the basis of an income statement or profit and loss account:

Income statement

- Revenue

- Costs and expenses

- Net profit before tax

- Tax

- Net profit after tax

You may not understand how taxes work such as corporation or company tax, or transactional taxes such as Goods and Services Tax, and I do recommend that you learn. At the very least I suggest that you learn the book-keeping skills to keep a close track of what your business is doing in terms of its cash flow. If you are not sure what to do with relation to tax book a simple accrual based upon an estimate of what might be payable based upon a percentage of your profit. That way you should get no nasty surprises when your tax payments falls due at the end of the financial year.

Balance sheet

The other financial statements include a statement of financial position or balance sheet, which details:

• Cash

• Receivables or debtors (i.e. outstanding invoices to be paid by customers)

• Payables or creditors (e.g. loans, supplier liabilities)

• Tax liabilities

• Equity in the business (e.g. share capital)

• Accumulated profits or losses

As the name implies, your balance sheet should balance in accordance with principles of double entry book-keeping. The total of your assets less the total of your liabilities should be equal to your equity, being the initial share capital and the total accumulated profits of the business. And, thirdly you should maintain a...

Cash flow statement

A statement of cash flows reconciles the opening cash balance of the period to the closing cash balance through analysing:

• Opening cash

• Operating revenue received from customers

• Operating expenses paid

• Taxes paid

• Investment cash flows (e.g. purchase of a new laptop or office equipment)

• Financing cash flows such as loans taken out or loan repayments

• Closing cash

For larger companies there will be a host of other financial information which sits behind the primary financial statements in notes and points of disclosure, but for smaller and start-up businesses the above data covers the bulk of what is to be disclosed in a comprehensive set of accounts.

This is where an accountant immediately has an in-built advantage in small business over those who lack financial literacy. It is absolutely imperative that you understand the cash flows of your business. Therefore I recommend either learning the appropriate basic book-keeping skills to prepare the above data or engaging a book-keeper who can spend a few hours each month preparing at the very least the three financial statements listed above. You should also maintain detailed listings or sub-ledgers of:

- Customers or debtors who have still to pay you

- Invoices which you have raised and those which still need to be raised

- Client enquiries and leads to follow up

- Contact details of existing clients

While this may be one of the more tedious parts of being in business, it is imperative to be well organised so that you know which customers to contact and when. Remember that your existing customers can represent repeat business, or when you do great quality work for them, your existing clients can be your strongest points of referral for new leads.

Attracting and retaining the right customers

Ask anyone who is experienced in business and they will tell you that one of the key rules of success is to learn what your customer wants and then to exceed their expectations every time. One of my best mates of more than 25 years is a butcher named Roy. This might seem unusual given that I know longer eat meat, though I did in fact often visit his shop as a customer often back in my younger years! Roy explains that one of the most important things to learn in his line of work is to get to know and learn exactly what each customer wants in terms of product and service, and then to deliver this to them each and every time they visit the shop, without needing to be prompted. This is absolutely true no matter what industry you operate in.

If you want to be successful in any field, aim to add more value than you are paid for every time.

This is largely about getting your product and the customer service right. My friend Roy the butcher has a couple of long-term customers which have been ordering the same cut of lamb every weekend for more than 25 years, so he always ensures that he has those ready in advance of their arrival. Other customers, explains Roy, want to feel as though they are receiving a special service and engage in a short conversation each week, so for those customers it is vital to remember their name and what you discussed with them last time they visited. Roy always knows what they ordered last time they were in the shop and never fails to make a point of asking him how they enjoyed their cut of meat during the week.

In this day and age customers could easily opt for convenience and choose to do all of their food shopping under one roof at the local supermarket. Yet instead Roy's butcher business continues to thrive because he knows what his customers want and they come back for a superior quality of meat every week without fail as a result. People today have greater disposable incomes than ever before and will also pay a premium for quality and outstanding service. A butcher like Roy will put on a great show of preparing meat for each customer individually because he wants them to see that the customer receives outstanding quality of product and service every time. And it works.

Who are your ideal customers?

The 80/20 Principle also tells you that:

> 80 percent of your company's profits are likely to come from 20 percent of your customers.[4]

What this means, of course, is that it is important to focus on finding those key customers which will provide the majority of your revenue streams and profits. Perhaps you do not need to worry too much about the smaller customers? Of course it is acknowledged here that running a successful business is all about reputation, and therefore you should never provide a bad service to a customer - it may be better to provide no service at all than a sub-standard one.

My business partner Paddy and I quickly understood that finding wealthy clients to buy investment property is a profitable activity. Firstly, this is because these types of clients are likely to be repeat customers who see the big picture rather than get lost in the details, and perhaps they may buy a property every year. And secondly, wealthy clients tend to mix with other wealthy clients and therefore can refer new business. Another fast route to success can be to find a residential investment fund which can commit to investing millions of dollars with you per year, every year. We therefore targeted several investment funds which took a great deal of time and effort up front.

Even more than this the 80/20 Principle holds that when you find customers who have been profitable for you, double down on your success. That is to say, take a step back and think: how can I find even more customers like these? And don't forget repeat sales! If you are short on leads, customers and sales never forget to go back to your biggest and best clients to see if you can do more business for them. This is certainly true in real estate where customers who have received an outstanding service come back to invest with our company a second and third time, but it is surprisingly often the case in other industries too.

Difficult customers

Unfortunately, the 80/20 Principle also holds that:

> 80 percent of your complaints are also likely to come from 20 percent of your customers...and probably not the same 20 percent of customers which are generating your profits!

There are essentially two ways to resolve customer complaints. Firstly, identify the root causes of complaints, since the majority of them are likely to come from a minority of problems, and aim to solve or eliminate these issues. Alternatively, considering jettisoning the customers that are causing your headaches, since something in the process is not working correctly, either for you or for them.

The solution is either to *trim the bottom* – to get rid of those customers that are providing most of your headaches and comparatively little of your revenue – or to find the 20 percent of problems that are causing 80 percent of the complaints and eliminate those problems! The answer depends upon the type of business you are in the process of building, but either way you will find that business is far more pleasurable and successful both for you and your clients if you can eliminate the root causes of customer complaints.

Dealing with different people

One of the most difficult skills for an entrepreneur to master is the ability to interact successfully with a wide range of people. I strongly suspect the reason I was able to do this well was that when I was growing up my family moved around a lot, and I went to four very different schools in very different parts of the country.

Perhaps by necessity I became something of a chameleon and found that I became able to mix comfortably with people from a wide range of different backgrounds. This can be an invaluable skill to have in your armoury as an entrepreneur because a successful business owner needs to be able to work with all different types of people. In an international business like ours, we work with people from countries all over the world too, particularly from Europe, Asia, Australasia and America.

Entrepreneurs need strong and versatile people skills.

How can you work with such a wide range of people successfully without upsetting them or saying the wrong thing? The answer is that you need to have the ability to quickly establish other people's *values* in order to establish a sound relationship with them. People become upset when you unintentionally clash with their rules for living, so you need to first establish and understand what their rules are. This may seem like a tough task, but once you are aware of this fact, successful relationships can more easily be formed on a common ground.

If you get this wrong and continually break or violate the rules and values of other people they will quickly disengage and may begin to become upset and perhaps resentful. Even if they do not communicate this to you verbally, you may begin to feel or sense their negative vibes. The key to building successful relationships in business and in life is through clarity of communication. Let others know your own rules and values and therefore they can easily meet them, while you can encourage them to be similarly open to presenting their own rules and values. This way you can build trust and work towards win-win outcomes.

Breaking down into small targets

How can it be possible for someone starting out to possibly imagine building a business which they enjoy running without creating undue stress, yet allows money to flow to them? It may not seem at the outset as though such an outcome could ever be achieved. The secret, as you have no doubt guessed from the paragraph header, is to start small and to compound your business - slowly but surely building your expertise and knowledge, leveraging your networks, spreading your profile through word of mouth and client testimonials.

If you are planning to build a business which sells physical products, aim to start small with products that do not require large sums of cash outlay up front or in advance. You will need to find products which can command a reasonably high *margin* between the costs and the sales price leading to an acceptably high profit on each sale you make.

Look for high profit margins on your products.

If you start out by planning to emulate Microsoft, you will fail. Larger businesses have huge advantages and economies of scale allowing them to crush competition through superior branding, advertising and research and development techniques. So how can small business ever compete with larger firms? Through focus, expertise and delivering an outstanding bespoke service. A small, niche business can offer customers a superior experience which the right customers will pay handsomely for.

The only proven way to reach huge goals is to set smaller goals and targets which can lead you forward. If you have a goal of making $100,000 in sales in a month then you may feel that you have failed before you have started. Of course, I am not saying that every business can make $100,000 of sales in a month – some cannot – but what is certainly the case is that if you believe that the goal is not achievable then you will not be able to reach it.

If I was to set myself a target of increasing the turnover in my business of $100,000 in just one month, the way in which I would do so would be to break the target down into smaller and thus more achievable tasks. $100,000 of revenue for me might mean finding seven new customers or clients who will pay $15,000 each for an outstanding service. Seven customers already sounds like a more achievable goal than conjuring $100,000 of revenue out of thin air! How can I go about finding seven new customers? If this is a goal I want to achieve, lots of ways:

- Mailshot my previous clients to ask if they are interested in repeat business
- Give incentives to existing customers to use your service or buy your product again
- Ask existing clients whether they may have any referrals
- Run a short advertising campaign in a trade magazine
- Follow up all previous enquiries that have been made to our business
- Get yourself in the media through sheer persistence!
- Smile and dial - make 100 phone calls to target clients (it may not be easy to do, but it can definitely work)
- Offer to speak for free at events or at businesses or trade organisations
- Attend networking events or use affiliate marketing
- Frequent social media sites
- Contribute to chat forums
- Find out what larger businesses are doing to win clients - and do it better than them
- And much more...

I have barely begin to consider here of the many possible ways in which you could look to generate new leads. Of course, revenue does not come for free – you then have to deliver the service or product! But even just quickly brainstorming some of the methods which could be used to generate new leads makes me realise just how few of them we have pursued to the greatest of their potential.

We have been fortunate in that our business generated enquiries without us needing to advertise widely or use challenging sales techniques. This is perhaps unusual for a young business, but I can tell you that situation did not arise for free or by accident. Over the years I have spent thousands of hours effectively working for free and raising my profile through publishing books, writing media articles and undertaking press interviews, appearing on television and radio shows and so on.

My goal was to first raise my expertise to a level that was equal to or above that of all equivalent experts in my specialist field, then to demonstrate that knowledge via media work, social media and my books. Through doing this consistently over time you can convey to potential customers your level of expertise in your field that they will gladly pay to use, because you can add genuine value to the quality of their lives. So while it may appear that success came easily for our business, in effect it did not because I invested thousands of hours in advance by raising my own profile and expertise.

Acting big

While most businesses start out small, it is generally not a great idea to communicate to your clients that you are a tin pot operation, even if that is what you actually are when you start out.

Website contact details

The first point of interaction with your business for many of your customers will be your website. If your website looks cheap, they will assume that you are cheap. It can be patently obvious when you look at the contact details page for a small business when they are pretending to be something that they are not. For example, when there are 23 email addresses including for sales, marketing, promotion, support, information, accounts, media…and so on. If the business has only been in existence for a week, you would hardly be fooling anyone that all of these emails are not going to be feeding into one bloke's email account.

However, you do not want your business website to be directing queries to amateur-looking email accounts such as jimmy123@hotmail.com either. As previously noted when we set up our business, in the early days we simply had our own email accounts and a handful of enquiry email accounts on the company website which fed back to us. This represents plenty of accounts for a start-up venture.

When you are starting out in business you may be working from home, but home telephone numbers on a website are generally not a good idea. Potentially you could include your mobile number, although personally I am not convinced that this looks too flash either. Our solution in the early days was to use serviced offices which come with a receptionist service included. This way you have a landline number and if you are out of the office then the receptionist can easily forward the call through to your mobile phone.

Serviced offices

Serviced offices will become increasingly common hubs for small businesses in the future. The basic concept is that you pay a moderate monthly fee for shared office space with common areas, business lounges and work stations where you can base yourself and undertake your work. I found this to be a great solution in the early days of our business and the costs need not be too prohibitive. The idea of working from home may sound appealing but I never really liked the idea – I like to get out and about and there are too many distractions at home anyway, such as satellite television.

A serviced office package should include your business having a unique telephone number which the reception recognises when incoming calls are received - the receptionist therefore knows to answer with your business name. This is infinitely more professional than you needing to answer your phone while driving or standing in the lunchtime sandwich queue. The receptionist can then take a message or forward the call to your work station or to your mobile phone.

If you have clients who want to come in to your office for a meeting then there may be an additional charge to book a meeting room space for the period of time within which you intend to use it. Serviced offices are a great solution for fledgling businesses because they do not cost the earth but they do offer you a range of very useful and professional services.

Tenacity

I was not sure where to put this section of the book, but it does need to be written somewhere so I will simply drop it in here.

If you want to be successful in business you have to be tenacious.

If you are unable to display tenacity in business or self-employment, you will certainly fail to maximise your potential. This may seem a harsh assessment, but it is nevertheless a true statement. In the paid workforce you can delegate, seek support from colleagues, or if things get really bad at work you can simply change jobs. A start-up business venture affords few such luxuries.

It is a simple truth that in small business you will have good days and bad days when you are fed up and feel like you have had enough. And you will have days when you have arguments, frustrations, disappointments and miserable outcomes. There will be great successes too and days when your heart bursts with pride or excitement. However, as I have already said in this book, it is how you deal with the times of adversity which will ultimately determine the level of your success. Some people do not cope well with the tough times and dark days and their business will inevitably fold.

It is an unfortunate fact that when you decide to chase your dreams and embark upon the road less travelled there will be those who try to hold you back, criticise you or tell you that you are doing the wrong thing. This is definitely the case when it comes to investing, and the same is true when it comes to starting out in business.

> There will be good days and bad days – it is how you respond to the tough times that counts.

Friends, family and your peer group may be uncomfortable with the idea of you reaching for the stars or taking a different path, partly because it causes them to question their own beliefs and preconceptions and sometimes out of a genuine concern for your wellbeing. Generally, people are far more comfortable with you taking the same well-trodden path as them, and often are more comfortable with the idea of you being a moderate under-performer than a great success.

Think back to how people have reacted in the past towards you being thrifty and saving to achieve a goal – was it often vaguely disapproving, as though you are being something of a spoil-sport? But if you decide to spend hard on a luxury holiday or a big weekend on the town? Why not? Live for today! You are only young once! You need to understand why people react this way, but here is a small clue as a heads up: it is generally for their own benefit than it is for yours.

Another thing which you need to be ready for if you do any form of media work is adverse reaction which can range from mild disagreement, to strong criticism to outright abuse or even worse! My advice is to be ready for it, because if you have an online presence you will experience some or all of the above, and the level of intensity can be ratcheted up the further up the success ladder you move.

> To succeed in business you will need the mental strength to overcome negative feedback.

Some people say: 'If you don't like it, get out of the game' or 'if you cannot stand the heat, get out of the kitchen'. While this is to some extent true, I have found that it does not necessarily help you to cope with instant online feedback very well. Firstly, you need to understand that online comments and feedback are nothing more than simply words on a computer screen. It can feel personal, but when you stop to consider the sad keyboard warrior types who feel the need to abuse people from behind the anonymity of a computer screen, there really is little to fear or even concern yourself with at all.

As I write articles on real estate markets for the media, an emotive subject at the best of times (particularly for people who do not own any property), I have copped more than my fair share of abuse and even threats. Ridiculous and pathetic, yes, but nevertheless true. Of course I do not take abuse too seriously, but you may need to be able to find a coping mechanism as it affects some people significantly more than others.

I turned to one of my business and investing mentors Michael Yardney for advice on this very subject once after a bout of particularly nasty comments. Michael has been around the block for a long time and in the property business long enough to have seen it all more than once. Michael not only helped me to understand the psychology of people who write abuse online, but also offered me these wise words:

'You need to understand that abuse can be hurtful. But you will find that each time it happens the comments hurt just a little bit less and eventually you will develop a thicker skin. Of course, such matters will always hurt a little bit because we are human…and that's a good thing! But it is important to remember that the impact becomes just a little less each time.'

I found this to be very useful advice. Not only does adverse feedback become less hurtful each time it happens, you can even begin to use it as a motivational tool. The truth of the matter is that anyone with an increased media profile will see as an increased level of negative feedback. This is simply a sad part of modern life! These days I see most negative feedback as a positive – if I am getting a reaction then I must be progressing, and the more negative responses I get under my belt the more I must be making an impact.

Other bad days and genuine mistakes

When you are self-employed and responsible for all aspects of your business, you have to accept that some days you will not get things exactly right which can lead you to feel disappointment, hurt, embarrassment or end up taking good-natured or bad-natured criticism. Always aim to over-service customers and add more value than you charge for rather than ever risk under-delivering.

Raising your personal profile also comes with many such additional pressures. Some people have a fear of public speaking, while others are terrified of appearing on the radio or television or in news print. If you provide online content you can expect that some people will not like your views and will tell you so. Learning to deal with criticism and mistakes are part and parcel of having a public or media profile.

As someone who once committed the cardinal sin of gently mouthing part of a profanity live on a national breakfast show (and subsequently watched the clip played back more than once by a prime-time comedy production with a cleverly edited bleeped out audio - thank you kindly Channel Ten!), I feel that I can speak with a certain air of authority on this subject. The thing to remember is that what may seem to be of importance to you is unlikely to be quite so important for everyone else, and very few mistakes in life are of permanent or pervasive importance.

> Learn to accept worst-case scenarios and move beyond your limiting thought patterns.

What about genuine down days? In chapter 15 I already considered the important question of how to change your mood or state when you are experiencing negativity or unbearable frustration. Listening to music, going for walk, heading to the gym or for a run, phoning friends, playing sport… whatever it is that works for you, do some of that!

On some particularly dark days even these mood-changing choices may not feel like they are working. Ultimately to experience ongoing success in business and in life you need to bring this all back to the Pleasure-Pain Principle. You need to link massive pain to the notion of letting negative thoughts and feelings or the criticism of others stopping you from achieving your goals. One simple but effective thought which I kept coming back to was this one basic mantra.

> 'I will not let this stop me from achieving my goals of being successful in business. Not today and not ever!'

This sounds so very simple, but I found that it has definitely worked for me over the years. Even on the toughest days, make a decision to learn the lessons and messages that negative outcomes and emotions are sending you and resolve to come back stronger than ever before. Are you going to let small-minded criticism or negative emotions and feelings hold you back from achieving your goals? I will answer that question for you – no, you most sure as heck are not!

Getting support

Setting up a small business can be a surprisingly lonely affair at times. While you may spend much of your time out networking or talking to clients, engaging the services of others or outsourcing – all of which involve some form of human contact – being in business can be an all-encompassing experience and difficult to switch off from.

It is fairly likely, if not close to a certainty, that you will have days when you feel low and wonder whether you are doing the right thing, particularly when you are first starting out in business. I have already discussed earlier in the book that one thing you can do is write for yourself a long list of ways in which you can change your mood when you are feeling low or disheartened. I used to like going for a very long walk around Sydney's Botanical Gardens and the Opera House in the early days of my business travails, which I found helped quite a bit!

However, some days it can still seem almost impossible to shake off negative feelings. This is where some moral support can be invaluable. Having someone to bounce ideas off or get a second opinion from is absolutely priceless. Fortunately for me my wife Heather is also a Chartered Accountant with a good deal of experience in real estate – she owns a substantial property and share market portfolio of her own and also previously worked in the finance team of one of Australia's largest property development companies. In short, she knows her stuff and was always a rock of support and infinitely reassuring confidante.

Surround yourself with like minds and positive, supportive people.

When Heather fell pregnant she left the paid workforce and advised that she would be quite happy to take on some of the administrative tasks of my business such as invoicing and preparing our company accounts. This allowed me to concentrate on winning new business and executing contracts. It can be a case of all hands to the pump in the early days of a business, and any additional help you can pull in from friends, family or your other half can be very useful! In the start-up stage of our business I always found the support from my wife utterly invaluable.

Starting out in business can be extremely testing for anyone and having another person to bounce ideas off or provide another perspective can be priceless. I know that my business partner Paddy Allen said that when he set up our London office years ago found the process exciting but also extremely testing. The hours involved in small business can be challenging, and many business owners find it very difficult to switch off from work even after they have arrived home from the office. If you do not have a partner or friend to offer you moral support, find some from elsewhere. Why not join an entrepreneurs group or find a kindred spirit who you can share ideas and problems with?

In the middle of 2014 I recall my old mate Alastair Cook was being crucified in the British press after a string of poor results for the England cricket team. No fewer than eight former England cricket captains demanded that he resign from the post immediately, which is surely some kind of record! At the age of just 29 his career as England captain seemed to be hanging in the balance while the popular and tabloid media pilloried him for day after day.

'They say the darkest hour is right before the dawn' – Paul Kelly.

And then in July came a change of fortune! Suddenly, 'Cookie' was scoring big runs and England started winning, and not only by small margins. Captain Cook went from zero to hero in a matter of only two months. When I asked him over dinner one night how he had coped with being so relentlessly smashed by journalists and former players his answer was instructive. Ali advised that he had retreated to the farm owned by his in-laws and it was the calm and reasoned support of his wife and her family which had helped him to resolve to see it all through.

I believe that there are two valuable lessons to learn from this. Firstly, support can make all the difference. And secondly, no matter how much pressure one might be feeling, when I hark back to Ali's situation and the relentless tabloid intrusions, I realise that others will always be experiencing much worse! Interestingly my in-laws are also farmers and I found the same thing – sometimes getting away from it all to the bush to re-boot for a few days can pay handsome dividends when you return to work fully refreshed and enthused.

The good news is that when your business goes through lean patches – and it surely will – your failures and mistakes are unlikely to be plastered all over the popular media. Nevertheless, the impact of challenging times can feel just as lonely or even draining at times and at these times a sympathetic ear or some moral support can be absolutely invaluable.

Investing in yourself versus investing in your business

It is said that investing in yourself is the best investment you can make, for the positive effects can compound and flow on to your business, relationships, health and happiness. Yet small business owners are often so focused on business operations that they neglect to invest in their biggest asset of all — themselves! Let us take a short look at the principles of investment and how they can be applied to investing in both your business and yourself.

Assess your business costs and risks

Small business owners should think critically about each dollar spent and whether it is working optimally for their business. The balance of investment in your business or yourself to some extent comes back to why you set up your business in the first instance. Was it to follow your passion? To create financial security for yourself through recurring income? Or to build a business which could be sold as a turnkey operation? We will consider here a little about your investment options.

1. Investing in your business

There are other forms of investment in your business besides a bank loan or an equity injection. They include a promotional campaign, a new business equipment or a new staff member. In each case, the key consideration for a small business owner should always be the acceptable risk-adjusted return on your dollars invested. Some types of expenditure or investment may appear to be discretionary, and in these instances you must make a reasonable assessment of the likely benefits or return on the investment (ROI). If you plan to spend $1000 on an advertisement campaign, the promotion and exposure for your business or brand must add more than $1000 to the bottom line, with an acceptable margin of safety in excess of the cost of capital.

Other forms of investment are considered to be mandatory. As an author, I might deem an investment in a laptop as a necessity since I cannot readily write further books without one! In all cases, stick to the fundamental business principle: every dollar invested must deliver an acceptable risk-adjusted return.

2. Investing in yourself

With busy lifestyles today, too often folk neglect to invest in themselves. Your human capital can be defined as your skills, knowledge and experience, or *the sum value of your capacities*. A purely academic economist would advise that human capital is a measurement of the skill set of an employee or business owner — the more skills and experience you get under your belt, the greater your earnings capacity or potential.

Always remember that as an entrepreneur or small business owner, the greatest asset of all for your business can be your own talent. Investment in yourself can take multiple guises and usually involves some sort of cost, be it a financial cost such as payment to attend a business course or a time cost.

Six ways to invest in yourself

You may have decided to invest in yourself, but what does that actually mean? Here are six ways in which you can invest in yourself:

1. Invest in your health

Exercise and good nutrition may involve some time cost, but without wellbeing, only suboptimal results can ever be achieved. The greatest wealth, as the traditional saying goes, is health. Exercising has the great knock-on impact of improving both your physical and your mental health.

2. Grow your skill set

Take courses to improve your skills, particularly in the areas you perceive are your weakest suits. If you detest the idea of public speaking, consider joining a public speaking group. Or find a small business mentor and take a course. While this can sometimes involve a cash cost, a quality business course should generate a return on investment well in excess of the initial cash outlay.

3. Hire help

Hiring help such as a bookkeeper, an administrative staff member or a cleaner may come with a financial cost, but the principle of opportunity cost holds that these may be funds well spent if they free up time for you to focus on more important or productive matters.

4. Choose mentors

One of the greatest shortcuts to success — both in small business and in life — can involve identifying mentors who have already successfully accomplished what you want to achieve, and then resolve to learn from what has worked for them and what has not. Model those who have succeeded, and follow their path. Better still, why not decide to improve upon their path?

5. Read to learn

As Harry S. Truman famously said: 'Not all readers are leaders, but all leaders are readers'. When engrossed in day-to-day travails, it is frequently difficult to see the wood for the trees or acknowledge the bigger picture. This can be particularly so during the early growth phases of a small business, where the business owner can be covering a wide range of roles. Stepping away from the detail of your business to read about new ideas and strategies can be a highly effective blueprint. There are so many wonderful resources written by brilliant business people that it would be a shame if you didn't set some time aside for them.

6. Make time

In an ideal world we'd all resolve to invest in ourselves, yet many business owners don't because they don't have time. Yet, we all have 24 hours in a day and 7 days in a week, so by definition we all have the time! What we really mean is that we have other priorities.

How do you start investing in yourself?

Firstly, at the start of each day write a list of bullet points of what you want to achieve, and tick them off as you go. This alone should make your day more effective. Secondly, just for one day, keep a time diary of how you spend each hour of the day. Take a careful note of the time expended on activities of a low yield, such as checking for new emails or idly perusing social media. Through efficiency and focus you should be able to make the time to invest in both your business and in your most valuable asset of all: yourself!

Summary

The rewards for someone who can transition successfully from the workforce are immeasurable. You can be totally free from a boss or the requirement to work set hours, and be a true master of your own destiny. What a wonderful place that can be! Of course, little in life that is genuinely worth having comes easily, so achieving this goal will require enthusiasm and tenacity. All I can say is, it is worth the effort a thousand times over.

Chapter 20 summary

» You will need to demonstrate tenacity to succeed in business and resolve to never, ever give up

» The early days of business can be challenging, demoralising or even overwhelming at times – support, a sympathetic ear or just someone to talk to, can be priceless

» Ensure that you understand the importance of cash flow to your business

» You must get paid for what your business does and paid on a timely basis

» Make the time to invest in yourself and your own human capital as well as in your business

Part Five
Live It

21
Being Happy:
Healthy Body, Healthy Mind

21

*'Early to bed and early to rise, makes a man healthy
and wealthy and wise' – traditional.*

Why choose health?

The 80/20 Principle dictates that we should aim to get the bigger picture right but we do not have to live life perfectly all of the time. Which is just as well, because very few of us do! As the old Yorkshire saying goes:

*'There's only me and thee that's perfect, and
I'm not so sure about thee.'*

I do like to include a short section on health, happiness and nutrition in my books, which may seem a little esoteric to some people. It's not to me. Success in life is largely about feeling happy, nourished and fulfilled, and a big part of that can be achieved through healthy living. Indeed, it has been found that financial health, physical health and mental health when well managed act hand in hand, forming a virtuous circle, each feeding the other. If you want to live a great life, then heed this fact and feed yourself healthy nutrition for the body and the brain!

Skilled share traders have found that physical exercise improves their discipline, concentration and performance. Yet at the other end of the scale, people who are stressed, anxious, depressed and unfit can make poor financial decisions and are less likely to achieve optimal results in other fields of their lives. The point here is that the foundation of a wealthy and successful life is built upon good health. Without good physical and mental health, other areas of our lives cannot be as fulfilled as they might otherwise be.

Mental and physical health

Physical and mental health can be indelibly and inextricably linked, with one feeding from the other. Since this book aims to help you design a life of fulfilment that you enjoy living we should briefly consider here the importance of each. Recall the 80/20 rule. I have come to understand over the years the benefits and energy that can be derived from feeding your body the right fuel and exercising it appropriately.

A healthy lifestyle should include a balance between work, rest and play and the 80/20 rule holds that you should aim to get a high yield from each of these areas of your life in an efficient manner. Good physical health is perhaps 80 percent down to nutrition and the fuel which you provide to your body and 20 percent down to exercise. Meanwhile, the brain also needs to be fed appropriate fuel and regularly trained accordingly.

Nutrition is 80 percent of the battle

I said previously that we should be careful of the vocabulary and metaphors which we feed to our brains. Perhaps we should not say achieving a healthy lifestyle is a *battle*, rather we should see it as a *journey*! One easy way to kick-start nutritional health is to resolve to start each day by eating a healthy breakfast. Even if the rest of the day doesn't go so well, at least you will have one good nutritious meal under your belt.

The benefits of eating a good breakfast are many and well documented. Firstly, a breakfast gets your metabolism moving for the day, which is obviously helpful if weight control is an issue for you (as it certainly was for me in my younger years!). To keep your metabolism firing, aim to eat small, healthy snacks regularly between meals, aiming to eat once every three hours.

Be wary of low-fat diets particularly those that contain high levels of sugar. A balanced diet should see around 20 to 30 percent of calories derived from healthy fats. Attempt to limit the poisons that you put into your body which include excess levels of sugar, salt, fat and red meat. Applying some basic common sense to nutrition and learning to listen to what your body is telling you helps. Natural foods and raw foods tend to be beneficial, while food additives, sweeteners, MSG and colourings do not. It is now more than half a decade since I gave up meat and fish, and while the concept may take some getting used to, the benefits of this lifestyle can really start to grow and compound.

Aim to provide your body with the right fuel most of the time.

Now don't get me wrong, I may be a vegetarian but I can still enjoy junk food as much as the next person, and probably more so on occasions – few people can take as much pleasure in a curry with all the fried trimmings as much as I do. As noted, I am surely no role model for doing everything right all of the time, and indeed I would have great hesitations about someone who claimed to do so. Rather, in the true spirit of the 80/20 Principle, what I am a strong advocate of is getting the important stuff right *most* of the time.

There is no value in me using my book as a soap-box for vegetarianism, only to note that once people get into the groove of not eating meat, they often begin to wonder why they ever ate meat or fish in the first place. Much of what we do in life is about habit or living in the way which we are conditioned to believe is right. I encourage you to look carefully at your approach to diet and nutrition and consider healthy changes and alternatives that will improve your lifestyle.

Exercise – 20 percent of the journey

In the modern world with the inexorable rise of knowledge-based and service industries where sedentary lifestyles are increasingly the norm, regular exercise is a win-win, because it improves your physical health and has associated benefits for your mental health too. Exercise releases endorphins which can help to make you happier, help you to think more clearly, increase your metabolism and control your weight.

Does exercise represent pleasure or pain to you?

So if exercise makes us happy, improves our physical health and brings us vitality, why do we not all exercise regularly? Well, some people do! Part of the problem is that a significant percentage of people associate *pain* to exercise, because they have been relentlessly drilled with the erroneous message of 'no pain, no gain!' Exercise should be linked to *pleasure* and, if you are doing it right, exercise is a pleasurable experience. There is no need to associate a requirement to exercise with going out and immediately running 15 miles – if you are not in the practice of doing so regularly this would indeed be a dramatically pain-inducing exercise!

For a number of very sound reasons, starting out with a brisk power-walk is likely to lead to better outcomes all round. The key thing to remember is that health and fitness are not actually the same thing. It is also important to understand the difference between aerobic exercise (aerobic meaning *with air* or oxygen) and anaerobic exercise (*without air*). When you go from resting to sprinting you create an oxygen deficit in the blood and quickly become out of breath while your body will begin to burn its sugars. This will not be a very pleasant experience and nor is it likely to be particularly good for you.

If you are undertaking a cardiovascular workout on a cross-trainer, for example, while there is no exact way to calculate an ideal heart rate for exercising, the figure is likely to be approximately 175 minus your age (e.g. if you are 40, a heart rate of around 135). This way you should still be able to breathe and talk fairly easily, taking in plenty of oxygen and enjoying a pleasant *aerobic* exercise experience. The human body needs oxygen to survive and thrive, and your cells need oxygen in order to burn glucose, so what better way to get oxygen flowing than exercising aerobically? This can be particularly beneficial if you suffer from depression or anxiety.

You need to associate pleasure to daily exercise.

You should not deplete your oxygen levels unduly and *anaerobic* exercise burns also glycogen. Performing aerobic exercise with a lower heart rate can instead help to burn fat. If you can embrace the benefits of aerobic exercise, two excellent things happen. Firstly, you can begin to associate *pleasure* with exercising instead of *pain*, and thus you will almost certainly be more inclined to actually do more of it! And secondly, you will experience renewed vigour and physical vitality that cannot be achieved by those with a sedentary lifestyle.

Once you have formed a solid base using aerobic exercise you may then go on to develop fitness by incorporating *anaerobic* exercise too. This is a far better idea than leaping straight into vigorous exercise which you won't enjoy and may not be particularly good for you either. Exercise can be an addiction, but a positive one, and the best place to start is by creating an aerobic base. Of course, this is not a personal training handbook, rather it is book about getting the big decisions right, designing a fulfilling life and using your time as positively and efficiently as you can. If you really want to turn exercise into a win-win use of your time, why not listen to motivational tapes while undertaking aerobic exercise?

I have always found that an hour of aerobic exercise away from email, the internet and other distractions also provides wonderful clarity and potential positive thinking time. Gnawing business or client problems which seemed unsolvable and anxiety-provoking while I was snowed under with work at my desk can be seen in their wider context while exercising and appear to be of less significance when viewed from something of a distance.

Finding time for a brisk walk

One of the problems with exercise is that it can take up a fair chunk of your time. Something which I have found is that exercise can be the perfect time for thinking things through. As a small business owner, work can seem at times to become all-encompassing and as the old adage goes, it can be difficult to see the wood for the trees.

There is no better way that I know of for sorting through your mental to-do list than to go for a brisk walk in the fresh air. Walking fast enough to get your heart rate up into the fat-burning zone, but not so fast that you become out of breath, gives your body a chance to move which is great for your mental health, but also time for you to *think* in a considered manner about important tasks that you need to do. What can seem overwhelming when you are sitting at your desk being pestered on your mobile phone or by email can become much more manageable when viewed at a distance.

An alternative is to hop onto a cross-trainer for an hour, which is a low-impact exercise (and not as bad for your knees as jogging on a tarmac road) and use that time to listen to motivational or educational tapes. Or simply to listen to music if that is what you find helps you to relax. Remember, you do not need to run yourself into the ground while exercising. Instead you can see an hour of exercise each day as a pleasurable time for you to enjoy your own thoughts while reaping the benefits of endorphin release and happiness that regular exercise provides.

Fresh air

With the rise of the services sector and the internet, more and more work is based around the computer, the office or a study. If you want to achieve balance in life, you need some fresh air too. One consideration is whether you should fit your home or working environment with an air purifier. This is also a strong argument in favour of taking a brisk outdoor walk as part of your exercise routine.

Walking is a great pursuit to undertake with a friend of partner because it fulfils another human need for connection and genuine interaction. Increasingly communication today takes place electronically or in front of a television or computer screen. You might be able to air a few of your day-to-day business gripes too and get some of those off your chest. You can actually enjoy meaningful conversations which rarely happen in front of the television or laptop. For this reason, I like to live within walking distance of my office. I find that a 30 minute walk to the office is the most wonderful way to start the day by walking around sunny Sydney harbour (the Opera House and Harbour Bridge always makes my heart beat a little faster – what a glorious spectacle) and the Botanical Gardens, instead of being crammed in on a bus or train somewhere, or worse, being stuck in a traffic queue!

Step to it - what gets measured gets done!

Whether it comes to your personal finances, investments, your business, succeeding at sport or your health, it is a key rule of success that *what gets measured gets done*. For example people will shambolic personal finances rarely analyse their bank statements in any detail because deep down they know that the transactions will make for depressing reading and so they do not consider them in any detail. In many cases, the bank statements will be tossed in the bin! What is certainly the case, is that someone who measures their results retains superior odds of success than a person who does not.

As accountant by profession of course I recommend finding ways to measure your progress. One simple and cost-effective idea is to buy a pedometer which measures how many steps you take in day. Most people should cover 8000 to 12,000 steps per day, although those with active lifestyles or occupations will find this easier than those who sit in an office for most of the day.[1] As what gets measured gets done, a useful investment to make is in a pedometer which measures how many steps you take in a day. An extra 1000 steps in a day burns around 50 additional calories and probably takes around ten minutes of time.[2]

'Away from' motivation

One of the interesting things about human motivation is how we are driven to behave in a certain manner by conflicting forces. When it comes to exercise, for example, many of us are driven by an *away from* motivation, such as wanting to 'get away' from being overweight or out of shape. We diet and exercise intensively for a period of time until we get back to a level that we are comfortable with, and then return to a semi-sedentary lifestyle. The results therefore tend to oscillate between rising to mediocrity and sinking under par again.

Can you see the similarities here with the way in which we unconsciously set our own financial thermostat? Because that is exactly what we do in terms of our financial health too. Commonly we work hard until we rise to a level which are comfortable with and then we ease off, or if we have become uncomfortable with the level of our success we unconsciously find a way to sabotage our success.

The greatest results in life are achieved when we set ourselves big and exciting goals and then set ourselves a specific and measurable plan to work towards those goals. This is 'towards' motivation which tends to be a more powerful motivating factor. If you want to get fit, challenging yourself to climb Mt Kilimanjaro for a charitable cause which has meaning to you is likely to be a stronger motivating factor than aiming to remain below an arbitrary weight on the scales.

Chapter 21 summary

» The 80/20 rule holds that we should aim to eat well most of the time

» Regular aerobic exercise brings great physical and mental health benefits

» Use your understanding of the Pleasure-Pain Principle to bring more pleasure to your life through exercise

» Use exercise time as valuable *thinking* time, or to listen to music or motivational tapes

» As in all areas of your life, set yourself some exciting targets and goals

» Be happy!

22
Giving It Back

22

Find a cause with meaning to you

We have talked at some length in this book about finding your passion and considering how you can make your passion your business, and use this vehicle in order to add value to as many people as possible. I now would like to encourage you to use these same principles to consider how you can give something back to the society you have benefited from living in. Accumulation of wealth is not really a worthy goal in and of itself. Wealth can, however, be of real worth if it used to make the world a better place.

Just as your business should be something which excites you and gives you a reason to jump out of bed each morning raring to go, so it should be with the process of giving back. Find a cause with meaning to you. In my case, close friends of mine have been impacted by cancer, so this became a cause which I was passionate about and has a very strong meaning to me. Similarly, having lived in East Timor, there are causes in that beautiful country which I feel very passionately about too.

> Find a cause you are passionate about.

Of course, there are thousands of deserving charities and causes out there. How to weigh up which is more deserving than another? There is no easy answer to that question, and I suspect it is one which has given people like Bill Gates great cause for deep thought over the years. The answer, I believe, is that just as in business you will be a greater success at something which you are passionate about so it is with giving back. If there is a cause which you feel passionate about and has a deeper meaning to you, you will automatically lean towards travelling the extra mile, making the additional effort and adding more value. You will be more effective at delivering for the cause as you will be passionate enough to make it so!

Tithing

The concept of tithing – gifting a tenth of your income or produce – is centuries old, and has a rich history. The word *tithe* derives from Old English, meaning a one-tenth part of something, and was referred to in the New Testament. In fact, tithing has been practised across a wide range of cultures, religions and countries. Of course, you may not be religious yourself, but tithing today need not be related to the church, or indeed any religion. Instead, you can choose a charity to donate to.

You can also donate your time to worthy causes as well as money.

If you don't have enough surplus cash to donate yet, you can always donate your time. There are so many charities out there which would dearly love more support from volunteers. In truth, we all know that we should donate time or money to charity. In many cases, folk donate to charity when they are put under social pressure to do so, but less so at other times. Money is often considered too tight. We are too busy. We already pay too much in taxes, so why donate more?

First of all, qualifying donations to registered charities are tax deductible from your income! Secondly, we all have the same amount of time in a week, so is it really true that you do not have time? On a psychological level, tithing can actually increase both your spiritual and financial wealth. Gifting a tenth of your income teaches your brain that you have more than enough, which can automatically raise your financial thermostat.[1]

We have looked in some detail at how financial success is largely a result of belief systems, self-worth and mind-set programming. Well, this is a fine example. You will often find that the truly wealthiest people are those with a strong drive to give more back and make a positive difference to the world.

'For every one lifter, there are twenty who lean'
– Ella Wheeler Wilcox.

The reverse is also true. In life, there are lifters and leaners. You can argue over the exact percentages but it seems likely to me that much more than 80 percent of the heavy lifting in this world is done by a minority of people, probably much less than 20 percent. Perhaps the ratio is more like 90/10 or even 95/5. Meanwhile, the vast majority are leaners, expecting much of the hard graft to be undertaken on their behalf.

Of course we have all been in both categories being both lifters and leaners at various moments in our lives, but as previously noted, one of the important facets of the 80/20 Principle is that you don't have to be perfect and get everything right all of the time. However, you do need to get the big things right most of the time, and your state of mind is definitely one of these things. People who are eternally pessimistic are rarely successful at anything of note, except being eternally pessimistic.

Sadly there will always be a certain percentage of the population who see it as their right to complain, whinge, carp and rant about how unfair the world is. This will never change, for it is simply in-built into some people. The cost of living is too high. Shares are too risky, which is unfair. Houses are too expensive and they should be cheaper. Interest rates are too low, so money in the bank does not earn enough. This also unfair. The boss is unfair too. Greedy rich people earn too much. Interest rates are moving higher which will push the cost of housing up. It is *all* unfair and anything and everything must be whinged about in perpetuity.

> 'Always look on the bright side of life'
> – Eric Idle, *Monty Python's Life of Brian.*

If you want to find problems in the world, there will certainly always be something to whinge and whine about. But if that represents your outlook on life, then you can expect to continue getting what you have always got and achieve less than your fullest potential, because we view the world as we are, not as it is.

To conclude this penultimate chapter of the book, I would like to divert your attention to one final key rule of success. If you do not learn to associate pleasure to building success and wealth, you will probably not maintain your levels of success or growth over the long term. And that is one reason why I recommend finding a higher purpose for yourself, one which has a meaning to you and one which will bring you the ultimate satisfaction of helping the lives of others. Success will then be fulfilling to you, and therefore it will be sustained.

Chapter 22 summary

» As with all areas of life you will achieve more when motivated to do so

» Find a cause or a higher purpose with great meaning to you

» Tithing – the practice of donating a tenth of your income to a cause with meaning to you – is one of the most spiritually rewarding practices there is

» Charitable donations can take the form of time as well as money

» Set yourself some big and exciting contribution goals

23
Living The Life Of
Your Dreams

23

Putting the 3 golden rules into practice

I noted right at the beginning of this book that all of us have a dream of the way we would like our life to be. All of us want to experience happiness and to lead a great quality of life. You now understand exactly how to action the changes you need to make in order to live the life that you once dreamed was possible. You need to change the beliefs that have been holding you back from maximising results and implement specific new strategies that can help you to achieve your ultimate goals. Set huge and exciting goals and then devise a plan of action to reach them.

You now know that there are 3 golden rules which you can use to multiply your results, not just in investing, but in business and in all areas of your life. If you can master these three golden rules, what you can achieve is almost limitless.

- Golden Rule #1: **The 80/20 Principle**

- Golden Rule #2: **Snowballing** your results

- Golden Rule #3: **The Pleasure-Pain Principle.**

Nearly there!

And so, we are nearly at the end of another book. As ever, space is finite and I have tried my best to cram a vast range of information into a necessarily limited number of pages. Of course, there is always more to learn, there are more details to be discussed, and financial markets and the world will continue to subtly change over time. Hopefully by now I have successfully encouraged you to get out there and take control of your life, for that is what is to be done.

Too many folk in the modern era are living unsatisfactory lives. They have insufficient time to do what they want, never seem to have enough money, they find their jobs unfulfilling but do not have the drive or the tools to do anything positive about these challenges. You do not have to live life that way. Through setting yourself big, exciting and inspiring goals and then designing and implementing a plan to reach those goals you can wake up each morning excited and inspired that you are living your passion, chasing your dreams and, most importantly of all, enjoying the journey.

What next?

Thank you for taking the time to read this book. I hope that you found it interesting and that you discovered some new ideas that will inspire you on to great things. Most of all, my hope is that this book has provided you with the enthusiasm and the motivation to be the best you that you can be!

So, what next? In the **Recommended Further Reading** section at the end of this book I have listed a few other books which might make for useful and interesting reading for you. If you want to know what is happening in the economy, property and financial markets as well as whatever else I am thinking about on a daily basis, then check out my free blog at http://petewargent.blogspot.com

My contact details are on my blog page too so please do email me to let me know how you are going with your quest for fulfilment. I look forward to hearing about your successes and how you are continuing to improve the quality of your life while making the world a better place. Now is the time to design your ideal future and to go right ahead and live it. Remember to think big and to use the awesome combined powers of 80/20 thinking, the Pleasure-Pain Principle and compounding growth. And above all, make absolutely certain that you have some fun along your journey. All the best, and start that snowball rolling!

Chapter 23

References

Chapter 1 – What Do You Desire?

1   *Who Moved My Cheese? An Amazing Way to Deal with Change in Your Work and in Your Life,* Dr. Stanley Johnson (G.P. Putnam & Sons, New York, 2008)

Chapert 2 – Golden Rule #1 - Living The 80/20 Way

1   *The 80/20 Principle: The Secret of Achieving More with Less,* Richard Koch (Nicholas Brearley, London, 2007)

2   ibid.

3   *Think like a Billionaire: Everything You Need to Know about Success, Real Estate and Life,* Donald Trump (Ballantine, New York, 2005)

4   www.michaelyardney.com

5   *Motivated Money: You've Invested Well? Compared to What?* Peter Thornhill (Motivated Money, Sydney, 2003)

Chapter 3 – Golden Rule #2 - The Snowball

1   *The Snowball: Warren Buffett and the Business of Life,* Alice Schroeder (Bantam Dell, New York, 2008)

2   ibid.

3   ibid.

4   Nationwide House Price Index, www.nationwide.co.uk

5   RP Data, www.rpdata.com.au

Chapter 4 – Golden Rule #3 - The Pleasure-Pain Principle

1   *The J.K. Rowling Story,* article in *The Scotsman* by Steve Dening, 16 June 2003

2   *Awaken the Giant Within,* Anthony Robbins (Simon & Schuster, New York, 1991)

3   *Lest We Forget - Why We Had a Financial Crisis,* Forbes article, 11 December 2011

4   'What if Money were no Object?' - recording of Alan Watts speaking (2013)

5   ibid.

Chapter 5 – Mind-Set Reprogramming

1   *Humble Pie,* Gordon Ramsay (Harper Collins, United Kingdom, 2008)

2   ibid.

3   ibid.

4   *Outsiders: Studies in the Sociology of Deviance,* Howard S. Becker (Free Press, New York, 1963)

5   ibid.

6   *Awaken the Giant Within,* Anthony Robbins (Simon & Schuster, New York, 1991)

7   *Out of My Comfort Zone,* Steve Waugh (Penguin, Australia, 2005)

8   *The Millionaire Next Door: Surprising Secrets of America's Wealthy,* Thomas J. Stanley and William D. Danko (Simon & Schuster, New York, 1996)

9.   ibid.

10   ibid.

Chapter 6 – The Psychology Of Wealth Creation

1 *Thriving not just Surviving in Changing Times*, Michael Yardney (Wilkinson, Melbourne, 2009)
2 ibid.
3 *Trading for a Living: Psychology, Trading Tactics, Money Management*, Dr. Alexander Elder (John Wiley & Sons, USA, 1993)
4 ibid.
5 ibid.

Chapter 7 – Choose Your Own Adventure: Big Goals...Inspiring Goals!

1 *Why Things Always Go Wrong*, Laurence J. Peter and Raymond Hull (Harper Collins, New York, 1969)
2 ibid.
3 *The Magic of Thinking Big*, David J. Schwartz (Simon & Schuster, New York, 2008)
4 ibid.

Chapter 8 - A New Attitude To Debt

1 *Let's Get Real About Money*, Eric Tyson (Pearson Education, New Jersey, 2008)
2 *The Millionaire Next Door: Surprising Secrets of America's Wealthy*, Thomas J. Stanley and William D. Danko (Simon & Schuster, New York, 1996)
3 ibid.

Chapter 9 - Automated Investing

1 Warren Buffett, Chairman of Berkshire Hathaway, speech in July 2001 as referenced in *Fortune* on 12 October 2001
2 ibid.
3 ibid.
4 ibid.
5 ibid.
6 *Get a Financial Grip: a simple plan for financial freedom*, Pete Wargent (Big Sky, Sydney, 2012)
7 Berkshire Hathaway *Letter to Shareholders* (2011)
8 ibid.
9 ibid.
10 *The Intelligent Investor: A Book of Practical Counsel*, Benjamin Graham (Harper & Brothers, New York, 1949)
11 ibid.
12 *Rich Dad's Guide to Investing: What the Rich Invest in that the Poor and Middle Class Do Not*, Robert T. Kiyosaki and Sharon L. Lechter (Warner, New York, 2000)
13 *The Intelligent Investor: A Book of Practical Counsel*, Benjamin Graham (Harper & Brothers, New York, 1949)

Chapter 10 - Shares: Get Rich Slow

1 *Get a Financial Grip: a simple plan for financial freedom*, Pete Wargent (Big Sky, Sydney, 2012)
2 *The Warren Buffett Portfolio: Unleash the Power of the Focus Strategy*, Robert G. Hagstrom (John Wiley & Sons, USA, 1999)
3 *Motivated Money: You've Invested Well? Compared to What?* Peter Thornhill (Motivated Money, Sydney, 2003)
4 ibid.
5 ibid.
6 ibid.

Chapter 11 - Real Weath Through Real Estate

1 *Property, Prosper, Retire*, Kevin Young (Goko, Australia, 2008)

2 Nationwide House Price Index, www.nationwide.co.uk

Chapter 12 - Be Your Own Property Buyer's Agent

1 *Household Income and Expenditure 1301.0*, Australian Bureau of Statistics, www.abs.gov.au

2 *Australian Demographic Statistics 3101.0*, Australian Bureau of Statistics, www.abs.gov.au

3 *2011 Census*, Office for National Statistics. www.ons.gov.uk

4 *The Construction Industry's Linkages with the Economy*, 2002 Year Book 1301.0, Australian Bureau of Statistics, www.abs.gov.au

5 *Mapping Australia's Economy: Cities as Engines of Prosperity*, Grattan Institute, Report No. 2014-9, July 2014

6 ibid.

7 *'Space and Stability: Some Reflections on the Housing-Finance System'*, speech by Luci Ellis of the Reserve Bank of Australia in May 2014, www.rba.gov.au

8 *Mapping Australia's Economy: Cities as Engines of Prosperity*, Grattan Institute, Report No. 2014-9, July 2014

9 *Household and Family Projections 3236.0*, Australian Bureau of Statistics, www.abs.gov.au

10 *The Construction Industry's Linkages with the Economy*, 2002 Year Book 1301.0, Australian Bureau of Statistics, www.abs.gov.au

11 - *'9 reasons developer costs jumped...and what they're planning to do about it'*, http://petewargent. blogspot.com

12 *Location and land use: general theory of land rent*, William Alonso (Harvard Press, US, 1964)

13 *Four Green Houses and a Red Hotel: new strategies for creating wealth through property*, Pete Wargent (Big Sky, Sydney, 2013)

14 ibid.

15 *Economics, Planning and Housing*, Michael Oxley (Palgrave MacMillan, United Kingdom, 2009)

Chapter 13 - How To Build A Multi-Million Dollar Property Portfolio...Safely

1 Data sources including:
   Australian Bureau of Statistics
   Reserve Bank of Australia
   Australian Securities Exchange
   Residex
   RP Data
   SQM Research

Chapter 14 - Getting Started: The End Of Mass Consumption

1 *50 Economic Ideas You Really Need to Know*, Edmund Conway (Quercus, London, 2009)

2 *2011 Census*, Australian Bureau of Statistics, www.abs.gov.au

3 *Household and Family Projections 3236.0*, Australian Bureau of Statistics, www.abs.gov.au

4 *Australian Demographic Statistics 3101.0*, Australian Bureau of Statistics, www.abs.gov.au

5 *The End of Growth: Adapting to Our New Economic Reality*, Richard Heinberg (New Society, Canada, 2011)

6 *Economic Analysis and the Hunt Silver Case*, Jeffrey C. Williams (Cambridge University Press, New York, 1995)

7 ibid.

8 *Think and Grow Rich*, Napoleon Hill (Wilder, US, 2007)

9 *Let's Get Real About Money*, Eric Tyson (Pearson Education, New Jersey, 2008)

10 ibid.

11 *Restoring Economic Equilibrium: Human Capital in the Modernizing Economy*, Theodore Schultz (Blackwell, US, 1990)

12 *The Intelligent Investor: A Book of Practical Counsel*, Benjamin Graham (Harper & Brothers, New York, 1949)

13 *Natural Health Magazine* (Australia, April 2014)

Chapter 15 - When It Doesn't Go Well (Not 'If'!)

1 *Awaken the Giant Within*, Anthony Robbins (Simon & Schuster, New York, 1991)

2 ibid.

Chapter 16 - Recognising Market Cycles

1 *Building Wealth in the Stock Market: A Proven Plan for Finding the Best Stocks and Managing Risk*, Colin Nicholson (John Wiley & Sons, Milton QLD, 2009)

2 *Australian Demographic Statistics 3101.0*, Australian Bureau of Statistics, www.abs.gov.au

3 http://petewargent.blogspot.com

4 *Economics, Planning and Housing*, Michael Oxley (Palgrave MacMillan, United Kingdom, 2009)

5 *The Warren Buffett Portfolio: Unleash the Power of the Focus Strategy*, Robert G. Hagstrom (John Wiley & Sons, USA, 1999)

Chapter 17 - Don't Give It All To The Taxman!

1 *The Warren Buffett Portfolio: Unleash the Power of the Focus Strategy*, Robert G. Hagstrom (John Wiley & Sons, USA, 1999)

2 *Get a Financial Grip; A simple plan for financial freedom*, Pete Wargent (Big Sky, Sydney, 2012)

Chapter 18 - Making Your Vacation Your Vocation

1 *The Zulu Principle: Making Extraordinary profits from Ordinary Shares*, Jim Slater (Orion, London, 1992).

2 ibid.

3 ibid.

4 ibid.

5 Refer to *Crossrail* project website, crossrail.co.uk

6 *Think and Grow Rich*, Napoleon Hill (Wilder, US, 2007)

7 Australian Taxation Office - www.ato.gov.au, Her Majesty's Revenue & Customs - www.hmrc.gov.uk

8 *Obedience to Authority: An Experimental View*, Stanley Millgram (Harper & Row, New York, 1974)

9 ibid.

10 ibid.

11 *The World at Your Feet: The Book that's empowering the Lives of Young People*, Dale Beaumont and Brent Williams (Learning Worldwide, Sydney, 2002)

Chapter 19 - How To Get Started In Business

1 *The 80/20 Principle: The Secret of Achieving More with Less*, Richard Koch (Nicholas Brearley, London, 2007)

2 ibid.

3 *The Warren Buffett Portfolio: Unleash the Power of the Focus Strategy*, Robert G. Hagstrom (John Wiley & Sons, USA, 1999)

4   *Australia Small Business: Key Statistics and Analysis,* www.treasury.gov.au (2012)

5   ibid.

6   *How to Start a Business without any Money*, Rachel Bridge (Random House, London, 2012)

7   ibid.

8   RBA Financial Aggregates, rba.gov.au

9   *How to Start a Business without any Money*, Rachel Bridge (Random House, London, 2012)

10 ibid.

11 Bloomberg, www.bloomberg.com

12 Customer Return, customerreturn.com.au

Chapter 20 - Minding Your Own Business

1   *The 80/20 Principle: The Secret of Achieving More with Less*, Richard Koch (Nicholas Brearley, London, 2007)

2   ibid.

3   *How to Start a Business without any Money*, Rachel Bridge (Random House, London, 2012)

4   *The 80/20 Principle: The Secret of Achieving More with Less*, Richard Koch (Nicholas Brearley, London, 2007)

Chapter 21 - Being Happy: Healthy Body, Healthy Mind

1   *Powerful Beyond Measure*, Andrew Jobling (Melbourne, 2008)

2   ibid.

Chapter 22 - Giving It Back

Awaken the Giant Within, Anthony Robbins (Simon & Schuster, New York, 1991)

Glossary Of Terms

Accumulation fund – a fund where the investor receives their benefit from contributions made plus investment returns less fees, insurance premiums and taxes.

Asset protection – a type of planning designed to protect assets from claims by creditors, such as lawsuits or other claims.

Bad debt – in business a bad debt is a receivable which cannot be recovered from a customer or other debtor. Today the term bad debt is also used to describe consumer or personal debt which is taken out for purposes other than investment i.e. debt which does not generate investment returns.

Bid-rent theory – a geographical economic theory which holds that greater competition for land closer to the centre of a city will result in higher land rents in inner locations.

Bundling – a marketing strategy which sees an aggregation of products tied together (e.g. mortgages) for the purposes of selling them on to investors as a single combined unit.

Blue chip – investments of the highest quality such as a quality, reliable company with strong and consistent earnings. In residential real estate may refer to dwellings in premium suburbs in prime locations.

Brokerage fee – a fee charged by an agent in order to facilitate transactions between buyers and sellers.

Bull trap – a false signal which appears to show that a declining trend has reversed when in fact it is only a blip or interruption in a continuing downtrend.

Business angels – angel investors tend to be affluent or high net-worth individuals who provide funding for small businesses or start-up ventures often in the form of convertible debt or a share of the equity of the business.

Buy and hold – strategy of buying assets with the intention of retaining them for the long term which works on the theory that despite volatility the long-term trend in markets is upwards.

Buyer's agent – a real estate advocate or agent who works solely on the behalf of the buyer.

Capital gains tax – a form of tax which is levied on the sale on profit of an asset or property net of legitimate deductions.

Capital growth – the increase in market value of an asset of portfolio of assets over time.

Central bank – the national bank which provides financial and banking services for the government of a country and its commercial banking system. The central bank is also responsible for well as implementing monetary policy, issuing the currency and financial stability.

Compound growth – the year-on-year growth rate of an asset or investment over time. Where a consistent growth rate is achieved gains will snowball over time.

Counter-cyclical investing – an investment strategy which aims to profit from the business cycle by buying when sentiment is at a low ebb and assets cheap.

Defined benefit scheme – a pension scheme where the employer determines the final benefit to be paid based upon age, seniority, earnings and years of service.

Defined contribution scheme – pension scheme whereby the employer and employee make regular contributions, with the final pension balance to be determined by investment returns net of costs as opposed to a pre-determined benefit.

Dividends – a sum of money paid regularly by a company to its shareholders out of its profits.

Dividend reinvestment plan or *DRP* – a scheme which allows participants to re-invest their cash dividends through acquiring further shares in the company at each dividend date.

Dividend yield – a dividend expressed as a percentage of the prevailing share price.

Dollar cost averaging – an investment strategy whereby the investor places a fixed dollar amount into a given investment on at regular intervals (e.g. monthly) regardless of what is occurring in the financial markets.

Economic moat – a competitive advantage of a business or company which is difficult for competitors to copy or emulate. Economic moats can take the form of a powerful brand or a niche technology, for example.

Entrepreneur – one who sets up a business venture with the aim of generating profit.

Equity – may have several definitions, including the value of shares in a company, or the amount of funds in a business contributed by the owners plus retained earnings or profits (also known as shareholders' equity). A real estate investor refers to equity as the value of a property asset less mortgage debt against the asset.

Equities – securities such as stocks and shares which carry no fixed interest.

Focus investing – a strategy which aims not to diversify too widely instead focusing on a few individual stocks or investments.

Flipping – a real estate strategy which aims to involve buying and sell properties quickly profit.

Gross National Product - the total annual value of goods produced and services provided by a country which is equal to the Gross Domestic Product (GDP) plus the net income from foreign investments.

Human capital – the sum total of skills, knowledge and experience for an individual or an organisation.

Index funds – a type of fund designed to mimic the performance of a stock market index.

Inflation – a general increase in prices and corresponding fall in the value of a currency.

Inflation hedge – investment in hard assets with intrinsic value such as oil or natural resources. Can sometimes apply to certain real estate investments dependent upon type and location.

Kaizen – Japanese business philosophy of continuous improvements in business practices and personal efficiency.

Labelling theory – theory self-identity and the behaviour of individuals which may be determined or influenced by the terms used to describe or classify them. Labelling theory is closely associated with the concepts of the self-fulfilling prophecy and stereotyping.

Leverage – the use of borrowed capital or funds for the purposes of some form of investment with the expectation that the returns will exceed the interest payable.

Listed Investment Companies or *LICs* – a closed end investment scheme in Australia. Investors can buy shares in LICs which in turn hold investments in a range of other companies and trusts.

Liquidity – the availability of liquid or tradable assets in a market or company.

Macroeconomic – branch of economics associated with broad trends and market forces such as interest rates or other general economic factors.

Malthusian trap – a popular theory which led that with population growth outstripping agricultural growth the growth of the population must be capped.

Management expense ratio (MER) - a measurement of what it costs a listed investment company or fund to operate, calculated by dividing annual costs by the value of assets under management.

Millgram experiments – a series of psychology experiments designed to test human obedience to authority which concluded that the majority of people adhere to instructions.

Net worth – the value of total assets less total liabilities. Sometimes also referred to as *net wealth.*

Non-tradables inflation – increase in prices of goods and services which are consumed domestically which face no foreign competition.

Opportunity cost – the loss of other alternatives when one choice or strategy is made or taken.

Overtrading – engaging in or taking on more business than can be sustained by the resources available.

Pareto's Law – a principle which notes unequal distribution between inputs and outputs. For many phenomena 80 percent or more of the outputs are accounted for by 20 percent or fewer of the inputs.

Price-Earnings ratio or *PE ratio* – an equity valuation multiple calculated as price per share divided by earnings per share.

SEC – regulatory agency of the US federal government, the Securities and Exchange Commission.

State final demand – measure of economic activity within a state which excludes exports.

Technical recession – an economy which experiences consecutive quarters of negative economic growth is said to be in technical recession.

Tithing – the practice of donating one tenth of income to a cause. In the modern era this might be a charitable cause which may have further implications for the reduction of taxable income.

Trailing price-earnings ratio or *trailing PE ratio* – see price-earnings ratio, based upon the most recently reported earnings figures as opposed to forward price-earnings ratio which is calculated based upon projected earnings in the forthcoming reporting period.

Tradables inflation – an increase in prices of goods or services which that are imported or are in competition with foreign goods and services either in the domestic of foreign market.

Venture capital – capital which is invested in small businesses or start-up ventures with a perceived high risk but potential for rapid growth.

Yield – a percentage measurement of income from an investment calculated as the current annual income divided by the capital value.

Yield curve – a series of yields plotted across a range of time horizons from a fixed interest security to maturity. Used as one potential indicator for market expectations of future interest rate behaviours.

Yield trap – investment strategy deficiency caused by a failure to understand the difference between the importance of yield (a spot figure calculate as a percentage terms) and ongoing income.

Zulu principle – the concept that it is possible to become an expert in a specific field relatively quickly through focusing on one area of expertise.

Recommended Further Reading

At the end of each of my books, I recommend a series of other books as further reading. Here are four further books for you to check out.

Personal finance and investing in the share markets

Get a Financial Grip: a simple plan for financial freedom – Pete Wargent (Big Sky, Sydney 2012).

This was my first book which looks in more depth at managing your personal finances and the various different approaches to share market investing as well as the importance of asset allocation in your portfolio, including property.

Applying the 80/20 Principle to business

The 80/20 Principle – The Secret of Achieving More with Less – Richard Koch (Nicholas Brearley, London, 1997).

A huge best-selling book, Koch's book is a business classic which addresses practical suggestions of how you can achieve more with less in business and, through more effective use of your time, and your life.

How and where to invest in property

Four Green Houses and a Red Hotel: new strategies for creating wealth through property - Pete Wargent (Big Sky, Sydney, 2013).

My second book considers all of the various property markets across Australia, and which are likely to deliver the best long-term results for property investors.

Starting small in business

How to Start a Business without any Money – Rachel Bridge (Random House, United Kingdom 2012).

Rachel Bridge takes a look at how entrepreneurs can start out in business on a shoestring. The book is filled with practical suggestions on how starting out in business need not require a huge budget, and also considers numerous real life examples of successful start-ups.

Also By The Author

Get a Financial Grip: a simple plan for financial freedom (Big Sky, Sydney, 2012). Rated in the Top 10 Finance books of 2012 by *Money Magazine* and *Dymocks*.

'Pete Wargent gives you a simple plan for achieving financial freedom at any age' – Chris Gray, author and TV presenter of *Your Money Your Call* and Channel 10's *The Renovators*.

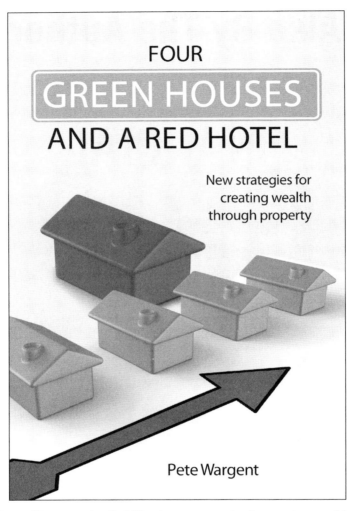

Four Green Houses and a Red Hotel: new strategies for creating wealth through property (Big Sky, Sydney, 2013).

'Writing a book which is new and interesting yet relevant to our changing times is a tough gig. But Pete Wargent, one of Australia's finest young financial commentators, achieves this in his book, sharing a wealth of information. I have been investing for over 40 years and read nearly every book on property ever written, yet still learned new concepts in this book.' – Michael Yardney, Amazon #1 best-selling author and Australia's leading expert in wealth creation through property.

About The Author

Pete Wargent is a finance and investment expert and the co-founder of *AllenWargent* property buyers with offices in London, Sydney, and Brisbane. By profession Pete trained as a Chartered Accountant and having worked for a number of financial institutions and listed companies he holds a range of other top financial qualifications including being a Chartered Secretary, and holding Diplomas in Financial Planning and Applied Corporate Governance.

Pete quit his full time job at the age of 33 having achieved financial freedom through investing in shares, index funds and investment properties. He is a keen blogger and posts his thoughts on finance, investment, the markets and much more daily on his free blog at http://petewargent.blogspot.com

Pete is the author of the 2012 investment book Get a Financial Grip: a simple plan for financial freedom which was rated as one of the top 10 finance books of 2012 by *Dymocks* and *Money Magazine*. Pete is also the author of 2013 investment book Four Green Houses and a Red Hotel: new strategies for creating wealth through property..